CU00828118

¿CLUELESS CHRISTIANITY?

~ loving Christians

in a

postChristian

something

by

Gary Davis

¿CLUELESS CHRISTIANITY?

ISBN:061550986X
ISBN-13:9780615509860

LCCN:

DEDICATIONS

~ to those who claim the Name of Jesus Christ who have decided to live out their faith *within* the matrix of our *post*Christian society instead of merely going to church

~ to my wife Starr Lynn Davis, who is the finest wife anyone could want this side of eternity

~ to our children, Joshua and Bethany, who are working out their faith with fear and trembling

~ to my mother, Florence Adelene Andersen Davis, who left her home on the plains of Nebraska to marry my dad, Earl Carlton Davis, in Baltimore, MD. Now she lives with us.

You each gave me more than you could ever imagine

¿CLUELESS CHRISTIANITY?

TABLE OF CONTENTS

¿CLUELESS CHRISTIANITY?
~ loving Christians in a postChristian something

Do or Do Not…, there is no Try.

-Jedi Master Yoda,
<u>The Empire Strikes Back</u>

ACKNOWLEDGEMENTS

As I write these acknowledgments at this point in the development of this work I am keenly aware that it has already become an historical document; poured over by a slew of editors, proof readers, reviewers, my wife, my mother, a "cohesiveness editor," teenage "consultants," the Board of Directors of NEED*inc*, who coerced me to take up this venture (ouch), too many other published authors who deemed my stuff worthy of a look, and numerous others who had to put up with my plodding questions about this and that and how everything worked together, or not. Thank you all! Because of you I did not lose my sanity over the efforts required to produce what follows. I merely lost any ability to think in short sentences and hold more than two thoughts together at the same time.

ALL deserve honorable mention, public acclaim, and a place at the Table right next to Jesus. But you have all read those lists of people whom writers of dreams cannot live without. And you ask, *Who are these people?* Let me name a few who played major roles in morphing this scribble to actual useful publishable writ.

First, my wife Starr, has been God's gift to me throughout the entire process. I could not have done it without her. AND, she let me live. (Thank you.) Then, Mrs. Tom Dowdy, a.k.a.- Beverly (Duke University Library). Every writers dream! Her services as a researcher, writer, re-writer, editor, re-editor, critic, and in general a great friend were an inspiration to me like no other.

Enough tribute cannot be paid to those suffering women who tolerated my mood swings in writing, who played the roles of Special Assistant to the President (SAP) of NEED*inc*. Notably— Lynne Smith (Galbraith), Ashley Donovan (Church), Alexis Kumar (Williams) and her insightful husband Hari, Ashley Baglow (who oft threw things at me), counselor/guides Dr Bob & Judy Cassell, and the amazing Melanie Lamere (who also threw things at me in the office and re-titled her position— Sinister Apprentice to the Problem—SAP). And, yes..., I was. Feel the Love!

And then cover artist Sophie Theroux popped out of nowhere. WOW! Guess we're having "fish" for dinner.

Thank you! May God honor you for your sacrifice and tolerance. You let me live.

Gary

Dr. Gary W. Davis

¿CLUELESS CHRISTIANITY?

INTRODUCTION

I don't think we're in Kansas anymore, Toto.

~ Dorothy, <u>Wizard of Oz</u>, *1939*

Remember when you were a kid…, well, unless you still *are* a kid, in which case what are you doing reading a book like this!? Anyway, remember when you were a kid? What do you remember? Think about it. The stuff of your childhood rumbles about in your brain in images from curiosity to wonder to pain. They pop up every now and again to make you laugh, cry, and remember with fondness, or, with regret. Memories— the way it was.

Today, you are sitting in your office, or living room, or at a mountain (ocean, lake, desert) retreat somewhere starting to read this book, thinking back to your childhood. There are things you wish you had done differently. There are things you wish you could do over again. Come on, they're *your* unique memories—conjure them up. R-e-m-e-m-b-e-r. Think back. There's a lot back there, isn't there. And sometimes you wish you could go back. Go back to those simpler days, when you felt safer and didn't have to be so responsible for so much.

Good news, bad news: you can't. That is the reality of growing older. Your world, whatever it has become, is *your* world. But you can change what is to come, what might come *NEXT*.

¿CLUELESS CHRISTIANITY?

Now think back with me for a bit. In the 1939 movie *The Wizard of Oz*, two shifts took place; one revolutionized the film industry forever. The first shift stunned audiences as a modest black-and-white Dorothy (Judy Garland) was transformed into a living color Dorothy in the magical Land of Oz. There, she met the scarecrow, the tin-man and the lion, also in living color. The second shift slipped into the movie with a bit more subtlety. Dorothy's first words, as she scanned the horizon of this strange new land called Oz were *"I don't think we're in Kansas anymore, Toto!"* Truer words could not have been spoken. North American audiences were wowed at the vibrancy of color movies for the first time. And Dorothy's scripted words heralded an era that would become prophecy fulfilled some 30 years later.

Look around you today and you find a world substantially different than the one you grew up in. Whether you grew up in the 60s, 70s or the 90s, or 00s the world has taken a turn around a corner that cannot be retraced. The last century saw two of the worst wars imaginable, a flu epidemic that annihilated 30,000,000 of the world's population in 1918-1919, the nationalizing and unification of Europe, the rise and fall of Soviet Communism, the isolation of the great sleeping giant, China (and then its reintegration into the world economy at the turn of the last century), the proliferation of the automobile, and the introduction of mobile phones to the world's teenagers. Politically, nationalism gave way to global commerce and communication. In the field of art, reticent Impressionists succumbed to the *dada influences.* The century ended with streaming video and a questionable reality— *what IS real,* in a new art form, FX movies like The Matrix. And we

¿CLUELESS CHRISTIANITY?

drove to see it in vehicles that the earlier 1900s could never have imagined.

Time did not stand still. To the contrary, technology accelerated it. From its humble beginnings in the mid 1940s government enclaves, to its wide spread popularization as Macs/Apples, and PCs in the early 80s, to its utility transformation, later woven into "the World Wide Web," the personal computer overran not only the western world, but ALL of the world. Just as the automobile changed the way we worked and lived in the first decades of the 1900s, so computerized communications have affected everything from national defense systems to personal privacy, to interpersonal (read cyber) relationships.

It's a different world out there. The way people think, talk, travel, communicate, eat, and live have all changed over the past 50 years, and especially within the last 20 years. Some things have definitely gotten better; nonetheless, something has been lost—a way of living, a *paradigm* of living has been lost. Therefore..., this book. The title, **Clueless Christianity**, came to clarity as I reflected on our continuing (if not complete) inability to integrate our beliefs, faith practices, and Christian *life-style* into the ever expanding pluralistic, and often antagonistic, culture around us.

So, why write it? Briefly put, because of all of the above and more. This book needs to exist, and to be read, by you. Why... because of the changes raining down on us daily. You need a clearer grasp of what lies ahead. To get there you need a clear understanding of what is out there, now, in the present world. And to understand our present you need a brief history lesson on well, history. This book will address all of this and more. But its main purpose is to offer you some principles and practices on how you can become a more adaptable, more comfortable (sorta), more influential Christian in a world that has far less understanding of who Jesus Christ is and what the Christian faith is.

I would like to think that certain kinds of people are reading this book. As I wrote it I had this profile in mind.

- You think, you feel, you are alive to life

- You want to do something to change things—you are a *change agent*

- You are a Christian in the truest sense of the word

- You seek the company of like minds when it comes to increasing the influence of the Christian faith in the world

- You are frustrated with the expressions of the Christian faith that you find around you

- You are not afraid of being different (well, maybe you are afraid, but you will still stand by your convictions)

- You are excited about the times in which we live; you are not afraid of them

- You know that we are not in Kansas anymore, at least in regards to where the church sits in the western world

- You are frustrated by the impasse between the normal world and the Christian world

- You believe it is time we (*genuine* Christians) have a voice when it comes to setting the cultural agenda

¿CLUELESS CHRISTIANITY?

If this is you, thank you for buying this book. If this is you *in process*, thank you for buying this book. I hope it helps you gain a clearer grasp of what it means to be a Christian in this rapidly changing, shrinking, pluralizing, diverse world of ours.

The first chapters start with a statement of the problem— namely, that the Christian community has lost the right to be heard in contemporary society. These chapters will also trace a history of how we got ourselves into this predicament. The next chapters will offer some clarity as to the nature and feel of our world today with emphasis on our world's disregard for the Christian faith. The last few chapters will offer some thoughts on how Christians can address the present post-modern issues as well as learn how to express their faith in ways that can be understood. [For more in-depth guidance read *How to Read this Book*.]

So, again, thank you for reading this book—just, please, go DO something about it when you've finished. You don't get any points for knowing, just for doing. I'll really be thankful to you then. I'll owe you big time!

Honor God, honor people…, make a difference,

Gary W. Davis

¿CLUELESS CHRISTIANITY?

¿CLUELESS CHRISTIANITY?

> *"If it works, it's obsolete."*
> -Marshall McLuhan

How to Read this Book

Some time ago I read a book by Rodney Clapp, BORDER CROSSINGS: Christian trespasses on popular culture and public affairs, and, besides finding it most helpful in gaining insights on how Christians could position themselves in/near the public arena, one of his intros was most captivating. It was titled A NONLINEAR READING GUIDE TO THIS BOOK. His section was, and will remain a true classic. It gave me the idea that the same kind of guide might be helpful to you, the reader, as you search which sections to read in this book. Because, let's face it, some of you don't have enough time to read this whole thing. So, I hope this little reading guide helps.

1. If you've ever been lost on a back country road in the great prairies of North America— Kansas, Wyoming, Alberta, Manitoba, or you really think we have a problem finding our way anywhere in life, **read the first chapter— NEW MAPS-OLD ROADS:--*a revised printing*. .**

2. If you think in global, galactic, yea verily even universal terms, and love all kinds of trivial tidbits from history, and you need to see the really B-I-G picture, **read the second chapter— A BRIEF HISTORY OF REALITY: *from mystery to email*.** This chapter is a truly arrogant attempt at brevity!

3. If you want to know about the changes that have overtaken North America in the last 100 years or so, and you need to understand how people think these days, go right to **Chapter three— READY FIRE AIM:** *the future isn't what it used to be*.

4. But if you've ever had funny thoughts about the question "What is truth?" you need to **jump to Chapter four— RETHINKING THINKING:** *the non-propositional nature of Truth*.

5. Tired of postmodern analysis? Here's where we make a shift. If you have found that all your knowledge about your faith has only reinforced your guilt, even though you know so much more than the next guy, hit **Chapter five— OF PASSION & PROPOSITIONS:** *growing a non-balanced faith*. It's freeing, eh!

6. If you sing hymns and can't understand the words, or you really don't like your father's Buick (?), go right to **Chapter six— BEING A CHRISTIAN IN A NEW ERA:** *a generational thing*. Hey, there's room for everybody.

7. Ever had one of those periods where your faith in Christ felt like it hadn't kept up with the rest of your life? Kind of a kindergarten faith in a Master of Arts body? Or if you've wondered how *"that old time religion"* can be good enough for you, you'll find some help in the **seventh chapter— UPGRADING YOUR FAITH:** *reformatting the expressions of faith*.

8. But really, if all you want are some ideas on how to live your Christian life in a postChristian society (and we are there, believe me; but you already know that), zoom over to **Chapter eight— GETTING FROM HERE TO THERE:** *what to do, what to do…?* This chapter is the real reason you bought this book anyway. No

analysis or digging into historical stuff—just the facts, mam. Solutions, solutions.

9. So much of our credibility in society is tied to our authenticity and open-mindedness toward people who live differently than us. It's about being non-judgmental, forgiving, and truly loving. Save yourself some more time, go right to **Chapter nine— A Christian Message for a postChristian Heart**.

10. Finally, I remembered some things that are in the back of my brain that need to be in the back of yours if you are going to make any sense of your Christian faith in this world. So read **Chapter ten— After*Thoughts*: *my best ideas come to me in the shower*.**

Now, if you actually *read* the whole book I will be most flattered. My goal throughout everything, though, is that you will start to make some sense out of being a *loving* Christian in a culture that has little patience with it. I hope you will come away after reading and think "*Yeah, I can do this*." and start to live out your faith in Christ in more appropriate ways for postmodern/postChristian people to perceive.

It's really been fun for me to write this book…, well, actually it's been rough too. So I do hope you'll do something with it in *your* life and in the lives of those around you.

Honor God, honor people…, make a difference,

Gary

Dr. Gary Davis, journeyman, guide & author

Go for it!

¿CLUELESS CHRISTIANITY?

¿CLUELESS CHRISTIANITY?

Remember, wherever you go, there you are.

-Buckaroo Banzai in the Sixth Dimension

Chapter 1. New Maps-Old Roads

— a *revised* printing.

My last few months as a senior in college I worked as the Athletic Director for the local YMCA. Since it was a somewhat smaller Y, I was responsible for just about everything. But it did have one perk I had not quite counted upon—the summer tour! So, the summer between college days and my first year of grad school found me working as a swimming coach for the YMCA on tour throughout North America. Our team hit national and local parks and swimming clubs across the United States, Canada, and Mexico. We competed with local outcroppings of the Y and anybody else who wanted to swim against us. One of the places we toured was Jackson Hole, Wyoming. Now, growing up as an inner city kid in Baltimore, MD, I could never have imagined a place so majestic, so alive, so grand. Jackson Hole got to me. I fell in love with the town, the people, and, of course, Grand Teton National Park. I vowed that I would return yearly!

For the most part I was able to do so, until the onslaught of kids eight years into our marriage. But in our early marriage Starr (my dangerous wife) and I made the 2,400 mile trek from the East Coast to the Tetons an annual pilgrimage. For a couple of years we tried to see if we could find our way to Wyoming without ever opening a road map. I was guided by my heart, by my passion for the West, by my memory, and by a small piece of paper with route numbers. Yup, you got it, never missed a turn; well, okay, maybe a few where we had to back track.

Until, one day, the Wyoming Department of Roads put in a NEW road, then redirected and renamed the old ones. I was forced into unfamiliar territory. You guessed it; we got totally lost. Old roads now had new route numbers; and there were now new roads where before there had been only buffalo and antelope. Now I'm not one of these guys who is afraid to ask directions. By humorist Dave Barry's standards I may not be a "real guy," but at least I don't stay lost long, either. I ask for help. Saves time and frustration.

You need to do the same. When you're lost..., ask directions.

The point of this chapter is this— unless you are consciously living your life continually immersed within contemporary culture, you need help finding your way. It is harder to find your way when new roads overrun the old ones. Simply put, you need a new map. Your cultural map is out of date; you think the old route, but find new signs that make you go "HUH?" You're on the wrong road, even though you want it to be the right one. *What happened*, you think? *You've been buffaloed* (sorry, old Wyoming joke).

Let's start by twisting our necks around to look back. Where did Christians get culturally lost? Where did the road take new turns? What happens when we insist on following old maps?

> **The Bad News:** *how Christianity marginalized itself*—So much changed in the 20th century it was virtually impossible to keep track of it. The acceleration of industry, expansion of population and mass migration had a tremendous impact. Technology and communication grew to the point of vertical take-off. For some people, namely North American Christian conservatives, the rate of change was simply too much. So many of us isolated ourselves and our families into protective cocoons and from a culture that we perceived as increasingly complex, a bad influence, and even an evil influence.[i] Conservative Christians in North America started the 20th century skeptical of such things as electricity, artificial light, mechanized forms of transportation, and, later, radio and TV. We **ALL** finished the 20th century with reservations about the Internet, fear of *M*TV, and skeptical of *e*-lationships *"Come on, how can you feel close to someone you've only met on a computer!?"* (Ever hear that one?)

The conservative withdrawal was driven by the need to feel safe again, secure within our church walls, our small groups, and our Bible studies. Though it appeared that the conservative Christian community was assimilating into society in reality it was merely running parallel with society, along its own track. Not surprisingly, the result of our actions, was that the rest of the world simply moved on. We were set aside by the western world; but in a real sense we sidelined ourselves. We positioned ourselves in opposition to the rest of society and developed our own Christian kingdom, safely confined within church walls. Secular society took the upper cultural hand, but not without criticism or commentary from the religious right. In the end, the conservative tongue was clipped, her voice was stifled, and her philosophical position was silenced.

➢ **Whiplash Effect**— A number of cultural factors contributed to the marginalizing (setting aside) of conservative Christians. It is not so much that Western society turned its back on the veracity of the Christian faith. It was society's response to Christianity's *ill-mannered* activities around the world. To list a few of the earlier historical events that even now drive people from the church—

- **The Crusades** (1095-1291). Though these wars date back one thousand years, they nevertheless laid the groundwork for an attitude of *us vs. them* that has continued in the *collective* consciousness to this day. The search for the Holy Grail, the liberation of the Promised Land, and the annihilation of the heathen Muslims in Jerusalem all seemed to our Christian forebears to be of honorable intent. This was perceived by the *unbelieving* world as something quite different, something quite aggressive and egregiously evil.

- **The Inquisition** (1291-1522) (primarily Spanish, but throughout Europe) An example of Christianity at its worst. In the name of theological purity the Holy Roman Catholic Church tortured, maimed, and executed many who did not tow the party line. Branded *heretic,* many genuine Christians were burned at the stake in the name of Christ. The effects of The Inquisition rippled throughout all Europe and the East. The Christian Faith was perceived to be an unforgiving violent faith, and often a treacherous religion.

- **The Protestant Reformation** (1564+). In the beginning the Reformation appeared hopeful to the populations of Europe, offering a richer, deeper faith. Those within the Roman Catholic Church protested the sale of salvation (a.k.a. Indulgences) via monetary dues paid to the Church. They protested the abuses of the clergy, the secularization of the church and its sins in acquiring its wealth and political power. One protesting priest, Martin Luther, was held in contempt, put on trial, and defrocked.

Jumping ahead to the 20th century we find more recent, memorable events that the world interpreted as Christian stupidity. The highlights are:

- The **rejection of technological innovation** in the early 1900s: the automobile, the electric light, flight, and radio were all seen as instruments of the Devil, presaging the End Times.

- The **First World War** fought between "Christian nations" did little for our spiritual persona worldwide.

- The **abuses and extremes** of the early Pentecostal movement. (Personality cults, snakes, anti-intellectualism.)

- **The Scopes Trials** (1923), with its confrontation between Darwinism and the Bible. [We lost.]

- The **Second World War;** the remnants of Christendom at war with each other again. And yet a new manifestation of the centuries old war between East and West (Japan).

¿CLUELESS CHRISTIANITY?

- **The Holocaust** and the public Christian silence concerning its atrocities.

- Equating the **American dream** and a conservative life-style with **evangelical Christian theology**.

- **Opposing the election of John F. Kennedy** to become the first Catholic President of the United States (Al Smith, also Catholic, ran in 1924 but lost).

- **Jonestown Massacre.** Beginning as a social justice movement in the San Francisco Bay Area, and claiming to be Christian in nature, the People's Temple soon declined to the demigod worship of one man—the Rev. Jim Jones. The November 18, 1978 mass suicide of 913 members of The People's Temple, embedded itself in the minds of North Americans as a prime example of the Christian fundamentalist-right extremism.

- **The Televangelist financial scandals of 1987**. Thank you, Jimmy Swaggert; thank you Jim Baker.

- **The Moral Majority**. Founded by Rev Jerry Falwell in 1979 as a political movement to return America to its "Christian roots." Many Americans saw the MM as a ploy to re-Christianize our country, thus eliminating pluralism.

- **"Sexual misconduct"** by numerous evangelical leaders in the early 21st century (Ted Haggard, John Edwards, etc.).

- **Sex scandals of Roman Catholic Priests in Boston**. Reaching back 25 years earlier, Investigators uncovered hetero/homosexual misbehavior and assault by Catholic priests on alter boys and school girls. All covered over in secrecy 'till the early twenty-first century revelations by Cardinal Bernard Law.

This history, no matter how accurately recalled today, has planted the seeds of ridicule and rejection in the mindset of contemporary people. They view the Christian faith as irrelevant and as an object of scorn. Not a pretty picture, is it? I can remember an evening in my favorite Buffalo Wings hangout, THE HANGER, in Amherst, MA where I was catching up on life with an old friend. At one point he asked if I still did things like that "Billy Graham guy." Without invitation, another couple sitting one table over chimed in with *"Billy Graham!? Isn't he that boring TV evangelist?"* I responded *"Boring? How long did you listen to him?"* *"Not long, 2-3 minutes at most. That's all I could take."* I suggested to the couple that they might want to give him at least a five-minute hearing before they passed judgment next time. This experience reinforced the fact that people start from skepticism if not outright prejudice about the Christian faith today. A prejudice that has been increasing over time.

We must see this. We must keep peoples' preconceived ideas and assumptions in mind before we proudly boast of being CHRISTIAN. Their connotation of the word *Christian* may be quite different from ours. We must admit that Christians have done things in the past, in the name of God, that, were horrible acts of destruction and deceit. To use a Biblical injunction, we are to confess our sins to one another, especially to those outside the Body of Christ. If we do not, be sure that they will point them out to us with little hesitation. Far too often we have bombed our own road to reconciliation. We have wrecked the highway. We need new roads into the hearts and lives of people whose collective Christian consciousness no longer looks to us for hope in this life, let alone the next one.

Of course, many people who do not want the influence of God in their lives can erect some wonderfully clever barriers to the Christian faith themselves. Much of contemporary society functions intentionally as if there were no God, no divine governing principles, and no sense of responsibility owed to anyone but the SELF. Arguments and barriers flourish in this environment of hostility. There is a predisposed rejection of anything that smacks of Christian faith. This is far from the much admired position of *tolerance* for all beliefs. But it *is* western culture in the early 21st century.

Taking all this into account, our only option is to build new roads and craft new spiritual and cultural maps to communicate our faith to a people who have moved far beyond any remembrance of the beliefs, contributions and values of the Christian faith of the past.

➤ **The Good News: how the Global Village can eliminate Christian Isolationism**— The last quarter century has seen a new twist in the road of modern culture flowing out of the advances in communication and transportation. Over the past 60+ years the world has grown smaller, bringing worlds and peoples together. The fact that a Second World War (1939-1945) on the European continent (alongside the war in the Pacific) would have such imminent implications for life on the North American continent illustrates just how much our world has closed in on itself. Although fought in the Western Pacific rim and in Western Europe, both World War theaters involved the continent in the middle— North America, lying some 3,000 miles away from both conflicts. Following WWII the Cold War standoff between NATO and the Warsaw Pact nations produced the specter of total global annihilation. What was the flight time of an Intercontinental Ballistic Missile (ICBM) in the sixties — 30 minutes? Short trip to oblivion, eh!? Fortunately, it never came to that.[ii]

The early 50s saw a blossoming in technological growth that challenged the very fiber of the way we live. With the proliferation of the telephone (beginning with 1950s basic black, through the 60s Princess Phone, to the 90s Nokia mobile phone, through the Apple iPhone, RIM's BlackBerry and tablet PCs, with due tribute to Apple's early iPad) we could now stay in touch much more conveniently and more frequently. With the proliferation of the automobile, and the best Interstate Highway system in the world, we could live where we wanted and work elsewhere. With the proliferation of the Internet and the World Wide Web (WWW) we could stay at home, stay in touch, and work everywhere.

As the 60s and 70s melted into the *détente* of the 80s, an odd '50s catalyst was mixed into the pot of world politics. It was a dynamic element that ignited a unilateral connection between all western cultures and numerous non-western cultures— rock 'n roll! Don't believe it? Listen to Paul Simon's GRACELAND, recorded jointly with the South African group Ladysmith Black Mambazo. On the heels of John Denver's duet with Luciano Pavarotti, U2's Bono teamed up with Pavarotti in 1995 on Miss Sarajevo. This was followed in 1999 by Celine Dion, a popular singer from Quebec, pairing with Italian operatic tenor Andrea Bocelli for one of the finest duets ever performed: The Prayer.

Things were also changing inside the church in North America. The early part of the last century (1900-) saw the rise of the Pentecostal movement. The core of the movement wasn't so much a new theology as it was a culturally expressive reflection of the new freedom found in the Americas. It allowed people to worship God with their whole being, not just their minds.[iii] The outstanding contribution the Pentecostal movement offered the American church was the reintegration of mind and spirit in worship. It took until the very end of the 20th century for it to become mainstream in contemporary worship. Pioneer groups like The Spears, The Blackwood Brothers Quartet, Larry Norman, Michael W Smith, Sandi Patti and "The Gaithers" forged the cultural groundwork for, Keith Green, Michael Card, Amy Grant, Delirious, Passion, Sonicflood, and Burlap to Cashmere.[iv] I was once in Vancouver, British Columbia, where I was to address a number of Salvation Army groups, from Millennial teens to emerging Army officers. Before I spoke we held a time of worship together. To my surprise, it was one of the most contemporary worship services I have ever attended. Teens, Boomers, Busters, and even a number of the Silent Generation (those who fought in Korea) were praising God as they sang, raised their hands, and danced…, yes, danced. This was not some kind of far right charismatic group. It was The Salvation Army. THE SALVATION ARMY! Can you imagine a more conservative group— dancing!? Dancing to Christian groups like Casting Crowns and News Boys, and

Christian artists like Toby Mac, Switchfoot, Steven Curtis Chapman, and Jeremy Camp.

In a sense this experience taught me that, indeed, the ethos of worship had caught up with the ethos of the culture, the new roads of the culture. But this is only one instance and one form of worship. Most Christian worship lags a generation or two (or three or four) behind the prevalent culture. Worship should be consistent with the expressions of each generation of people within a culture. Yet it remains the ongoing battleground of the old making room for the young.

Yet this experience is representative of something else as well. When it comes to Christians expressing our faith in life and worship both are *generationally delimited.* That is, people born in the same era, who share common experiences or social class (but not limited to class), generally express their faith in similar ways. There is a certain *personality* of Christian expression that shifts from one generation to the next. Always has, always will; get used to it. We dare not try to force the emerging generations of Christians into the formats of expression of their parents, grandparents, or other historical ancestors. How we express our Christian faith must be upgraded with every new generation.

Looking over the past 60 years (1950-2010), we have witnessed a shift in Christian circles from *renewing your mind* to *expressing your heart.* Emotion has been reintroduced to worship.[v] This has had both a positive and a negative effect on the Christian world. On the plus side, we have regained a wholeness in worship and in being. No longer is worship so exclusively cerebral in nature, with "the sermon" as centerpiece; we have reintegrated the brain with body and spirit. On the minus side we have grown a Christian generation of *responders* with very little Biblical understanding. Faith precedes fact it seems. Still, fact can always be added later to explain the empowering of faith in an individual. This returns the *sermon* to a pedagogical position of importance in bringing young believers to maturity in their minds as music in worship draws them into the heart of the God they love. In numerous encounters with younger new believers I have found it necessary to put (*new*) words to the expression of their faith. God had worked in them: now they needed some definition of His work. *Yeah, that's it! That's what happened to me!* is their consistent mantra.[vi]

This is entirely in keeping with the general flow of the cultural shift in North America. *Personal experience* has become the touchstone of verification. People are more expressive, more diverse, and more exclusively trusting in their own experiences than in some external truth about something. Experiencing life is tantamount across Western culture, no longer limited to generational groupings. Seventy-five year olds are hiking, rock climbing, kayaking, and even break-dancing (believe it); sixteen year olds are learning 1940s Swing-dancing and founding Internet businesses. Generational and intra-cultural barriers are being bridged in new ways, with new maps to guide you there. And although we still compartmentalize our generations (young, youth, married people, established, old people), our technology and communications are giving each of them common experiences and therefore a more laterally common understanding and perception of our world. It is almost as if we are experiencing both *generational blending* and *generational consolidation* at the same time. Go figure. [Canadians read *Go figure, eh.*]

> **Paradigm Blending**— Let's look at this era of *paradigm blending*[vii] a bit. One example of *paradigm blending* in our culture can be seen in the early 2001 movie <u>SAVE THE LAST DANCE</u>. Set in urban Chicago, Sarah is a young white girl who has lost her mother in a terrible auto accident. She must now adjust to the hip-hop climate of a Black/Hispanic inner city culture. Sarah longed to be a ballerina and attend the Julliard School of Performing Arts. Instead, she found herself struggling to learn the moves of hip-hop in a club called STEPS. Coming to her aid is Darrell, an intelligent, street-smart inner city black man, a fellow high school student who wants to be a surgeon. From Darrell, Sarah learns the intricate moves of hip-hop. In the end, Sarah blends the moves of hip-hop with ballet training for a second Julliard audition that is truly incredible. Not surprisingly, Julliard accepts her.

Another surprise hit me in a 2003 visit to Macau, China. Once settled in my hotel room, I turned on the TV to find the Chinese (Portuguese?) had their own version of MTV simply titled "V." There, to my amazement, performed ENERGY, the hottest sensation representing American RAP music. (Again, go figure.) Paradigm blending at its finest!

> **Music 'n Stuff**— Drawing together all of the above, two strains have emerged throughout Western society that are bonding much of both genX and Millennial cultures. They are *music* and *consumerism*. Through the rise of MTV and music videos a basic coupling, a paradigm blending, has taken place; sight and sound have joined to bring visual expression to what before was only audio. Before, people either read books, OR listened to music, OR watched TV. Now, these three media resources have blended into a single *image-experience* that

moves conscious-thought into the realm of experiential stimulation. Reading once called on the reader to create the images: TV and cinema now create them for you. Listening to music once drew the listener to heights of glory in classical inspiration or excited the senses in a hype/jive rock 'n roll beat. No longer. Now, listening or watching music (over radio, on an iPhone or Smartphone) *recalls* the images in the video. People have begun to *think* in music; experiential blending has *supplanted* analytic thought. Because music/visual images are beginning to replace mental assessment, it is also true that active critical analysis has given way to a more passive, music-reflective level of thinking (if you can even call it thinking); this is more like *reactive* thought versus *proactive* thought. Nonetheless, musical/visual reference points have displaced methodical, mental analysis.

Western music and video have permeated almost the entire world. All continents seem to be listening to common themes, and therefore mass-marketed ideologies, in music. Regional and national differences aside, there is now a worldwide homogeneity through music that is uniting a generation across national and even political boundaries. For example, in France, or the Netherlands, or Germany GenXers (who hate the self-definer) no longer think of themselves as French, or Dutch or German; they think of themselves as European. Hey, the EURO, remember!?

The other glue that is uniting generations, and even continents, is stuff. STUFF, STUFF, and MORE STUFF. Our world is becoming a global village of STUFF— consumerism. What is the saying? *He who dies with the most toys wins.* I remember watching a man buy a Cadillac; he was smoking on a mondo-big Havana cigar while the car salesman counted out his $68,000 in $100 bills— CASH. STUFF. There is a woman whom I know is on welfare and Medicare. She lives in state subsidized housing. She goes to Florida for a month every January and has a ball. How do I know? Because she tapes it on her digital Camcorder and shows it to me on her 42" HD flat screen TV. If these two illustrations don't convince you of western society's lust for stuff allow me to point you to The Robb Report, December Issue. Every year it comes out with recommendations for the world's most elaborate gifts— like a $485,000 watch, or a $1 million special edition Mercedes, or an $8 million dollar boat (boat?). But there are also items for poorer types (like me, or you); a $10,000 fountain pen, for example (ink-well included, of course).

You can find inner city "poor" teenagers in $250 Cross-Training Shoes, or a back-bush Maasai tribesmen with his iPAD wandering the bush. Australian singer Olivia Newton-John (played Sandy, opposite John Travolta in Grease) put it best in her 70s song NEVER ENOUGH..., *O it's never enough, simply never enough. Why is all that we have simply never enough."*

STUFF. Never enough. God help us all.

➤ **How do North Americans view the Christian faith?** With all these wanderings across cultures, continents, and centuries we need to come to the question *"Just how do North Americans view the Christian faith?"* To assume that there is one unilateral response would be simplistic. But even a cursory, general observation seems to yield three rudimentary responses—

1. According to polls (2007) conducted by Gallup Group in Princeton, NJ, roughly 40% of Americans assent to some form of Christian faith. But sociologist Stanley Presser, of the University of Maryland, through a study of peoples' *personal diaries*, calculated that from the mid '60s through the early '90s many Americans claimed to be in church on a regular basis. Only 26% were actually there. In Canada, 40% claim to be in church weekly. The actual percentage is nearer 10%. The researchers simply commented "Canadians lied." [viii]

2. **You won't like this one, but easily 25% of Americans are angry with Christianity.** Some of their anger is warranted; some of it is ignorant presumption or misperception. In a number of conversations with people who have had some past connection with a church (or with a parachurch group) there are overarching themes that challenge the form of existence of those churches or groups. Comments like *"The church just seems out of it; like it's from another century or galaxy,"* or *"Yeah, I was in InterVarsity when I was in college; but they never really answered my questions."* These comments should challenge the Christian community to ask the question, *"**Just what questions were we answering that were not their questions**?"* That's an answer worth knowing, don't you think? Political scientist Ronald Inglehart, of the Institute for Social Research at the University of Michigan states—

> *Although church attendance is
> declining in nearly all advanced industrial
> societies, spiritual concerns more broadly
> defined are not. In fact, in most industrial
> societies, a growing share of the population is
> spending time thinking about the meaning and
> purpose of life.*[ix]

How will people find the answers about the meaning and
purpose of life if we don't even understand their questions,
but, instead, merely give them OUR answers, in OUR life-
context?

3.   Finally, from surveys conducted by NEEDinc in
     Amherst, MA, it has become apparent that between
     30% to 40% of North Americans[x] know virtually little
     to absolutely NOTHING about the Christian faith.
     Though some have some illusory sense of *the
     Christian religion*, most have no preconceptions, no
     prejudice, no inkling of what it is all about
     whatsoever. They see *"the church"* as *"that building,"*
     somewhat similar to a solid, square block sitting on a
     street corner. Christianity has no content, no meaning,
     no nothing; only a sidelined presence in people's daily
     lives, to be visited or called upon only at times of
     family weddings or personal tragedy.

     I often overhear the comments of younger
     people as they leave a church service. *"Well, that was
     interesting." "What was that all about?" "Did you get
     any of that?"* And from some older people who come
     back to visit, *"Well, now I remember why I don't go to
     church anymore."* Those who attend church regularly

said *"Well, that was a good message;"* but they could not give me a summary of the content of the sermon within just 10 minutes of its conclusion.

What has taken place to bring about these kinds of reactions to the Christian faith? Beside the *historical cultural consciousness* delineated earlier, it comes down to the Christian's need for new road maps. We simply do not know how to get through to this new set of people. I recently learned of a pastor in the Midwest who preached a series Sunday mornings on "The Shift to Postmodernism." The sermons were very well received by his congregation. They felt they now understood this new generation a little bit better. In the closing moments of his final sermon the pastor admitted, *"Frankly, I don't know how to reach this new generation of postmoderns."* NOT encouraging. He could only *follow* the old road maps even though he had a *new* road map in front of him.

The cultural and spiritual roads of North America have changed significantly over the past 20 years; even more so in the last 50 years. But, more significantly, the critical factor is actually something that has NOT changed. Can you guess what it is? Right…, it's *us*— the church of Jesus Christ in North America. By and large the formats we are using to express our faith are the same as they were in 1950. Only, today, thanks to computers and in-house desktop publishing, they look better in print; thanks to great PA systems they also sound better in worship services. We still train Christians to "witness" to people as if they are asking the same kinds of questions that they were in 1950. The reality is, those questions, seeking answers in linear sequential logic or scientific verification, are barely asked in our colleges and universities. **Less than 1% of**

the U.S. population have intellectual questions about Christianity. The majority of Americans are NOT asking intellectual questions about the Christian faith. They are looking at the lives of those who claim the name of Jesus Christ as a definer for their life; they are looking to see if a relationship with him makes any difference at all. So, when they look at you, at me, what do they see?

➤ **How should Christians view their fellow North Americans?** Taking all this into consideration, how should Christians in North America look at their society? To start, we need to remember that a great deal of our world has changed. Christians are no longer the dominant influence forming either political platforms or societal mores, however much we would like to be. To live as if this is not so would be to deny a new reality that has overtaken the Western World. There is little understanding of genuine Christian faith. Once this hits home it must affect how we view our friends, neighbors, and work associates. They simply do not "get us."

At the very least, to relate to them in any way at all, we need first to BE in their world. That may sound like stating the obvious; most of us work in the marketplaces of life 5-6 days a week. But do we work there as *Christians*? In general, we do not, except maybe privately, secretly hiding our faith (out of fear?) because we might not know the answers to some of their questions. If we were more transparent about our faith I dare say Christian influence would jump exponentially. Instead, we've become *closet Christians* in the living rooms of the world. Many of us isolate ourselves within an evangelical or main line church world, venturing into "the world" as *Christians*, as infrequently as possible. We may work in this world, earn a living, raise our kids, shop for food and clothes, pump gas, go on vacations and vote for the candidate of our choice; we just don't interface with the people we meet as transparent Christians— more as non-descript Christians, with little or no Christian definition or expression to our lives. This is not good. It is almost as if we are afraid of being identified as Christians; it is almost as if being "Christian" brands us with a kind of societal stigmata. And, to a great extent, given the revelations of recent "Christian" evangelists, preachers, and other leaders, there is some truth in this.

But what if we were REAL in our Christian faith; what if we talked casually about our faith, answers to prayer, and about the difficulties we have sometimes with our faith, our lives, or our church? What if we talked about being upset over something our kids did that infuriated us, or the inner embarrassment and frustration we feel over our divorce as a bad expression of our faith? What if we were REAL in our relationships with people? What do you think; is that okay? Is it okay to, dare I use the word, *fail*, in our life of faith? Dare we tell people who are not Christians about our failures? I tend to think that people who are not believers in Christ will find our transparency surprisingly refreshing. Why? Because they are looking for faith to be real, to reflect the way we all deal with the issues of everyday life. They are looking for a faith that reflects a real relationship with a real God who does something for people in the real world. They are looking for TRUTH to be reflected in the joys, struggles, failures and triumphs of everyday life. If it doesn't do that, on what level are we living out our Christian faith anyway? Does your faith hang in a sort of limbo *above* the struggles and successes of everyday life, only to drop down to earth when you feel that the definition of something works? Come on, now... is that *really* your faith? To me, that's excluding God from life so that we can feel good about what we've accomplished. Then, when things don't work out, we turn on God as if he has failed us. Not good again.

Frankly, I find no replacement for genuine Christians, living transparently before their friends, neighbors, work associates, and relatives. I do *not* mean before their Christian friends, Christian neighbors, Christian work associates, and Christian relatives: I mean the people who never darken the door of a church, who have never had a Christian thought. Don't believe they're not out there; don't kid yourself. You just can't see them; but they are there. We need to open our eyes to see the world around us in a new light— the light of the glory of Christ, clarifying our lives and opening a window to God in the lives of those who cannot see him. Oh, by the bye, that window is YOU. So, if you're NOT there, in their world, what do you think they see of God the Father? Get the point? For us to have any Christian effect on any of our friends the first thing we need to do is actually have friends who are not Christians. We need to cultivate friendships with the "normal" people around us. But we need to do so not as a set-up for the presentation of some gospel outline, but so they will be able to see the God we love present in us in the daily issues of life. And, frankly, with all the advances in transportation, communication, medicine, technology, and the realigning of the residential/marketplace, it still comes down to people. It comes down to Christians, walking along side of people, normal people, so they can see with their own eyes what *real* Christianity is all about.

¿CLUELESS CHRISTIANITY?

When I was an undergraduate at Nyack College in Nyack, NY, I used to walk down to the Hudson River to a small park below the Palisades. I would often walk deep into the park where a tree had been blown over, half falling into the river. Astonishingly, it flourished there, hanging into the water's edge. When I needed to ponder life's issues, what girl I would date, whether or not I wanted to stay Christian, or just to escape for a moment from life's discouragements, I would climb out on that tree, and think. I would pray, cry, laugh at myself, and come away with a clearer perspective on who I was and what I needed to do in life. Some years later, the Northeast had a particularly cold winter that created a devastating ice flow on the Hudson. It took my tree away in one simple, cold sweep. I couldn't go there anymore. My place to sort things through was gone.

In a similar way the traditional pathways which the church established to reach the surrounding culture (social-gospel/four-point gospel outlines) have been swept away by the rapidly moving cultural currents. The paths have become outdated through misuse; the roads rerouted with not quite so clear detour signs around the flood waters and ice blocks. The Christian community needs to establish new routes into their surrounding world. We need to chart new maps with clearly marked road signs so that people can learn about our faith and come to embrace it or reject it. Following the directions of the past will only get us lost and confused. *"Take the second left after the Guernsey Cow Farm on the right"* is out: *GPS Navigation* is in. Get used to it. New roads: new kinds of directions.

Want some more good news? There are already some roads that run between the church and the world, but they are few and have yet to be surveyed, or opened, let alone traveled. Some new pathways have been carved out between the Christian faith and her surrounding culture; but those paths are hard to follow and often overgrown with fears of possible compromise. The rest of this book will serve as a surveyor's guide. The guide is for those who would like to lay some new roads into the new cultures of Western society. Cool, huh?. The next chapter deals with A Brief History of Reality— *from mystery to email..., texting & beyond.* Let's get to it!

¿CLUELESS CHRISTIANITY?

Try this—

1. Watch a Gulf War movie (Three Kings) with your grandparents. Research your roots (ancestry, heritage). [Internet sites abound to help in this.]

2. Identify the different nationalities in your community (not city or town, just your immediate community).

3. Draw a LINE MAP of your life, delineating the different stages brought about by its "change-points." What were you like *before* the change point: how were you different *afterward*?

4. Talk to any two people in the neXt Generation (born since 1990). Ask them how they use their time. What TV do they watch, what kind of music do they listen to, and do with their friends?

5. Read a brief history book. [Not Kenneth Scott Latourette's, unless you have a spare lifetime or two.] Remember, though, "history is written by the victors."

6. Go to a Starbucks or micro-brewery and listen to the conversations. See if you can guess some of the life-forming experiences of people who are engaged in conversation. Join in, if you dare.

¿CLUELESS CHRISTIANITY?

All that is solid melts into air.

-Karl Marx

Chapter 2: A Brief History of Reality:
from mystery to email, texting & beyond

Hopefully you didn't find the first chapter unduly negative. There are some perceptual realities about Christian faith that lie just beneath the surface for many North Americans. We need to be aware of their place in influencing the attitudes of people as they consider our faith. To some, we are naïve, to others, we are duped, to still others, we are seen as a negative influence on society and must be kept in our own Christian world. We are not seen as offering meaning or hope to a society that seems to change its values and definitions every quarter generation.[xi] Actually, we are seen more as a part of the problem than as part of the solution; but there is some encouraging evidence that this scenario is about to change. Unfortunately you will have to read this entire chapter for this change to make sense.

First, a disclaimer; I am one of those people who need to see the big picture. It is hard for me to think in terms of step 1, step 2, step 3, etc. I rather *imagine* a scenario all at once. For example, if you would say the word *baseball*, some people would immediately think of batting, or pitching, or fielding a ball, or the baseball itself; others will remember an experience they had attending or playing a game. I visualize the entire game as a complete entity... and then I taste the hotdogs. For me, this kind of *visualization* of the whole clarifies the different parts of the game and gives them a context.[xii] This broad-view visualization will serve this chapter well as we embark on a Shaefferian-like overview of a massive chunk of history— from *mystery* to *email*. But do not despair, I will not attempt to be exhaustive (or exhausting) on the subject; it will be brief. Well, maybe. Just don't expect Latourette.

Take your mind back; journey back before September 11th, 2001, before the Gulf War, before personal computers, before Vietnam, before two World Wars, before America, before Europe, even before the Roman Empire and the Greeks. Journey back into prehistory when nomads wandered the earth searching for sustenance and shelter. It was a time when there existed a clear understanding that the gods ruled the fates of men[xiii] and everything happened for a purpose. It was a time of evil spirits and good spirits, of fear and majesty, of power and mystery. This was the period of time before time, when recorded history had not yet begun; people were in touch with their spirits, with their need to appease the gods in the heavens; where every tribe and clan and "family" had their own deity to protect and guide them. It was pre-Classical period, before Socrates, Hercules, the Mycenaeans, and Abraham. It was a time of mystery— when the world held little definition or comprehension. But one thing was clear; there was a sense that a Divine Being, or Beings, ruled the earth and all therein. It is here we will begin to paint, draw, no, sketch our brief history of reality.

¿CLUELESS CHRISTIANITY?

PREHISTORIC ERA

➤ **Daryl Hannah at an Early Age**— This may seem a strange way to start; but if your mind could search the WEB in the mid 1980s film world you will discover a movie with Daryl Hannah titled *The Clan of the Cave Bear* (1986). Granted, it was a dismal Hollywood amalgamation of *Quest for Fire* with cave-babe Raquel Welch's *One Million Years B.C.*, interspersed with a weird kind of 1980s retro-feminism. But its presentation of what might be denoted as *pre-thought* existence illustrated a lucid glimpse of an era wherein all life was understood as the will of the spirits. The spirits of fire, of the wind, of the earth, and of the cave made their way clear to the clan through the authority of the head-of-the-clan. An individual's life was without meaning or context outside the clan. Life had no value other than that defined by the clan or directed by the spirits. Meaning was derived from the contexts of life's interplay with the four primary elements— earth, wind, water, and fire. It was through these four elements that the clan received its direction from the spirits. Clan shaman would consult everything from the stages of the moon to the lay of animal bones to determine the will of the spirits. Spiritual beliefs, merged as guiding principles for the tribe and for the individual. As tribes banded together for protection and divisions of labor (more hunters, more food; more cooks, more meals) so also did their "deities" mate and mix.

By 2,500 BCE, in Egypt, religion had risen to dominate all life. Through numerous military conquests millions of slaves and skilled laborers from many lands were mixed into the flow of everyday life. In their capture, they brought with them their own deities and their faiths. Truly pluralistic, Egyptian deities melted with the nuances of beliefs about other deities. Egyptian common culture became infused with the practices of many religions. Every family had its own personal god(s) it worshiped: every community grew its own shape of explanation for life as they found it. Egyptian, Hittite, Phoenician, and Sumerian beliefs flowed as converging religious streams into one pluralistic culture known as Egypt.

Yet surpassing all other religious beliefs, the worship of Pharaoh as the god-king grew to regional prominence and ran the length of the Nile River. In the Pharaoh, god became man, merged into one entity to be worshiped. He is one with all gods, their younger brother, who would join them upon his crossing of the River of Life. As a corollary, the worship of Isis and Osiris gained popularity because of its emphasis on the resurrection of the dead; mankind can live beyond the grave. All of life became the preparation for the life to come. Ishtar (Astarte, & later Aphrodite) emerges to become the goddess of love, sexuality, fertility, and war.[xiv] This fascination of *crossing over* grew to such dominance in the Nile Valley that all life is seen as a fore-shadow of the life to come.

➤ An Era of Majesty (2,000 BCE – 1,000 BCE)

This model of *life-as-preparatory-for-the-next-life* grew to magnificent proportions during the ensuing millennium. Throughout Egypt *THE BOOK OF THE DEAD* prescribed the rites and procedures for proper interment for the life-beyond. Thutmose I[st] built the first tomb in the Valley of the Kings. He was followed by Amenhotep IV (Ikanton), who issued a decree to abolish all gods, save Aton, the sun god, as the only true god. In ancient Babylon, Hammurabi set forth the first book of medical, criminal, and judicial law [Code of Hammurabi], while Babylon's astronomers developed geometry for measuring distances between the stars (zodiac). Moses received the Ten Commandments on Mount Sinai for the people of the Exodus who would become the nation of Israel. All the ancient world seemed to come to a unilateral comprehension that the will of the gods can be discerned or divined, then set down in written form. The will of the gods is now man's law. The technological discoveries in metallurgy, mathematics, astronomy, architecture, and written literature were paralleled by the institutionalizing of religious beliefs that, in turn, established a platform for these new, "scientific," innovations. Scientific discoveries became the subordinate offspring of the religious establishment: religious beliefs were bolstered by scientific and technological advancements.

PreModern Era

➤ **The Classical Era (1,000 BCE – 400 CE)—** The term *Classical Period* refers to the Greco-Roman influence (read domination) around the Mediterranean Rim, with significant expansion both east and west. As King David was succeeded by his son Solomon in Israel, classic Paganism[xv] was in full bloom throughout Greece. As the Chaos spawned Uranus and Gaea (heaven & earth), the gods toyed with the destinies of men (and women). Zeus, Hera, Poseidon, Demeter, Apollo, Athena, Artemis, Ares, Aphrodite and Hermes looked down on their creation as if it were a grand toy. During this time-period Homer penned the Iliad and the Odyssey.

Before Alexander the Great defeated the Persian Empire (325 BCE), Socrates, Plato, and Aristotle debated the efficacies of logic and pondered the world of men *without gods*. Alexander's conquests were, no doubt, aided by the invention of the catapult (300 BCE). Greek Tragedies, Comedies, and Plato's Republic all reflected a culture that swept across the Mediterranean, and then to Persia. Hellenistic culture was forced upon the conquered to various degrees. But it laid the foundation for its own demise at the tips of Macedonian swords.[xvi] Alexander's death in 323 BCE left the Greek world no leader of equal stature. Greece declined to become little more than a series of skirmishes between rival generals and city-states.

The Romans then supplanted the Greeks as the conquerors of the ancient world. Starting with their conquest of the Etruscan town of Perusia (310 BCE), through the Punic Wars (First- 264-241 BCE: Second- 219-201 BCE: Third- 149-146 BCE), onto the war between Rome and Macedon (172-168 BCE, where Rome suffered defeat at the hands of Perseus), to the consolidation (read capitulation) of Italian provinces, the "Roman Empire" encompassed Sicily, Sardinia, Corsica, the two Spains, Gallia, Transalpina, northern Africa, and Macedonia. The Roman Empire built its glory on the rubble of its conquered. But dissention among Roman leadership spawned corruption that spread throughout the Empire— a politics of position and greed. The empire had planted its own seeds of destruction.

In both the Greek and Roman Empires there existed a double standard. Officially, there was the belief that the gods determined the destiny of the individual (most individuals) and that of the State. Unofficially, the Empires were ruled with the swords of men that only paid tribute to the gods to preserve their reign.

It was into this milieu that one called Jesus was born (4-6 BCE, after calendar adjustment) to a middle aged man and his betrothed in a little known town named Bethlehem, in an eastern Province of the Roman Empire (Judea). Slightly fifty years after the greatest compilation of knowledge and literature ever assembled was burned to the ground (Ptolemy's Library at Alexandria), a small child made his entrance onto the stage of history. Who would have imagined that by the birth of this boy in an insignificant town in the eastern reaches of an Empire the paradigms of history would be forged anew?

In the world at large, little changed. The next years would see the influence of the Roman Empire falter because of internal political positioning. It began with the poisoning of Claudius (34 CE, by his wife Agrippina), and was followed by the rise of the Emperor Nero. Nero's treachery took the life of not only his enemies but also of his wife and mother. His suicide in 68 CE ended a reign of terror that forced this great empire to stumble. It wasn't until the Emperor Trajan (98-116 CE), under whose leadership the Empire reached its greatest geographical reign, that Rome regained its greatness.

Within all these cataclysmic, history-forging events an unknown Jew, one Saul of Tarsus [Paul], converted to Christianity, penned some letters to small groups of new followers of Christ throughout the Roman empire that would clarify the raison d'être of emerging Christian religion. Theological clarification— how Christ fulfilled Jewish law, the procedure for Christian ritual/celebration, principles of behavior, rules for conduct inside and outside of the church, forgiveness for a slave (Onesimus), and guidance for a young minister (Timothy), all became the standard by which Christians throughout subsequent times would govern their lives, faith, and communities.

As Buddhism grew in influence in China, the Roman Emperor Constantine the Great was baptized Christian (337 CE), granting new status to Christian faith. By the end of the fifth century the Roman Empire was devastated by Visigoths and Vandals, two strong, warring, Germanic tribes. The history of Rome soon became the split history of the Eastern and the Western Empires. But the devastation had already served to splatter the greatness of Rome into ruin. It was in this context that the Christian faith gained influence over warring tribes in a most unusual way. The Christians who had come to positions of respect in the Roman Empire were taken to the distant regions of Europe as slaves. These Christ-followers influenced their Germanic, Irish, and Nordic masters to believe in their God, Jesus Christ. While the line of the Apostle Peter was creating a priesthood in the former Roman Empire (with the Bishop of Rome rising to lead the Church), captured Christian slaves were influencing the whole of Europe and Asia through their lives, character, and deaths.

The rising tide of followers of Allah, and of Mohammed his prophet, were the next great challenge to the West. Following the conquest of Jerusalem in 637 Islam swept across the east (engulfing Egypt, Mesopotamia and Syria in the swell) and then into Western Europe where Christianity had established a stronghold. The spread of Islam was so great that by 715 the Muslim Empire extended from the Pyrenees (separating modern day Spain and France) to the borders of

China. It wasn't until Charles Martel (mayor of the Frankish court) defeated the Arabs at the Battle of Tours (aka- Poitiers, Oct. 10, 732) that the western spread of Islam was halted.

Europe was in constant turmoil as fiefdom fought fiefdom after fiefdom— after which they fought the Muslims. It wasn't until Charles the Great (Charlemagne) became sole ruler of the Frankish kingdoms in 771 that societal order was to return to the western European landscape. Even with Charlemagne's powerful "Christian" rule and his attempt to reestablish order in Europe, considerable unrest and transition awaited Europe and the Britannia. Remember the Vikings? So do the Brits. From about 792 onward they wreaked havoc throughout the British Isles and much of Europe. In 845 they pillaged Hamburg and penetrated deep into Germany, leaving a wake of slaughter in their path. But Islam was not yet finished with Europe either. In 838 Muslims sacked Marseilles. In 846 they sacked Rome. For the next 1,000 years Europe was engulfed in war; seemingly uninterrupted war between Christians and Muslims, Roman Church and emerging Kingdoms, kingdom versus kingdom. [In a somewhat anachronistic move Otto was crowned Emperor of the "Holy Roman Empire" by Pope John XII in 962. Oddly, this title of Emperor of the Holy Roman Empire (which was never any of the three) continued in existence until 1806.[xvii]]

Through conquest, annexation, and marriage, and then more conquest and annexation, Europe was somewhat solidified by the year 1000. Semi-permanent national boundaries were in place, as well as established lineages of leadership in both Church and State. It was in this state of modest solidarity that the first CRUSADE was launched in

1095. The Crusades were a series of assaults on the Holy Land (Israel, Palestine, Syria, etc.), by Christians, whose end was to deliver it from the occupation of the Muslims. This first Crusade, which ended in 1101, was followed by seven more, the last one in 1270. Europe became enamored with its own greatness. Her kingdoms each saw their reign as grants from Almighty God [Divine Right of...]. Their quest— to rid the Holy Land of the Infidels. Lofty, yes: Christian, no. What first seen as noble would later be seen as wholesale slaughter in the name of God. Sound familiar? In the midst of this the "Black Death," the Plague, devastated Europe between 1347-1352, claiming the lives of over 75 million people, nearly a third of the population.

This 500 year period witnessed the building of the great cathedrals and castles of Europe (Winchester, St. Albans, the Tower of London); also the first hospital was founded in Bologna. Abelard wrote of his love for Héloïse, tea first conquered the English, alcohol is used to sterilize wounds in battle (and for..., well, you know), and cotton is manufactured in Spain (1225). Great strides in education saw the founding of universities across Europe: great strides in architecture led to the expansion of the greatest cities of the western world. Europe was growing in its national solidifications and urban establishments. Enter the devastation of the Inquisition— a vicious reinterpretation of the Christian faith. But in England the Inquisition held little sway; Henry II ordering only the execution of Sir Thomas Becket, Archbishop of Canterbury.

If I might be so bold as to wrap up the rest of this European era[xviii] somewhat simply, for the sake of brevity, the whole of the western world during this period was in constant turmoil. England invaded France, France attacked England; the Inquisition in Spain (and beyond) was in full expression, the last vestiges of the Crusades depleted the ranks of the righteous, and, of course, the Plague(s), all left Europe in shambles…, on one hand. On the other hand a more stable Europe emerged— one with more education (at least for the nobility), more law, more centralized-markets in her great cities, better communication and commerce, and a [slightly] higher standard of living for many of the formerly impoverished peasants. The times were ripe for change, for new invention, for hope, and for the world to enter a new way of perceiving and a new way of doing. Enter the modern era.

THE MODERN ERA (1450 – 1950)

➢ **The 15th and 16th Century**— If any event ushered in what we refer to as the Modern Era it would have to be Johannes Gutenberg's movable type printing press in 1452. Little could Gutenberg have imagined the informational, industrial, and social revolution that his invention would have on subsequent generations. Gutenberg first conceived a movable, metal type printing press in 1436. Its grand debut would be the first printed "42 Line Bible" (known as the Gutenberg Bible) in 1455. The first movable type printed literature was mostly produced for the Church, then for business (contracts). With moveable type, every letter was the same size, and of course, moveable. It could be re-used, thus allowing books to be printed at far less cost. The modern era dawned slowly as a revolution and proliferated only as distribution and marketing mechanisms developed. These newly mass produced books enabled not only learning, but the dissemination of information across Europe, resulting in a new interaction between young students and seasoned scholars, financiers and novice inventors, clergy and commoner.[xix] The future had been forged..., laid in movable steel/wood type set in old, screw-type, wine presses. ... *the mother of invention!*.

This was a new era of discovery, of invention, of breakthroughs in art, astronomy, and communication. The desolation of the Great Plague and the tide of religious persecution under the Inquisition may have slowed the interest in scientific discovery and global exploration, but it could not halt it.

The last half of the 15th century saw inventions from the common screwdriver (used first to screw knights into their armor), to the Anemometer (wind measurement), to the earliest world globe built by Martin Behaim in 1492 (it was, to say the least, somewhat inaccurate), to the magnificent collections of inventions of Italian entrepreneur Leonardo Da Vinci. Da Vinci (1452-1519), an inventor, artist and scientist, had an interest in engineering and made detailed sketches of the airplane, the helicopter, the parachute, the submarine, the armored car, the ballista (a giant crossbow), rapid-fire guns, the centrifugal pump (designed to drain wet areas, like marshes), ball bearings, and the worm gear.[xx]

Another early innovator of the modern era was Galileo Galilei (1564-1642), who invented the thermometer (1593). He was also credited as the first to use a telescope to observe the heavens (1609). The following year he discovered the rings of Saturn and the four moons of Jupiter. His studies of the heavens led him to believe, like Copernicus in his 1512 paper Commentariolus, that the Sun was the center of the solar system rather than the earth; thus was he accused of heresy by the Inquisition in 1633. Nonetheless, his discoveries paved the way for further interest in exploring the skies.

In a realm of exploration more down to earth, Christopher Columbus discovered the "new world" (actually Watling Island, now San Salvador, in the Bahamas), on October 12, 1492. Balboa crossed the Isthmus of Panama and was the first European to see the Pacific Ocean (1513). Two years later Dias (de Solis) began searching for a route to the Pacific at the mouth of the Rio de la Plata in Argentina. Hernando Cortes entered Tenochtitlan, capital of Mexico in 1519 and was warmly welcomed by Aztec ruler Montezuma. Jacques Cartier explored the St. Lawrence River (1535), Hernando de Soto tramped through the peninsula of Florida (1539) and was the first European to set foot in the Mississippi River. The discovery of this new world opened lands and peoples to Europeans that was never before imagined. This fed a new sense of individual independence and human grandeur.

This *renaissance* spirit was also reflected in the world of art (to a lesser degree), due to the patronage of the Church. The early modern era witnessed the creations of Donatello, Michelangelo, Botticelli, and Albrecht Dürer. Dürer's (1471-1528) woodcuts for the Gutenberg Bible (1453) further solidified the relationship between art and the printed page.

The fifteenth century saw cataclysmic changes in the church. The Council of Constance (1414-1417) ended the embarrassment of having 2-3 popes at a time. John Hus was burned at the stake as a heretic; John Wycliffe, also, was condemned as a heretic— *after* he was dead. Yet during the same time Thomas a' Kempis wrote the *Imitation of Christ*.

¿CLUELESS CHRISTIANITY?

The same year that the first Bible was printed on a Gutenberg press the Turks captured Constantinople and turned St. Sophia's Basilica into a mosque. In Italy, Savonarola, the greatest preacher for reform in the church, was burned at the stake. The Medici's, one of the most powerful families in Florence, increased their financial and positional support for the increasingly worldly papacy.

Two oddities of the period— Christopher Columbus (1451-1506), a flamboyant, renegade Genoan, son of a wool merchant and a weaver, won a grant from Ferdinand & Isabela of Spain to explore the possibility of a western passage to India. And French astrologer Nostradamus (1503-1566) releases his predictions [in 942 Quatrains (1547)] about the future of life on earth. These two men carved their niche as shapers of the new world. Columbus, by *discovering* America: Nostradamus, by suggesting the possibility of predicting future events. Quite interesting, from a post 2011+ mindset, that these two vastly different individuals should have had such an effect on postModern thinking.

In Christendom, the Church was going through major upheaval. On October 31, 1517, a little known priest protested the sale of Indulgences by posting his "95 Thesis" on some of the practices of the Catholic Church, to which he took exception, on the door of the Palast Church in Wittenberg, Germany. He refused to recant, thus starting something that could not be stopped— the Reformation. [Others had tried what Luther did earlier but were imprisoned and failed. Luther succeeded because he had the protection of the German princes.] That same year, Pope Leo X published a Papal bull (a particular type of letter-patent) calling for peace through all

Christendom. To this writer, his timing seemed a bit askew. Luther was excommunicated as a heretic in 1520; in response, Luther burned the bull, which declared him a heretic, publicly. From Luther swept a tide of leaders and their followers who denounced the practices of the Catholic Church across Europe— Ulrich Zwingli in Switzerland, John Calvin in France, William Tyndale in England, John Knox in Scotland. It seemed an odd mis-alignment— great discovery and invention and art in one world while political/ecclesiastical turmoil embroiled bitterness and controversy in the Church. It seemed that there was a Renaissance in science and society with newfound discoveries and freedoms: on the other hand, the Church was enmeshed in her own struggles. The progress of the world outside seemed left to its own. I've often wondered if the church could not cope with our world's discoveries and inventions and so directed her energies inward. Control issues & political positioning— no doubt. Such isolation & obliviousness seems not uncommon in the church.

➤ **The 17th Century**— The 17th century witnessed continued advancements in art, exploration, philosophy, scientific methodology (& discovery), and invention. As mentioned earlier, Galileo Galilei, astronomer/physicist , constructed a telescope (1609) through which he observed our solar system. Those observations that led him to conclude the earth revolved around the sun, challenged the Ecclesiastical cosmology with the earth being the center of the universe.[xxi] Following the work of Galileo, in 1620 Francis Bacon (1561-1626) proposed a theory of reasoning that revolutionized scientific inquiry. It stressed *observation* and *experimentation* instead of *a priori* belief and church tradition. It emphasized concrete scientific research and *empirical* observation to support philosophical theory instead of Church pronouncement. This began what we now know as the modern Scientific Method.[xxii] Religion's control was beginning to falter.

In the realm of philosophy, a French born Jesuit scholar, Réne Descartes (1596-1650), challenged widely accepted philosophical ideas and coined the phrase "*Cogito Ergo Sum* (I think, therefore I am.)," in his work *Discours de la Méthode*, 1637. Searching for the origin of human knowledge, he reasoned that one must start with *doubt* instead of faith. He concluded that the physical universe, aside from God and the human soul, was mechanical and therefore subject to the laws of mechanics.[xxiii] In 1690 John Locke (1632-1704), an Oxford scholar, medical researcher and physician, political operative, economist and ideologue for a revolutionary movement, published his two most important works - "*An Essay Concerning Human Understanding*" and "*Two Treatises on Civil Government*". He advanced the idea that the human mind is born blank (*tabula rasa*)[xxiv] and only formed by experience. Locke further maintained that all human beings were equal and free to pursue life, health, liberty and possessions— a belief that formed the basis of constitutional democracy.

In 1600, the formation of the British East India Company allowed for the major exportation of textiles and tea from India. The company began intervening in Indian political matters to expedite trade. This intervention was a prelude to colonial rule of India by the British. Eventually, such colonization affected the political, economic, and social history of the entire world for the next 300+ years, especially on the continents of Africa and Asia.

¿CLUELESS CHRISTIANITY?

In 1607, Jamestown, Virginia was established as the first permanent colony in America. The New World was opened to be settled by Europeans. Millions immigrated in the centuries that followed. And through that immigration new ideas were born that tempered and challenged Old World ideologies. The American frontier and the melting pot of immigration had huge effects on democracy, social class, and race. In old Europe a new idea, especially when it impacted the state or the church, could mean death: in the New World it meant merely moving further west, to the ever expanding frontier.

The invention of the microscope (1680) displayed for the first time the complexity of the smallest organisms. By giving humans the ability to see what had previously been unseen, it debunked many unquestioned theories that existed since the Classical period. It's invention played a significant role in the start of the scientific revolution.

For the remainder of the highlights of the Modern Era, I am indebted to a multi-volume work, <u>Science and its Times: Understanding the Social Significance of Scientific Discovery</u>. Some of these are:

In 1628, William Harvey discovered the human circulatory system. He was able to illustrate the action of the heart, and clarify the pattern of blood circulation throughout the body. His use of the experimental method of scientific reasoning to do so was bold and unsettling to the medical community, which attacked and derided him. He would not accept mysticism, dialectics, or tradition as evidence. Only experiments that could be repeated multiple times over with the same result were accepted. His system completely altered the wide standing view that the liver was the source of blood in the body. Harvey thus created the starting point for modern physiology. But it was the printing press that allowed the greatest advances in medicine to go forward. Before printed texts all medical knowledge was transmitted by hand. Most medical treatments were transcribed in painstaking, elaborate manuscripts. Because they were so elaborate, they were difficult to reproduce. Once medical texts could be printed with accompanying drawings medical knowledge became widespread. Clearer diagrams and illustrations of surgical procedures, disease identification and anatomy could be included. Medical literature could now describe every detail including the color, smell and structure of diseases. Because a printing press could produce numerous exact duplicates of texts cheaply, medicine was brought to the masses.

In 1656, the invention of the Pendulum clock revolutionized timekeeping. Before, people had kept track of time with a variety of inaccurate tools such as sundials and spring-powered clocks. A uniform rate of oscillation was difficult to regulate in all of these devices. The pendulum clock was the first that produced an error of less than one minute a day. In the nautical world this meant that navigation became much more accurate, lessening the cost of a voyage.

But the seventeenth century's greatest challenge to the Church's hold over Europe was, oddly, Sir Isaac Newton's discovery of the law of gravity. Newton realized that the force holding any object to the earth is the same as the force holding the moon and planets in their orbits. He created a mathematical equation that defined the gravitational pull between any two objects. It was a profound insight into the mechanics of the natural world. It became the model for the future development of physical law, and was a powerful verification that the entire cosmos could yield to inductive reasoning. Because his law was so mathematically precise, it strengthened the idea that all laws describing the universe could be mathematical. It was perfect in describing a clockwork-universe that was knowable and predictable, sweeping away any need for the supernatural.

➢ **The 18ᵗʰ Century—** Newton's discoveries continued to draw favor in this century as well, spinning off even more paradigm-shifting inventions. The publication of Isaac Newton's _Opticks_ in 1704 brought about a rise in scientific experimentation across Europe. Newton's account of his own experiments found a wide audience, who began to be convinced that nature could be understood by observation, and more importantly, controlled. Enthusiasm for experimentation spread from elite circles of the educated to the general public. Public lectures on scientific experiments began to be attended by tradesmen and entrepreneurs who applied these ideas to practical problems. As Newton's physics began to be applied to the construction of various machines, commercial life began to be transformed. The science of engineering emerged. Throughout the eighteenth century the world of construction and building moved from guesswork and approximation to precise calculations. Before the discipline of engineering, nature always had the upper hand. Builders had always gauged by what they could see, with some exception to the Greek Classical Period. There was no systematic knowledge to draw on. It had been lost. Investigations into nature, its forces, and the chemistry of materials meant that designers could have a degree of control over their constructions. The knowledge which began to be codified into engineering made it possible to build models of buildings, bridges and other structures before building them full-scale.

At the same time a revolution was taking form on the farm, brought about mainly by three inventions: the seed drill, the threshing machine and the cotton gin. The seed drill began to be used in 1701. It set seeds into the ground in straight rows at a uniform depth and covered them. This was a much more efficient method of planting than scattering onto the soil by hand which wasted much of the seed. The resulting neat rows allowed farmers to weed the ground between the rows, saving time and effort. In 1788, a threshing machine was invented which removed husks from grain In 1793, the cotton gin began to be used in the American South: making cotton farming highly profitable. The resulting increase in the food supply from these inventions, among others, was incredible. Prices of food dropped, and the varieties of food in the normal person's diet increased. The increase allowed the farmer to sell a greater percentage of his crops, so more roads, canals and bridges were built to enable him to get them to the various markets. Better diets caused an increase in population. The resulting agricultural advances laid the foundations for the Industrial Revolution.

In 1712, Thomas Newcomen, an English blacksmith, connected all the separate components of what would become the first steam engine; but it was James Watt who modified the design and patented it. This machine provided an immense source of power. The steam engine established the place and importance of the machine in the modern world, where machine power replaced muscle power. The steam engine and the subsequent development of a railway system [in the 19th century] on which to run the steam-powered trains provided the transportation the Industrial Revolution needed to deliver all its newly manufactured goods to new markets. The steam engine and its railway system *literally* paved the way for the Industrial Revolution more than a century later. People moved in masses from the farms to cities. Western society thus shifted from an agrarian base to an urban one. The economy changed from a local mill and shop to one based on huge central factories and the wide distribution of goods.

By mid-nineteenth century the Industrial Revolution had changed the daily work environment of the majority of people of Europe, and then of America. It changed both the landscape and populations of cities. It moved economies from an agricultural base to a manufacturing base. This new economy created a new environment for the common worker. Work forces were moved indoors; they were no longer in open fields. The pace of work was greatly accelerated. The seasonal cycle no longer dictated the production of goods (though they still governed planting and harvest). Adults were expected to work 12 to 14 hours every day, all year long. Laborers eventually were seen to be interchangeable, just like the machines they ran. Human dignity and worth, based in Christian faith, was supplanted. Urban populations exploded since the workers now needed to live near their factories. The material wealth of Western nations was greatly increased. This helped to create the modern worldview that through technological applications of the sciences, greater productivity and a higher quality of life could be achieved. But sadly, any idea of connecting humanity's value to our position in Creation was displaced by the human industrial machine.

¿CLUELESS CHRISTIANITY?

In the Americas, the 13 colonies successful war of independence from Great Britain (1783) had a great influence on liberal thought throughout Europe, inspiring revolutions in France and in Spain's American colonies. France enjoyed a short domination over most of Europe, during which Napoleon instituted many administrative and legal reforms. He had no legal training, yet many of his innovations in law still endure. He established a council of state, a public accounts office, courts of justice, universities, and the rights of the national bank (1799). All of these served as restraints, as checks and balances, on democratic excesses.

The closing of the eighteenth century witnessed the beginnings of a power shift from Europe to America. The signing of the U.S. Constitution, in 1787, is the unqualified benchmark. Its four most important contributions to national governing were—

1. The introduction of the electoral process.

2. A system of checks and balances within the various bodies of federal government.

3. Federalization of government combined with both regional and sovereign-state control

4. A provision for the protection of all individual's personal, inalienable rights.

These initiatives, set forth in the Constitution, laid the groundwork, for Molly Wollstonecraft to publish "*Vindication of the Rights of Woman,*" (1792). This publication was the first great feminist document to stress the importance of educating women and providing them equal employment opportunities.

¿CLUELESS CHRISTIANITY?

The eighteenth century closed with a discovery in medicine that would enable people to actually express their rights and privileges through a longer life. In 1796, Edward Jenner stumbled upon a way to prevent smallpox when he noticed that milkmaids who developed cowpox didn't get the dreaded disease. His vaccine, made from the cowpox virus, virtually wiped out smallpox. This disease had claimed the lives of more than 60 million Europeans in the eighteenth century. Vaccines are now common, and death due to infectious diseases has seen a dramatic drop, with a corresponding increase in the human lifespan. This increase caused a corresponding increase in population in many nations. For the first time in human history, nearly every child born in a developed country could live long enough to reach a healthy adulthood. Vaccines saved many people from being crippled or injured by disease for much of their lives.

Not only did the eighteenth century see great advances in medicine, invention, and the dissemination of new ideas, it also ushered in the beginnings of an increase in the *rate of change*. Things were speeding-up, people were working longer, living longer, and experimenting with new technologies and ideas as never before. The die had been cast for the next century to refine and further improve on the last century's innovations.

➤ **The 19th Century—** In 1801, a French weaver, Joseph-Marie Jacquard (1752-1834), invented a weaving loom controlled by punch cards. [Sound prophetic?] In the first application of punch cards in history, he programmed the intricate weaving of patterns in textiles much more efficiently than humans could. Almost a century and a half later punch

47

cards were used to design the first automated calculators and eventually the earliest computers.

In 1844 refrigeration of foods was made possible through the use of an ice-making machine invented by Alexander Twiney. Refrigeration increased the lifespan of food, and the variety available year-round. It enabled workers in urban centers to buy food that was shipped in, instead of producing it themselves. Thus they were able to do work other than that of food production on farms. Farms could be located farther from population centers. The result was the end of a predominantly farm economy and the beginning of a predominately manufacturing economy. This, in turn, allowed for mass migrations from rural regions to cities, ever burgeoning with industry and income.

With this great influx of people to crowded urban areas, infectious diseases soon became a major concern. Water became the means of transmitting those diseases. Water could carry a multitude of diseases, including deadly typhoid and cholera. Clean water was highly important to human life in the urban setting. Many epidemics spread across crowded cities, especially during the Industrial Revolution. New living conditions were created by the industrial culture, which concentrated the poor in cities and towns. Urban workers moving from small towns often brought their livestock to live with them in the tenements; sewers became cesspools; refuse was shoveled by hand; and excrement often flung from windows. An entire neighborhood would draw its water from a single outdoor pump. In 1850 an English doctor named John Snow demonstrated that 500 cases of cholera in central London could be traced to a single source, which was a neighborhood water pump. Once Snow convinced authorities to close the pump, the cholera cases in London simply stopped. He concluded that disease had been transmitted through that one water supply. His discovery was the first step in public health and sanitation. The first water purification system for a public reservoir was installed at the Chelsea Water Works on London's Thames River. By the end of the 19th century, most cities in Europe had modern sewage and drainage systems. Of course, the local Pub remained, immutably, the primary source of liquid sustenance.

Four of the greatest inventions and discoveries of the nineteenth century were—

1. The first Photograph, taken by Joseph Nicephore Niepce, captured the world's first reflective image on an exposed plate. It was taken from a window in Burgundy (1825). It has allowed us to forever record people, events and places in time.

2. Anesthesia (1846) — Modern surgery was made possible by the development of anesthesia. For the first time, surgeons had the ability to go beyond the treatment of wounds, fractures and dislocations. They could perform life-saving procedures, and increase the lifespan and quality of life.

3. The Telephone— Alexander Graham Bell introduced the telephone to an amazed audience at America's Centennial Exposition. Within a year, he had installed 230 phones and established The Bell Telephone Company. The telephone changed the way people did business, communicated, and their perception of community.   One English businessman, touring

America in the 19th century, said he could understand the need for the telephone in the U.S. because towns were so far apart. He could envision a time when every TOWN would have one. But in London, there were more than enough messenger boys to do the job. In 1997, 643,000,000,000 calls were placed by people in the United States alone.

4. The Incandescent lamp— In 1879, after 1000 trials and $40,000, Thomas Edison introduced an inexpensive alternative to candles and gaslight. Using carbonized filaments from cotton thread, his light bulb burned for 2 days. [Similar to today's light bulbs.]

But it was through these new ideas and technologies that the *paradigm* of daily life shifted to a world where there was no longer a philosophical need for an external reference point (read God). In, 1848, Karl Marx and Frederich Engels made the claim that *economics*, not a divine plan, drove history. They proposed that economic disenfranchisement of the working class would lead to a revolution to seize control of the means of production— the idea upon which Socialism and Communism were built. From their ideological beginnings, millions lived and died under Communist ideologies throughout much of the 20th century.

But one of the great impacts to come out of the 19th century came in the form of a book. In 1859, Charles Darwin released his **"Origin of the Species."** Darwin explained that, over time, species adapt to the environment in order to survive and then passed along these acquired traits to future generations in a process known as "*natural selection*" (as opposed to *divine selection*). This new ideology up-ended the understanding of the orthodox religionists of the time. The automated nature of this process did not seem to include a divine being. If Christianity said all life was a gift, Darwin's theory emphasized the *randomness* of life. Natural selection seemed wasteful; divine direction was viewed as picturesque, but not scientifically pragmatic or efficient. Darwin's theory also took hold in the social world, where it was known as Social Darwinism. It argued that people, just like plants and animals, competed for success in life. They thus justified the status quo by claiming that those at the top of the social and economic heap *deserved* to be there. They had competed and had proven they were better than others. Darwin's ideology was used during the nineteenth century to justify racism and imperialism on a grand scale, not to mention the ever-widening disruptions of the Industrial Revolution. It even went so far as to suggest the *selective-breeding* of human beings.

One contribution that came out of the nineteenth century deserves particular mention— Gregor Mendel's discovery of the laws of heredity. In 1866, through his work crossbreeding different varieties of the garden pea, Austrian monk Gregor Mendel provided data that genetic traits are transferred from generation to generation by way of distinct units. He discovered the basic laws governing heredity. His work forever changed agriculture and livestock industries, as his laws were eventually proven true for both plant and animals, and can be found in genetic counseling as well as throughout every basic biology text. His laws became the framework for the field of genetics in the late 20th century.

Whereas Margaret Sanger (1879-1966) espoused the thinking of eugenicists— similar to Darwin's "survival of the fittest"— but related the concept to human society, concluding that the genetic makeup of the poor, and minorities, was inferior. Clearly, this was a form of social Darwinism. Therefore, society needed to establish a system of birth control to maintain a proper balance. She founded The American Birth Control League in 1921.

➤ **Chapter Coalescing**— Please accept my apologies for the brevity of this chapter, glibly panning most of recorded history in a matter of a few pages. It had to be written. What I hope you have gained from it is a sense of the grand picture, the cosmic drama of history (at least in the West). From these the twentieth century has drawn its roots of creativity and industry...; and, almost, global destruction. To be sure, not everyone needs a picture of history that is this sweeping. But to ignore the span of time and pivotal events, significant inventions, and innovative individuals who became the paradigm pioneers of our world is to reinvent reality. What should have become clear in such a hurried review are the events and innovations that produce major shifts in the way people perceive and live their lives.

The first move from a **prehistoric** subsistence, from hunter-gatherers and foragers to planter/harvesters, laid the foundations for kinship relationships and communal society. [Yes, Daryl Hannah, there is a place in the tribe for you after all.] Food supplies could be combined with those of others for the common good; and there was protection in numbers against the wild— potential predators and warring bands. The element of safety gave rise to the emergence of leaders within the group. This allowed the **time** for our earliest ancestors to ponder the universe and deduce their own origins. The coalescing of people groups into larger groups (cities) laid the foundation for an era of majesty in ancient Mesopotamia, Greece, and Rome. Today, in retrospect, we describe this era as ***pre-modern*** — that is, when the nature of reality gave credence to gods and spirits, both good and evil, who played an active role in the destinies of men. If, as is common today, we rationalize that the people of this era used the idea of a god, or divine direction/intervention, to explain what could not be explained, we have condemned ourselves. For reason, scientific discovery and rational thought are the products of the **modern era**, which discounted the works of God in society to direct or redeem, simply because that work was not quantifiable and could not be observed via the scientific method. The modern era created its own faith in science and continuing discovery to the exclusion of any faith in any deity outside its own, physical, quantifiable (controllable) universe. Now the burden of proof would rest on modern man to explain the universe without any reference to a divine being-who-governs external to it. Not a task I would relish.

But the modern era generated its own undoing in reductionism: reducing everything to the scientific method and electro-chemical reactions. Life without God fell to new heights of mechanization and created-meaning. There was no possibility that God had wound up the universe like a clock and was sitting back waiting for it to run down because there was no God: we had wound our own clock and lost track of the meaning of "clock." If I may recount a personal experience, one night in The Hangar, my favorite sports bar in Amherst, where I live, I found myself in a discussion with an owner, two waitresses and the bartender. I asked, somewhat baiting them, *"What do you believe God is designing you for?"* None were sure they knew except for one waitress, Kim. She quickly answered, *"I'm designing my own life. God has nothing to do with it."* At which point the other three pounced on her for not believing that God had a hand in our reality. So I chimed in with *"Are you the Supreme Being in the universe or do you think there might be another?"* At this they were all quick to agree that there just had to be a God out there, somewhere. They just weren't sure what, if any, role, he or she might play in their lives. I just left it there…, letting their clocks run on a bit. Later.

The shift to a **post-modern** universe is still in progress. We have not quite let go of the hope for a universe that makes sense: we are unwilling to get on board with a universe where the responsibility of destiny rests solely within us. In a very real sense it is one of the greatest shifts in the way life is lived and perceived. It is a paradigm shift of enormous proportions. But the final groundwork for this monumental paradigm shift would not be laid in the nineteenth century but in the twentieth. What you will find in the next chapter is a delineation of the events, both positive and negative, that laid the foundation for the present mistrust of well, everything. Read on if you dare.

"You really don't feel better

once you know you're wrong."

Chapter 3: READY FIRE AIM:
the future isn't what it used to be.

Life facts from 1902: *things that make you go hummm.*

1. The average life expectancy in the US was forty-seven years.
2. Only 14 Percent of the homes in the US had a bathtub.
3. Only 8 percent of the homes had a telephone. A three-minute call from Denver to New York City cost eleven dollars.
4. There were only 8,000 cars in the US and only 144 miles of paved roads.
5. The average wage in the US was 22 cents an hour.
6. The average US worker made between $200 and $400 per year.
7. More than 95 percent of all births in the US took place at home.
8. Ninety percent of all US physicians had no college education.
9. Sugar cost four cents a pound. Eggs were fourteen cents a dozen. Coffee cost fifteen cents a pound.

10. Most women only washed their hair once a month and used borax or egg yolks for shampoo.

11. The five leading causes of death in the US were:
    1) Pneumonia and influenza
    2) Tuberculous
    3) Diarrhea (most likely from contaminated food)
    4) Heart Disease
    5) Stroke

12. The population of Las Vegas, Nevada was 30 people.

13. Crossword puzzles, canned beer, and iced tea hadn't been invented.

14. One in ten US adults couldn't read or write. Only 6 percent of all Americans had graduated from high school.

15. Marijuana, heroin, and morphine were available over the counter at corner drugstores. According to one pharmacist, "*Heroin clears the complexion, gives buoyancy to the mind, regulates the stomach and the bowels, and is, in fact, a perfect guardian of health.*"

16. Eighteen percent of households in the US had at least one full-time servant or domestic.

17. There were only about 230 reported murders in the entire US. [xxv]

So, given the religious fun & fancies of the last 10,000 years, not to mention the incredible innovations that have taken place in the last 100 years, the question we are facing on this *postmodern/postChristian, text2text, family-redefining, iPoding,* Wii-*ing, touch-screen, Skyping-facetime* globe is—

¿CLUELESS CHRISTIANITY?

Who are we? or— **What are the definers of life and reality in a world** (western culture, in this case) **with so many value systems coexisting side by side?** In other words, how do we make sense of all the changes of the last years of the twentieth century and the few we have played with so far in the twenty-first? That is what this chapter will address.

Let's start with a metaphor from the early days of the wonderful world of computers. Can you say Ctrl+Alt+Del?[xxvi] You remember what that means, don't you? (Or not.) It's an old computer key combination for releasing a hard drive freeze up, a crash, a lock up…, call it what you will; personally, I remember it as *&@#$ frustrating. [Well, admit it. You feel it even if you don't say it. It's part of human nature to be frustrated by *all* things electronic.] We've all experienced that irritating situation where we are working along, just like we always do, and, for whatever reason, our computer's hard drive hits a wall, beyond which it will not work. Ctrl+Alt+Del. You have to REBOOT! And if you haven't bothered to save your work, or exit your application, or backup your work, well, bye-bye! Back to square one.

The point is that things don't always work the way they are intended. [Perhaps Microsoft *intends* their operating systems to work like this, but probably not. (*Why people buy Macs*)] So much has changed in the world it requires a focused determination (constant immersion) just to keep up. In the Western World (Europe, North America, parts of the Pacific Rim) the rate of change has accelerated to the point that we literally cannot keep up. For example, it used to be that if you ordered a computer from a distributor (DELL, GATEWAY, HP) by the time you paid it off it would be obsolete. Now, the joke goes (but not so far from the truth), that by the time it arrives it is obsolete. We are outpacing ourselves on a daily basis. The way we did something yesterday (made a phone call, turned on the TV, cooked dinner, "commuted" to work[xxvii]) is not the way we do it today.

In the mid-twentieth century products and goods were made to last; they could be counted on to be around for 5-10, even 15 years. They broke; you repaired them. Now it is use it & lose it. Material goods in the West are expendable; sometimes, so are the people. Company loyalty, holding onto your job, or having a single career for life have all been supplanted by upward mobility, "down-sizing," farming jobs overseas, and multitalented entrepreneurialism (read "*I want to do what I want to do*.").

For better or for worse, we have moved light-years past the modes of living at the turn of the nineteenth into the twentieth century. Imagine that world for a moment. Industrialization had taken over the cities, the family, and the father. Electricity was just becoming available to the masses. Most Americans used kerosene lamps for light. The automobile was crowding out the horse and buggy. Train travel was the rapid transit of the day; subways and trolleys were uniting workplace and home with greater efficiency. Back on the farm even the earliest mechanization of planting and harvesting was revolutionizing the agricultural process. The massive expansion of North America's roads enabled farmers to get their produce to more markets faster; the railroad transported goods and produce to yet further a-field markets, expanding trade and creating a hunger for exotic goods and tastes. On a world scale, old tribal conflicts were replaced by a new sense of nationalism. Europe had solidified under national monarchs. And it seemed that those American states had finally made it as a world power, even after the bloodiest of Civil and territorial wars. The world seemed poised for the entry of the greatest century ever, the Twentieth Century! Most Americans were giddy with what they had been told the new century would bring— science and technology freeing ordinary people from the demands of physical labor. And what an exceptional century it would be— both in greatness and in tragedy.

What were the definers of the Twentieth Century?

➤ **READY   AIM   FIRE**— *the way it used to be.* What inventions, creations, and events made a positive contribution to the enhancement of life in the West?

Mass production of Autos- Henry Ford's development of ASSEMBLY LINE (1908-09, significant improvement by 1926) manufacturing of automobiles enabled his fledgling company to initially turn out 365 cars a week, making the automobile both affordable ($400 - $700) and available to the general public. This wide-spread availability of cheap, individually mechanized transportation changed the way people lived and moved about forever. [Until, of course, the development of the traffic jam.]

Women's right to vote- (1920) With the heritage of the Nineteenth Century Women's Temperance Leagues, the Salvation Army, and WW1 employments, female suffrage laid the foundation for the emancipation of women from second class citizenship in western society. This western liberation seemed unfathomable to many other world cultures and societies where women were still considered property.

Unions protect workers- With the rise of industrialization came the inevitable misuse of large sectors of workers. Children often labored 12-15 hours a day in "sweat houses," men working swing shifts would rarely see the light of day. Women who worked in sewing shops and fabric mills were paid far less than their male counterparts. The unions established the rights of the worker in the face of industry's (often) tyrannical management. But by mid-century, they had evolved into a bureaucracy with a political agenda that existed for its own perpetuation.

The Commercialization of Air Travel- Following WW1, the proliferation of trained pilots gave rise to the establishment of postal routes via the air. Airmail was delivered from coast to coast in 32 hours, weather permitting. In 1926 four fledgling air companies came together to form United Airlines, carrying the first passengers in, well, interesting levels of comfort (first as part of the mail, then in wicker chairs in unheated cabins).

Penicillin (1928), heart transplants (1967), & genetic engineering (1997)- Advances in medicine in the Twentieth Century were unimaginable in the previous one. In 1900 the average life expectancy was 47; by 2000 it had risen to 75. In large measure this was due to the creation of Penicillin, other antibiotics and vaccines that put an end to infectious diseases in the West (unfortunately, though, not available in time for the 1919 Influenza epidemic). Later in the century, the replacement of lungs, stomachs, kidneys, hearts, and even hands, ushered in a new era. These advances opened the window for medical researchers to consider if the propensity for disease could not be addressed at the genetic level. The mapping of the Human Genome in 1999 introduced the West to the most amazing approach to medicine since the discovery of antibiotics. And then there were the cloning possibilities. Well, hello Dolly![xxviii]

Space flight: Moon landing- Though the Soviet Union (CCCP- now Russia) got into Space first with Sputnik (1957) and stayed there the longest (Mir Space Station- 14 years), the Space Race was soon dominated by the United States. The Russians learned how to lift heavier payloads earlier; the U.S. launched lighter payloads with superior technology. With the first manned MOON LANDING (1969) the sky was opened to think about exploration of the rest of the Solar System. If we put a man on the moon... .

Credit Cards- With the introduction of Credit Cards in the 1930s and their subsequent proliferation, via the DINERS CLUB CARD in 1950, the spending habits of North Americans took a radical shift. Where once only the poor used "layaway" to purchase material goods "on time," with a Credit Card everyone could purchase whatever they wanted whenever they wanted. By the end of March 2010 the revolving national credit card debt in the US exceeded $852 billion [that's b-i-l-l-i-o-n] a year.[xxix] The total consumer debt in that same period was $2.45 TRILLION. Into the early Twenty First Century the continual practice of overusing credit cards by North Americans continues to create a spiral of exaggerated wealth (read "*looks rich*"; think "*actually broke*") that, eventually, will force us all to pay the piper.[xxx] With the collapse of the banking institutions in late 2008, the subsequent government bail-out, and the numerous home foreclosures, it seemed that America's recession was in full swing. Nonetheless, banks are once again issuing credit cards to individuals who are defined as financial risks.

Music diversifies and goes Visual- Starting the century with residual Sousa dance music, American culture witnessed the rise of Rag, Jazz, Crooning, Bebop, Rock n' Roll, Soul, Folk, Heavy Metal, Rap, Latino [Santana, Gloria Estefan, Christina Aguilera, Ricky Martin) and Country & Western pop/crossover with the likes of Shania Twain, Kenny Chesney, and Faith Hill. The American music scene gave rise to a worldwide music culture, greatly influencing both emerging Arab and Asian youth cultures.

But the biggest shift in Western music came with the release of **music videos**. With ever-increasing broadcast band spectrum (cable or satellite) for TV, a new music channel was inevitable. MTV started in 1981[xxxi] and has revolutionized the presentation of music itself. Music could no longer be creative, innovative, and simply well-performed, it now had to be visually-artistically represented as well. Music videos produced a new culture of people who *imaged* and *thought* in music. It was this *imaging* that laid much of the groundwork for the shift from logical-sequential explanations of life to visual-experiential images of life. Stay tuned: more on this later.

Youth culture established- More than with any generation before, America's youth of the '50s and '60s were defined by music—specifically, Rock n' Roll. The adult population rejected this new definer of their children as unhealthy, wrong,

¿CLUELESS CHRISTIANITY?

and even demonic. "*Rock n' Roll is the Devil's music*," one DJ was noted as saying. But Rock n' Roll was here to stay; it prevailed to the end of the 20th century and with some redefinition, into the early 21st century. It played a major role in defining the youth of the white middle class. But it also offered a means of expression for America's Black culture; it brought their soulful expressions (Soul into Rap) into the mainstream of the urban cultural milieu. It eventually gave presence and respectability to Latino culture as well, allowing Puerto Rican and Mexican cultures a place in the American scene.

By 1980, fully 41% of the United States population was under the age of 25.[xxxii] A large percentage of products and services were marketed (PUSH marketing and technology) at this definitive youth culture. And why not!? Who has more discretionary $$$ to dispose of than teenagers!? Not me, that's for sure. I have to admit I enjoy teen culture. I like their exuberance, their hope for the future, their sense of indestructibility, their desire to make a difference, and, yeah, their music. Most of it. Like it or not, they *are* our future. What a great opportunity for adults like us to leave a legacy through the lives of this emerging generation. [**Note**— But will they take what we bequeath them? Is our "wisdom" wisdom to them? Do our stories of the way-it-used-to-be touch their hearts?]

Proliferation of artificial birth control (1966)- Though fiercely debated from Roman Catholic to Evangelical circles, the promise of "safe sex" through the Birth Control Pill ushered in a sexual revolution. It was now possible to separate the act of sex from the responsibilities of commitment,

63

marriage and parenthood. Sex could now stand alone as an activity unto itself. As expected, artificial birth control not only reflected a shift in the acceptance of divergent moral standards, it also contributed to a breakdown of commitment relationships throughout the Western World.[xxxiii]

Civil Rights Movement- During the 1960s, the consolidation of local civil rights action groups into a single Civil Rights Movement raised the awareness of the plight of and prejudice against Afro-Americans. Through the sacrifice of life by many American blacks, the civil rights taken for granted by the white population were eventually extended to blacks. No sacrifices were more keenly felt than for those who died in the Church burning in Birmingham, AL; the murder of Medgar Evers, and the assassination of Civil Rights leader Dr. Martin Luther King, Jr. These became the martyrs that united America's Afro-Americans behind one single movement—equal rights for *all* minorities.

Computerization of life- Though computers were developed as early as 1947, it was not until the 1980s that they became a major influence in North America. The proliferation of Radio Shack's TRS80s, KayPros, Commodores, Apples, IBMs, and Wangs made the "personal computer" available to the common man. Over the next 20 years computers revolutionized the business community and penetrated the home-life of North America. From basic word processing, spreadsheets, and simple games to integrated office suites, the business/personal computer became invaluable in both home and office. With public access to the World Wide Web (initially a network utilized by and for military purposes only) in the mid-90s, the computer became the tool of communication and marketing from preteens to CEOs. At this writing audio and video downloading over the Web are acceptable modes of connecting. I can't wait to get a video-conference call on my Blackberry mobile…, during my next trans-Arctic flight.

Collapse of Communism- To the surprise of the West, Mikhail Gorbachev laid the groundwork for the dissolution of the Soviet Union and the introduction of "democracy" to a people who had known nothing but totalitarian rule for more than 75 years. The dissolving of Communism in Russia opened an untouched market to an influx of Western influence and culture. This united two former enemies (the former USSR & USA) in a mutual cultural adaptation. Although much of Communist rule suppressed its absorbed protectorates, it also brought an end to centuries of ancient tribal warfare in the name of Slavic unification.

Worldwide Communications- The Twentieth Century started with the laying of the first reliable[xxxiv] transatlantic telephone cable connecting Europe with North America. It ended with instantaneous live TV coverage of every event imaginable, cell-phones, GPS, satellite uplinks, a World Wide Web and email exceeding all expectations. Technology took us from a world of isolated nations to a global village that assumes instantaneous communication as a given. Pen pals come of age (read *online buddies & instant messaging*). Tweet me!

Instant Internet Commerce- The development of Internet commerce/trade must have a place of its own as a major factor in the way both established and emerging nations have come to do business. From online trading to home investment brokering to getting anything you want, it all came down to a single mouse click. Purchasing products *online* supplanted the antiquated ordering from the Sears catalog of an earlier era.

The Twentieth Century witnessed an acceleration in the rate of change in industry, technology, globalization, and communications. The contributions in all facets of life forced us to rethink the answer to a question once put to Jesus— *"Who is my neighbor?"*

Answer pending.

➢**And Now for the Bad News**— With all the aspirations, inventiveness, wonder and greatness of the last century, there were also the unavoidable tragedies that lessened our joy and senses of greatness and reminded us of our "other side." The human race has not quite overcome its propensity to replace God. Below is a listing of some of the lower points of the Twentieth Century.

World War 1- "THE WAR TO END ALL WARS" it was called. But the First World War's continental extent, combined with new technologies —the Gatling Gun and Mustard Gas, made it the most devastating war known to date. The European arena knew death in the trenches as never before. More than 8.5 million people perished in this bloody conflict (with another 7.7 million missing). This was equal to 13% of the total mobilized armed forces of the war.[xxxv] [Dear God... .]

Russian Communism (1918) - As the First World War of the century drew to a close another bloody civil war erupted in Russia. The *new* Bolsheviks overthrew the centuries old Romanov dynasty, promising equality for all under one Socialist Society; this seemed far more appealing than the continued repression of the Czars. What emerged was just another repressive regime that feigned equality in the name of emancipation of the workers. Karl Marx's socialization of labor dreamed of equality of all classes— the total flat stratification of society. But when you are paid in Vodka (or often not paid at all) it becomes fairly clear that something is not working.

Influenza Epidemic (1918-1919)-[xxxvi] Though virtually forgotten by mid-century, a flu epidemic devastated the world's population following the end of World War 1. Starting in America the influenza spread around the globe through returning soldiers to almost every continent. Once contracted, the flu led to death within 7-10 days. There was no cure. More than 50,000,000 died worldwide. [3% of the world's population.]

Stock Market crash (1929)- The US Stock Market crash on October 29, 1929 created a global imbalance in banking and trade that took more than a decade to reestablish. Families and businesses found themselves in financial ruin with no recourse or hope for rebuilding. The crash brought about the ensuing Great Depression of the early 1930s, wherein American poverty reached record levels in urban and rural settings alike. By the Spring of 1932 New York City saw payrolls down more than $80 million a month; nonetheless, the city had to spend more than $4 million a month on relief. The effects were just as devastating in the American South. On a single day in 1932, ¼ of the State of Mississippi came under the auctioneer's hammer.[xxxvii] Going once... .

¿CLUELESS CHRISTIANITY?

World War II- Though the "War to End All Wars" had been fought just 21 years before, another war erupted in Europe which would eclipse any war heretofore. Hitler's invasion of Poland in September of 1939 and its ideology of a "master race" turned the Second World War into genocide. Jews, Christians, the mentally ill, gypsies, and homosexuals were all sought out and sent to the death camps. As it advanced its imperialistic conquests, it pushed across the European continent on both eastern and western fronts. The civilian and military cruelty of the War was unprecedented.

In the Pacific, the December 7th bombing of Pearl Harbor in 1941 drew the United States into the Global War in a way that stunned her people. Even though the attack on Pearl Harbor had been predicted by Col. Billy Mitchell in 1926, the shock of the attack so enraged the American people that her entire industry restructured itself, virtually overnight, to a wartime industrial machine. The wartime efforts of all combatants made World War II one of the most destructive, savage wars ever fought.

The Holocaust- A byproduct of World War II, the Holocaust deserves a mention because of the nature of the atrocities committed. More than six million civilians and non-combatants were murdered in Nazi Death Camps in Poland and Germany. Adolf Hitler's hatred of the Jews birthed a genocide unknown in world history. Six million. We will never forget. [Oh, I forgot, we already have— in Rwanda, Bosnia, Cambodia, East Timor... .]

Birth of Atomic Weapons- The development of the first nuclear device, an atomic bomb (code name- Manhattan

Project), culminated on July 16, 1945 at 5:45 a.m. in northern New Mexico in a blast of heat and light. Two more blasts occurred in the context of the war in the Pacific; Hiroshima and Nagasaki were decimated in an instant. Total vaporization spanned a ½ mile radius from ground zero. Today a typical 20-megaton bomb detonated at 17,500' would produce total vaporization for a radius of 9 miles. [Statistics on further destruction and desolation can be found on the Web.]

Collapse of World Economy – Following WWII, as North America grew in power so also it grew in wealth. America's "war machine,"— her industrial plants— were transformed once again; only now they produced goods (cars, kitchen appliances, furniture, houses, etc.) that could be bought by the average wage earner. But the global economic market was in ruins, especially in Europe and Japan. Europe needed total rebuilding, literally. Japan, as a conquered nation, had little strength to rebuild itself. In an attempt to return the world to some semblance of economic balance, the US undertook a large role in rebuilding of the economies of Europe and Japan.

But the lesson was forgotten as the next 50 years of world peace (that is, where there were no global wars were being waged; regional conflicts abounded still) created a grievous greediness in people. There was wholesale acceptance of overspending: credit card debt surged to unprecedented levels, international borrowing put many countries in hock to the United States far beyond their ability to ever repay; in the US, overspending in government, industry, business, and individually created a debt surge that is just now exhibiting its rebounding effects on society. (More on this in the section on the US national debt below. Do the math.).

¿CLUELESS CHRISTIANITY?

The Vietnam "conflict" leads to a loss of national confidence- If the McCarthy era[xxxviii] following the Second World War wasn't enough to unnerve the American spirit [xxxix] the Vietnam conflict (never a declared "war") put the lid on national trust in government in the US. In Canada, the government of Pierre Elliot Trudeau's (1968-1984) socialization of services (which isn't working to this day) and regional apartheid truly divided Canada between east and west. Or, as they say in Ottawa, "BC?"

AIDS threatens society- Though its route remains debatable, the virus that causes AIDS (**A**cquired **I**mmuno**d**eficiency **S**yndrome) was first identified in North America in 1981 among homosexual men. Though fatal in the West until the mid-90s, it remains a taker-of-life in all non-Western cultures, especially in Africa and Southeast Asia. During a conference at Princeton in October 2000 I met a South African who told me AIDS was so widespread in his country that a loss of 25% of their population was predicted by 2010.[xl] We're there.

Worldwide political assassinations and terrorism- Some of the people assassinated in the Twentieth Century were— President William McKinley shot in September 1901; Czar Nicholas II of Russia (along with his immediate family); Archduke Franz Ferdinand of the Austro-Hungarian Empire (igniting Europe into WW1); Mahatma Gandhi of India; Gamal Nassar, (first president of Egypt); Pierre La Pointe, Canadian Labor Minister by the Quebec Liberation Front terrorists (FLQ) in 1969; Anwar Sadat (Egypt). On May 13, 1981, Mehmet Ali Agca attempted to assassinate the Pope; the attempt failed. In the US— President John F. Kennedy, Senator Robert F. Kennedy, Rev. Dr. Martin Luther King, Jr., were all assassinated in the last 40 years of the Twentieth Century.

By the 1980s assassinations had been supplanted by a new wave of terrorism that introduced the United States into its devastation in the 1995 Oklahoma City bombing of the Alfred Murrah Federal Building by Timothy McVeigh. He killed 168 people, including children in daycare in the building. Following the iconic glory modeled in the Matrix Trilogy (movie series) his brand of terrorism spread from Columbine High School in Littleton, Colorado in 1999 to others. What a great way to end a Millennium.

Racial prejudice/violence- Though the American Civil War ended more than 135 years before, racial discrimination and prejudice persists. Though slavery was outlawed by Abraham Lincoln (Emancipation Proclamation- (1863), segregation and separation of Afro-Americans from the mainstream of society persisted well past the middle of the Twentieth Century. The Civil Rights Movement of the 1960s, founded on the pain of almost two centuries of injustice, finally brought the intervention of the US Federal government to enforce laws passed almost a century before.[xli] Enforcement remains irregular.   But it took the murders of black men such as Medger Evers, Malcolm X, and Martin Luther King, Jr. to fortify the resolve of the Afro-American community in its quest for racial equality.

Exorbitant national debts- From the introduction of the Diners Club Card in 1950 to the proliferation of Credit Cards over the next 40-50 years, North Americans piled up enormous personal debt. By the close of 2010, the average outstanding balance of individual credit card debt was $5,100..., per card.[xlii] Most individuals hold an average of 3 cards. On a national level The United States Federal Deficit merely reflected the spending patterns of the people, ringing in at $5.6 trillion by the end of the Twentieth Century.[xliii] Ten years later (2010), it had risen to almost $14 trillion; since Sept 28, 2007, it has increased on average $4.12 b-i-l-l-i-o-n a day.[xliv] Ka-ching! Unless something fiscally responsible is initiated in our immediate future this mounting sum will weigh heavily on the shoulders of our grandchildren, and their children, and their children.

Equalization of men and women- Although the Nineteenth Century Abolitionist Movement in the North and the Women's Temperance League across America did much to foster the position of women in the country, it wasn't until well after winning the right to vote that women gained (somewhat) equal status with men. The Feminist movement of the 1970s sought to bring more women into the workplace with pay equal to that of men. "Same work: same wage." (But no vodka.)

The sad part was that women saw being equal with men as something worth attaining. To me, this seemed to be a step down. Not only were home and child raising responsibilities now seen as second-class, the two-income family pushed the North American economy to extreme levels of inflation. [Costs rose to meet rising incomes.] Eventually, two incomes became a necessity instead of a luxury. Never again could a woman (or man) return to the home front without another member earning an enormous salary. And to make matters worse, women never did achieve equal pay in the Twentieth Century. The equalization of men and women did more to aggravate men and wear women down than it did to free either from the stereotypes and role definitions of the past. [Read THE SECOND SHIFT, by Arlie Hochschild, 1997] At this writing (late-2010), women still lag behind men in pay for equivalent jobs.[xlv] But it is getting better, sorta. Depends on who you ask.

Not a great start to a new millennium- September 11, 2001

Though not part of the twentieth century, the September 11th terrorist attacks on the United States have laid a foundation for a change in life assumptions in the West for the early twenty-first century. National security, the right to move about the country (the world) freely without thought of danger, the safety of the individual citizen, the responsibility of government to protect the homeland, and world economic stability have all come into question. The terrorist attacks have awakened the sleeping giant of democracy's defenses. Does the West unite with the rest of the world in a new war on terrorism? How long? How do you fight an enemy who is patient, hidden among us, fairly sophisticated in strategy and armament, and set on the destruction of western decadence?

The answers to these questions are still in the making. Initially, the focus was on the Taliban government of Afghanistan and ridding the world of an oppressive regime which harbored terrorist training camps. [At this writing, many of those training camps are now in Pakistan.]. Then allied forces invaded Iraq to uncover "weapons of mass destruction" hidden away by President Saddam Hussein as a threat against the West. [NONE were ever found.] The war against terrorism is again focused in Afghanistan. The Taliban, the Islamic radical fundamentalist group that had taken the country captive is once again entrenched and providing shelter and training for world terrorism.

But the War on Terrorism is just beginning. The world community will probably beat it; but "win?" Can there be such a thing? Terrorism, worldwide, is probably here to stay as long as there are people who hate people, no matter the root. For the immediate future, the world, as we have assumed it for 25-50 years, has changed. Will it return to "normalcy?" Define that for me please— we may be living in the *new* normal— for now. God help us all.

➤ **Know your history: dream the future**— I know this must have seemed a laborious review of the pluses and minuses of the twentieth century; but it was necessary if you are to grasp the significance of the changes taking place today in these early years of the twenty-first century. Isn't there a proverb— *If you would see the future, glance over your shoulder first?*[xlvi] Well, if there isn't, there should be. With the turn of this most recent century, 1999-2000[xlvii], you can see the effects of both the positive and negative influences carried over from the Twentieth Century. We live with technology in the West that has most definitely enhanced our lives; we also live with a memory of some of the greatest atrocities ever inflicted by humans on each other. But this is no longer a world of—

READY, AIM, FIRE.

The rate of change during the twentieth century had a greater velocity than any century before. If you feel like you can't seem to keep up, well, you're right. You can't. From here on out it's **READY…, FIRE…, AIM.**

¿CLUELESS CHRISTIANITY?

READY…, READY…, READY?

➤ **Well hello, dahlink!** – On a family drive from our home in Massachusetts to Townsends Inlet, New Jersey. we chose to save time by driving directly south on I-95 through New York City. For those of you who live in the northeast you already know that "save time" and "New York City" are an incompatible couplet. (For those of you who live elsewhere, trust me…, don't drive through NYC on a summer weekend.) On this particular trip, traffic was horrendous. It was a hot July day and we were stuck somewhere on the Cross Town Expressway (a true misnomer). All of a sudden our toddler daughter Bethany woke from a sound sleep and screeched "WELL, HELLO DAHLINK!" [*Dah-link* being the basic Brooklyn equivalent of "Darling."]. Where in the world did she get that!?! Her Brooklyn-ism struck me. Where had she connected with that phrase? Things are changing; people and ideas connecting. But you already know that. Just pick up your Smartphone and check your email, text-messages (Facebook or Twitter, etc.), or SKYPE call directly from your cell phone. Connect to your home or office computer from 20,000 miles away; then send a document to be printed while you play a game on your mobile device. If you are in Finland, the world's most wireless nation, buy yourself a Coke (again, with your phone) while you do your online-banking; and don't forget to open the door to your house for your kids after they get home from school—all from your mobile phone. Different!?! Not if you pick up this book up on an Online Used Book Store for $.99 (+S&H) a year after it's written. Change itself is changing; and the velocity of change is spiraling ever more rapidly. READY..., FIRE.

Before we examine the nature of our society today let's think together about that last idea— *change itself is changing.* Whether we are aware of it or not we all depend on *change* changing the same way. This is called *continuous change.* Things always change; we know that. We depend, though, on things changing in the future *in the same way* as they've changed in the past. For example, we expect changes in *style, travel, communication, etc.,* to follow the patterns they followed in the past. Models of cars modify yearly, mail is still mail, cooking with heat means turning on some kind of heater/burner. Governments go through transitions either through revolution and overthrow or some form of common election. That's History.

But the other side of the coin is *discontinuous change. Discontinuous change* is a change in *change* itself. In the early twentieth century travel went through monumental changes with the introduction of the automobile and airplane; telegrams gave way to the telephone; single teams building a clock, automobile, or radio gave way to assembly lines. As the century moved along at an ever increasing pace so also did *change*; human workmanship and control gave way to computer control with robotic arms doing the work; buying a home already built gave way, in some measure, to vast tracks of farmland being turned into housing "communities;" urban dwelling gave way to suburbia; and then urban dwellings rebounded through re-gentrification[xlviii]. Then there was the surge in the *neuvo rich* (*yuppies?*) —two income families meant more income—therefore, more money now available to be spent. So, INFLATION inflated. In other words prices of everything went up substantially, from houses to cars to bread. Single income families had a hard time of it by the early 70s. But the most influential change in *change* to effect the public sector, the private sector, and business in the West was the introduction of the personal computer into virtually every area of life. The computer changed the way people did business, kept financial records, wrote letters, structured filing systems, communicated, and played. It's a long way from PacMan™ to Laura Croft,™ baby. Wiiiiiiiiiiiiii! (Get the point?) *Change* changed, forever.[xlix]

Simple observation of any western society will mark a *stylistic* change about every 4-5 years. *Change*, itself, changes about every 20 years, with the emergence of each generation. Compare this to the rates of change in far eastern and emerging cultures. The nomadic tribes of the Sahara see change about every 300-400 years; the marsh dwellers of southern Iraq live much the same way as they did 1,000 years ago. Even with the intrusion of the gobbling machine of western industry, the Indian tribes of the Amazon in South America live much the same as their ancestors as far back as can be remembered. Albeit, the Inuit of the Northwest Territories and Nunavut have somehow managed to blend their ancient culture with mobile phones and cross trainers. I once watched a National Geographic Special on TV depicting a young Inuit teen dressed in a sealskin coat over a Hard Rock Café T-shirt. FIRE!

Which brings us to the main point of this chapter—READY FIRE AIM: *the future isn't what it used to be.* How do we make sense of all the changes that have taken place in the last few years of the twentieth century and the few we have played with so far in the twenty-first? Or, to quote my illustrious daughter, "*Well hello, dahlink!?!*"

➤**The Way We Were... doesn't matter**— Hello dahlink! Let me introduce you to the world we live in. It's not the world of the last century; it's a whole new world. It's a world whose values have gone through such major overhaul that it hardly bears any similarity to the world of 1900. It's a world that many have described as *post*Modern. If you're reading any cultural commentary you most likely have come across the word postmodern, or postmodernism. Strange nomenclature, to be sure, but one that describes present Western society in the context of its historical development. It's not that you have to know the past to understand the present; but doing so will give you a few cool clues about what's up next in the future.

➤*Pre*Modern, **Modern,** *post*Modern, *post*mortem: *what's in a name anyway*— As you read this section do not despair; you already know what these four terms describe. Well, maybe two outta the four, but, if you paid close attention to the preceding chapters, you understand at least three already. The **PreModern Period** was one wherein people generally saw things "*the way they are.*" The way they are, that is, if you believed that the world of the spirits and gods was every bit as real as the physical, visible, tangible world. Sociologist Earl Babbie puts it best—

> This view of reality has guided most of human history. Our early ancestors all assumed that they saw things as they really were. In fact, this assumption was so fundamental that they didn't even see it as an assumption.

No cave-mom said to her cave-kid, '*Our tribe makes an assumption that evil spirits reside in the Old Twisted Tree.*' No, she said, '*Stay out of that tree or you'll turn into a toad!*' As humans evolved and became aware of their diversity, they came to recognize that others did not always share their views of things. Thus they may have discovered that another tribe didn't buy the wicked tree thing; in fact, the second tribe felt the spirits in the tree were holy and beneficial. The discovery of this diversity led members of the first tribe to conclude that '*some tribes I could name are pretty stupid.*' For them, the tree was still wicked and they expected some misguided people were going to be moving to Toad City.[1]

The **PreModern** view of life understood that there were gods and spirits, good and evil forces, earthly beings and "other" beings, all playing together to run the earth and keep it in balance. Which spirits were good or evil was a matter of conjecture, or even of personal, tribal, or religious preference. The point is that life was understood as the interplay of good and evil, good spirits and evil spirits, men and gods. A methodical, empirical, "scientific" approach to life didn't exist.[li] It was not that things that could not be explained otherwise were explained in terms of the gods or spirits; it was simply this was the way reality actually was. It was as simple as that.

If I may be allowed to highlight some of the previous chapters, yet to *not* reiterate them, everything changed around 1440, with the invention of Johannes Guttenberg's printing press. This one invention made possible the dissemination of ideas and information to the masses.[lii] Not unexpectedly, the first major printing job was the Bible (1454). Country churches and monasteries could all possess their own copy of The Book (if they could afford it, that is). Information in the form of books were available now to all, no longer to dwell in the private collections of the wealthier nobles and lords, or in city cathedrals. The printing press revolutionized Europe, literally. Many fiefdoms fell because of the new ideas that were being heard for the first time. The **Modern Era** had arrived. The biggest revolution brought on by the printing press occurred, not unexpectedly, in the Church. It seemed that the practice of the Christian faith in the fifteenth century found itself somewhat at odds with the presentation of the Christian faith found printed in the Bible. Problem here, eh!

But for all the contributions of the Modern Era, philosophically a majority of its proponents sought to do away with any belief in anything supernatural *whatsoever*. They saw religion as a kind of boogieman to explain things wherein rational, logical explanation supported by science, of course, was decidedly preferred. Belief in the supernatural was a kind of escapism for the unexplainable. Eventually, Modernists held, science would explain all— especially this "god" thing. In their worldview there was no god, no divine realm, no world of the spirits, no spiritual explanation for anything. That which is real is ONLY that which can be verified empirically or scientifically. Therefore, historical belief systems (Judeo-Christian, Islam, Ba'hai, etc.), primitive or developed, were to be considered, at best, quaint. More seriously, they were to be considered as *beliefs*, not beliefs-grounded-in-historical-fact. Though they might be interesting to study, they were generally considered to be irrelevant to "modern" thinking.

In this modern period, that which is real is no more than that which can be perceived by the 5 senses (sight, touch, taste, hear, smell), or through their extensions— microscopes, telescopes, etc. There is no place for the spiritual. Now, at the risk of being rebuffed, if I might offer a mild criticism— for all the insight that humankind can gain from our senses, this perspective seems somewhat simplistic, arrogant, and naïve. It seems simplistic because it makes *us* the final determiner of all things and that seems a bit arrogant to me, naïvely so. How dare we set our human race as the centerpiece of reality's table!? There has to be more. There has to be!

Somewhere in the twentieth century (the 1960s?), somewhere between the greatest of accomplishments and a profound loss of cultural trust and integrity, modernism caved in. Not entirely, but mostly. It caved in on itself by not offering comprehensive explanations of *what is*. Why? Because in its predilection to ignore the ethereal or spiritual, it could offer no explanation of the mysterious, the miraculous, or the unusual. Not everything is *exactly* verifiable through logic or empirical/scientific examination. For example, prove you love me. Well, okay, not me, but someone you do love. Can you prove the emotion? Through actions, yes; but they may be false. Through body chemistry, yes; but that may be just that— merely chemical. Now try to prove anger. Or go further by trying to prove concepts— God, insight, wisdom, ESP, forgiveness, truth. READY? Maybe not.

And that brings us to ***post*modernism**. Postmodernism flips the modern era on its head. In this postmodern era, there is little trust in "reality." ***What is reality***? What we see, touch, hear, believe? Who's to say what is real and what isn't? In many ways, it's the old question of historical epistemology, *how do you know anything*? WE know we know things…, but with some complications— the acceleration in the rate of change; the invention of virtual realities— technological images that are *real, really,* in a manner of speaking; the increased pace of western life. Though *knowable,* their inclusion in our *new* reality rendered *thinking* about real-life issues almost impossible. This postmodern era has played a joke on us. Taking off on Rene Descartes' classical *"Cogito; ergo sum."* (*I think; therefore I exist*), postmodernism's joke would then be *"Cogito; ergo sum— cogito."* (*I think; therefore I exist— I think.*). Certainty is certainly getting harder to be certain about. AIM…, maybe.

➤ *So, hello dahlink!* **Some Observations on Postmodernism—** What are some of the characteristics of living in a postmodern, yea verily, a *post*Christian world? Allow me to offer some observations, with commentary.

Defining postmodernism is, at best, a shot in the dark. It is defining nothingness. Nevertheless there are some observations I'd like to make. Many cultural observers feel safer describing postmodernism in terms of what it is *not*. That withstanding, I'll take the risk of being perceived as arrogant and try to describe it in a more positive light.

Postmoderns trust in their own judgment rather than in traditional authority or group consensus.

With all the breakdowns in relationships, *"downsizing"* (yeah right), and marginalizing of historical institutions (read *the church*), people in every age category have grown exceedingly untrusting of any authority or group. Instead they rather rely on their own judgments to guide them through life's ebbs & flows. Now this would be just fine if *all* individuals had the wisdom of the ages and the insight of sages. But alas, a sort of generational-regional tunnel vision sets in that misguides people to construct their own ideas and values about life, somewhat naively, based upon their own limited experiences. And they do so with little regard for "real-reality" or consideration of anyone else. The end result of this process breeds a form of individualism that is as much heroic as it is patronizing of any other person's views or life values. This portends a kind of a pretentious respectfulness, or possibly a form of *extreme individualism* that allows little room for true friendships, mutually trusting relationships, or longevity of commitments.

Postmoderns conform to generational peer values.

Seemingly in opposition to the previous observation, people in their early postmodern years (ages 18-38 or so) crave acceptance from their friends. Come to think of it, the TV show FRIENDS was a fair representation of this. (Watch the reruns on hulu.com.) Amidst the convolution of individualism and personal values there remains this hunger to be accepted. Though there is no general unilateral value system to which they adhere, there is, among postmoderns, a sense in which personal acceptance is a pinnacle value in itself. "*I gotta be me!*" I gotta belong too.

Later Postmoderns, known as Millennials (born 1982 & later), are upbeat, positive, and do <u>not</u> like to be compared with GenX (late Busters). Actually, they do not like to be labeled at all.

As with any large group about which we make generalizations, there comes a time when some classification is necessary; but *"All teens are…" "All postmoderns are…"* just doesn't work. This observation came to fruition through watching our own son and daughter grow and mature. Josh is four years older than Bethany but they grew up on different planets. In his early 20s Josh sometimes acted as if the world owed him a living. He hated to have to work to earn his way. He seemed mad much of the time. [Now don't get me wrong. This is one of the greatest guys in the world, one of the finest young men I know. But he had grown jaded within his generation by his own culture.] Josh is now an Executive Chef in an upscale restaurant in Colorado who volunteers to serve those less fortunate. We are so proud of him! Ru, (or "Bethany Ruth" as she is listed on her birth certificate)— is quite different than her brother. When she was in her late teens she took life by the horns and ran with it. And the only time she'd wear black (GenX color of non-definition) was when she wanted to look, well, really, um…, good. She was a determined, spry spirit.[liii] Today she runs benefit motor-cycle rides to raise money for specialized dogs for disabled veterans. This is the generation that will shape our world.[liv] FIRE! AIM!

Postmoderns seek meaning in service, doing, living-life vs. becoming couch potatoes.[lv]

Postmoderns want to be part of a thriving, working society. They want to make a difference in our world, they want to have an impact, leave a mark. They are not as rebellious as Boomers or later Busters (GenX); they are more prone to changing the ills of our society than they are willing to sit by and wait to see what happens. With no internal guidelines to provide perimeters for behavior, most postmoderns perceive life as a challenge to be figured out, conquered, and shaped. *"Somehow we're going to make this work"* is their mantra. No loss of energy here! Present-day Recession not-withstanding, they will rise to the challenge and overcome. Do *any of us* have a choice!?

Postmoderns are more visual than linear-sequential. They *"think"* in music. They *visualize* life more than they analyze it.

The emerging generation in this early twenty-first century have grown up with TV, DVDs, iPods, MP3s, Smartphones with Twitter; and 3D movies with special FX (effects) that are way beyond those of the 60s - 70s. All has evolved to produce a truly visually-connected generation. Imagining or *"imaging"* a reality makes more sense to them than stating that reality in a logical, linear form. Words have lost their reference points for most postmoderns; unless they represent a visual image in their mental milieu. Furthermore, thanks to the omnipresence of MTV, VH1, YouTube, and other such visual offerings of audio sound stuff, younger postmoderns actually *think* in music. They don't think of lyrics set to tunes or of a base beat, they *image* lyrics with images with sound and impressions; it's a package deal. Visual music: musical thought: virtual realities indistinguishable from the real-real. [Thus have we returned to an *image* based representation of the Christian gospel once again. Logical explanations simply do not *explain* our faith as adequately.]

From this musical imaging has flowed the visualization of life. Image reality and real-reality (a la philosopher Francis Schaeffer of the 1960s) merge to become an integrated whole. Their lives combine a series of snap shots that merge into one continuous digital flow. So if one of the images doesn't fit the flow, say divorce or death, a religious belief, or unfulfilled expectation, the whole image (life) goes off kilter.

Postmoderns create personal truth-value systems to make sense of life.

Having witnessed the recent moral failures in the church and the ethical failures of our government and sports figures, most postmoderns have lost virtually all their confidence in external institutions to provide them with a basis for making sense of life. So they look within themselves to create *truth-value systems* that need only work for one individual, themself. Often, as in institutional faith or values, they find others of like-mind and they bond with them intimately. Until betrayed. But ultimately, it is their inner being that forms the final shape of their personally-validated beliefs for determining action and attitude. *Oh, you believe in a god/God? That's great; I'm glad it works for you. My personal truths/beliefs work for me too.* 'Nough said.

Postmoderns value experience-based truth over propositionally proclaimed truth.

One of the byproducts of an exclusive reliance on personal truth-value systems is an eventual abhorrence for anything nailed down, especially written. Writing something down makes it binding, authoritative, final. Postmoderns want to move with the flow, the immediate, the next, and the synthesis of the experiences and insights of life. [Though written in the last century, James Redfield's 1994 novel THE CELESTINE PROPHESY is a classic example of this. May I suggest an MP3 Download, or a CD version for a l-o-n-g drive.] Propositionally stated truth usually flows out of institutional conclaves; they are not to be trusted. Personal experience is the producer of truth and Truth (if there really is the latter). A rational explanation of life just is not as satisfying or relevant as that which is experienced firsthand. Experience wins out over proposition.

Postmoderns seek a spirituality <u>within</u> as a Life-Reference point, rather than outside of their inner world.

Alongside the previous rejections and creations of inner value-truth systems there lies, not unexpectedly, a form of inner spirituality. In a conversation with one of my 20-something friends I was taken aback by his surprise that I *"needed a god"* to support my spiritual self. *"I don't feel any need for an external reference point for my spirituality. It comes from within."* Postmoderns have little confidence in historical religions, especially Christianity. Not only do religions write everything down, [If this is true, Protestantism is in trouble with Bible-centric focus] it seems insistent on the supremacy of *words* over life. (You can see how this might affect the Christian's propensity to bring everything back to the Bible as the final authority. *Words* being merely representative of life— not the life itself.) Thus the church makes little sense to them. From a postmodern perspective *"It's all about money and peer approval. Christians don't seem capable of living life."* So postmoderns, late GenXers and Millennials turn within, again, to find their anchor in inward spirituality with no external reference point (*read God*). And you dare not challenge it.

Postmoderns resonate with transparent, caring people whose lives reflect an inner integrity.

Well, frankly, who doesn't like these kind of people? One of the greatest things about postmoderns is that they are some of the most congenial people you ever want to meet. They have a lightness about them that is infectious. Whether it is from some inner urge to escape and play or a zest for experiences that radiate with life they inspire those around them, even Boomers (who are often prone to a methodical melodrama). But this generation doesn't put up with any crap; they don't play the games of social niceties. They expect those they meet to be up front with them, honest about life, open with their ideas, even when it might elicit disagreement. They resonate with positive, upbeat, transparent people in *any* age category. (Informing them that they are *sinners before a Holy God* is NOT an understandable starting point. So then..., what would be?)

Earning their trust is just the same as in any generation; but to earn the trust of someone who is already suspicious of your Modernist stance (your linear-sequential perception base) will take some work. The only way I have found that postmoderns come to trust is if you are honest and transparent before them. No games, no false fronts, no condescension: honesty, openness, transparency. That's it. Anything less, any slip ups, and you are back to square one.

Postmoderns are very picky about how and with whom they spend their free time.

Got any free time with nothing to do? Right, neither do I. So also with the postmodern set. Life is f-u-l-l, VERY FULL! Every given chunk of time is packed with work, play, and appointments with whomever; food shopping, buying, going, going, going more and more and gone. The work-force set has very little time: take a number. The college/grad school set can't pack any more into their lives. And the junior/senior high school crew use the calendar sections on their cell-phones. Get the picture? To get into the life of anyone in the FaceBook/texting/Twitter generation you'd better have some great credentials and rock solid credibility. Otherwise, you're on the *"have a good-one, see ya later"* list.

➤**So… !?** Now, given all of the above, how can the Christian message ever make it into the lives of people who don't trust traditional institutions, *especially* the church, don't relate to linear/sequential propositional Truth, who construct value systems based on their own experiences (exclusively), who don't like the arrogant authority of written codes and beliefs, and who find a spirituality within themselves with no sense of a need for any external reference point? AND they don't have any time for you. Does the word *conundrum* come to mind? Hummm.

Well, please forgive me, but this conundrum excites me! What a great time to be alive! What a phenomenal challenge! What a great time to be a Christian in western society! We are living in what many commentators are now referring to as a postChristian era— a culture that thinks of institutional Christianity as having been tried already— and found wanting— an era where the Christian truth-value system has less effect than it did a millennium ago, even a century ago. So much has changed. If you are a Christian, and you are alive, you have an opportunity to make one of the greatest contributions to human history— to participate in reshaping the interface between the Christian world and our postmodern-postChristian culture. You've gotta love it!

But just how does the church of Jesus Christ make any difference in a world of people who don't even sense a need for any kind of relationship with Him? Ah, glad you asked. Because that's where we move in the next chapter. The present western cultural expressions of Christian faith were developed largely in the period we know as the Modern Period, following the establishment of the European states, within the context of the supremacy of the human ascendancy and the scientific method— ideas which were disseminated through the printing press across Europe and around the world. So in the next chapter we need to design the expressions and shape of our Christian faith in our rapidly evolving, and postChristian, society. Hopefully, it will also challenge you to rethink the way you think about your own Christian faith and how you express it to others. So, read on. It's time for more fun in the mind of faith.

"Cogito ergo sum." (I think therefore I exist.)

—Rene Decartes

"Cogito ergo sum..., cogito."

(I think therefore I exist..., I think.)

—unknown, I think

Chapter 4: Rethinking Thinking:
the *non-propositional* nature of truth.

By now you're probably thinking—

"Okay, are you suggesting that the way Christians have thought about their faith for hundreds of years no longer fits this postmodern culture? And what about this non-propositional Truth stuff? This is getting more than a little weird."

Actually, all Christians throughout history have articulated their faith differently, depending upon individual cultural setting. Some are more experiential than theological; some are more communally based than hierarchical; some have a minimal understanding of the theology of their faith-but hold a deep commitment to Christ in what they *do* know. So as we rethink the thinking about our faith in North American culture, we must to be careful to not create an historical assumption that things *"have always been the same."* We must to be willing to reexamine our present-day view of the Christian faith and how it is expressed and understood. Over time I have learned to not be so attached to my words. I even joke about it— *"Hey I could be wrong; I haven't made my mistake for this year yet!"* Nonetheless, to challenge the process of thinking does seem, even to me, a tad arrogant. I do so with a great sense of personal fear and large regret that a great era has past and could be lost forever. The Modern Era has given the world so much—from consolidated nations [*mostly*], to incredible scientific discoveries and never imagined medical breakthroughs, to established theological constructs for our faith, to world trade, and to even space exploration. During the Modern era the battle between religion and science won and lost, lost and won, on both sides.

One important point before we move on. In *science*, *truth* is *discovered* as observable data drawn from experiments that can be repeated with the same results. [Actually, that explains a huge difference in the pre-modern and modern eras. If something could be repeated with the same result every time, then there could be no "spirit" acting upon it.] Hypotheses are then drawn from these experiments. The *Scientific Method* refers to a body of techniques for investigating phenomena, acquiring new knowledge, or reexamining and integrating previous knowledge. To be termed scientific, a method of inquiry must be based on gathering observable, empirical and measurable evidence subject to specific principles of reasoning.[lvi] However, scientific method is not a simple recipe: it requires intelligence, imagination, and creativity.[lvii]

¿CLUELESS CHRISTIANITY?

➤ *"Two different worlds…, we live in two different worlds."*— Now it seems, at best, we live in a strangely dichotomized amalgam between religious *faith* and scientific *certainty*; religion for those who need subjective truth; science for those who need to feel "safer" with a more objective truth. Doesn't say much for any cohesiveness to life, does it? [In *philosophy* there is a distinction drawn between *certainty* and *certitude.* The former is absolute, irrefutably real: the latter is hypothesis, as close as possible to certainty, but not quite absolutely verifiable.] If anything, the unified thinking of the modern era (also referred to as *modernity*) has given way to a kind of *fractured* view of life. One wherein ideas don't necessarily have to make sense, don't have to fit together, don't even have to have cohesion to themselves. Beliefs, intuitions, and moods are *assembled* to create a workable-life relationship, regardless of their basis or reflection of any reality. Postmodern people weave a web of thoughts and ideas and life philosophies that don't necessarily need to hang together in any interconnected manner. They just *are*— existing in-and-of themselves, to be accessed when needed to prove a point, solve a mental problem, or cope with a stressful life situation. Other than that, the ideas, intuitions, reflections or beliefs sit unattended and dormant while life goes on, waiting for something to happen (as opposed to making something happen) to awaken a need for their resurgence. [Ou-blah-de, ou blah da… .[lviii]]

In a very real sense the whole process of thinking has been *rethought.* In the logical universe of the Modern era, things had to make sense *logically*, supporting the discoveries of science. That is no longer the case: our trust in reason and logic to provide us with the answers to life's riddles and mysteries is, for the most part, gone (albeit some still believe "Science" will answer *ALL* our questions about life..., eventually). Still, there is a logic to postmodern thought; as long as that logic is not based in—

$$A = B$$

$$B = C$$

Therefore— $A = C$

Postmodernism's "logic" is different. It is based not in sequential reasoning but rather in life experience, in intuition, in mood. In reflecting on Richard Weaver's 1948 book *IDEAS HAVE CONSEQUENCES*, Ken Myers, founder of MARS HILL AUDIO, noted these ships passing in the night. Starting with a quote from Weaver's book—

> *Every man participating in a culture has three levels of conscious reflection: his specific ideas about things, his general beliefs or convictions, and his metaphysical dream of the world.*

> *Many Christian apologists who talk about worldviews seem to have something less fundamental in mind than Weaver's "metaphysical dream of the world." They write as if worldview construction was simply a matter of deductive reasoning, moving from major premises derived from Biblical and theological sources to conclusions about human nature, history, art, politics, family life,*

> *and so on. These apologists either ignore or*
> *deny the power of the imaginative and*
> *affective matrix within which such deductive*
> *work takes place.*

Ken Myers comments… ,

> This is why so many champions of
> historic orthodoxy and traditional morality are
> stymied by the postmodern mood. They
> assume that postmodernism represents a
> defiantly capricious embrace of the irrational.
> In fact, the specific ideas about things and the
> general beliefs or convictions that characterize
> the postmodern sensibility are quite
> reasonable expressions of a metaphysical
> dream of the world that has been coalescing
> since the beginning of the modern period 500
> years ago.
>
> The publicists for the postmodern
> spirit will not be defeated by better, louder, or
> more popular arguments. <u>They didn't come to
> their position by a deductive process and they
> won't be defeated by one.</u>"[lix]

[Underlining, for emphasis, is mine.] Myers observation is that in this postmodern era, the modern thought process has been, well, rethought. Postmodern *thought* is based not on A=B=C deductive sequencing, but rather on an *intuition*, on our responses to life situations, to art, to social ideas, to political positioning, and so on. So for the Christian world to challenge postmodern thought in traditional apologetic terms, whether historical/evidential, presuppositional, or cultural, is to miss their point-of-reference entirely. Our ships just passed in the night. While we must still seek to point the postmodern individual to the Truth, our lack of realization that *that* concept for them (the idea of Truth existing in and of itself, standing objectively outside of their daily life experiences), seems arrogantly crazy to them. Or, as postmodern philosopher Richard Rorty asserts, *truth is made rather than found*. In an article written by Albert Mohler Jr., President of Southern Baptist Theological Seminary in Louisville, we learn—

> What has been understood and affirmed
> as truth, argue the postmodernists, is nothing
> more than a convenient structure of thought
> intended to oppress the powerless. Truth is
> not universal, for every culture establishes
> its own truth. Truth is not objectively real,
> for all truth is merely constructed—as Rorty
> stated, truth is *made,* not *found*.[lx]

Therefore the Christian idea of the *revelation of Truth* being given to us by a God who knew we couldn't figure it out by just looking around, seems absolutely ridiculous. Truth is not *discovered*, as Christians believe; "it is *made* as we need it," asserts the postmodernist.

➢ **Think about it**— If you updated this *thinking* and applied it to any religion, what you might find is a religion not entirely devoid of rational thought, but one where rational explanations of reality took their proper place *in back of* actual experiences. It *then* interpreted them in light of religious thought, revelation, or tradition.[lxi] For the past 350-500 years Western

¿CLUELESS CHRISTIANITY?

Christianity has been a reflection of modern, logical thought patterns. These thought patterns focused on "*defending the faith*," debating the opposition, and developing a cohesive world-and-life view which overshadowed the vibrant work of God in our midst. We have raised the Bible to such a divine level as to virtually eclipse the God of the Bible with the *words* that tell us about him! The wine glass has replaced the glory of the Wine.

Please hear me out on this point. Evangelicals are "*people of the Book*," we proudly proclaim. Not, mind you, that I am *not* a student of the Bible myself. It is the grass-roots of my faith sticking through my toes. It is the one, solely reliable source for Christians to learn about their faith, its foundations in Judaism, its founding, its history, and its implications for living before the God Who made us in this world He created. It is Truth revealed in writing. The Bible is no less, I repeat, than God telling us things He knew we would not be able to figure out from merely looking around. It sets forth the precepts, principles, and practice of what it means to truly be a follower of Jesus Christ. It is 66 individual books, letters, historical documents, collections of poetry, and future prophesies woven together over 4,000 years by 40 ± writers with one central theme— the redemption and fulfillment of the human race by the God who created us. That's no small feat. The Bible's internal consistencies, cohesiveness and congruency alone attest to its veracity. It is a book like no other ever written.

But as much as the Bible portrays the mighty works of God throughout history it is not the end-all of end-alls. When I was in college I majored in philosophy (duh). My specialization was *language philosophy*. I learned that, in any language, *words have referents*. That is, the word points to the object, the idea, the subject. It is NOT the object itself, it is the sign, the symbol, or the pictogram which represents the object. For example, when I say *cow*, your mind forms an image of the real thing. I do not know whether your mind's *cow* is black, brown, Guernsey or what. That would require you to ask "What kind of cow?" But you would have the basic cow image-idea down pat. Applying this simple linguistic principle to the Bible, it can be stated that the Bible, with its historical sections, poetry, prophesies, and letters, is the *tag* that points us to God. It describes God for us; it clarifies His conditions for us to live on this planet, it sets forth His rules of protection for human relationships; it informs us of the consequences of our actions, here and later; it sets forth Truth as God defines it.

So, in one sense, the Bible, the Word of God, *is* the Truth; but in another sense it is *only* the Truth-Tag, the reference-work, the word, that points us all to the object of The Word— Jesus Christ, God Himself. *"And the Word became flesh and dwelt among us."*[lxii] In the modern era, with a common acceptance of logical-sequential thought, this simple observation was not particularly important; but in a postmodern era, where the logical process has moved from its basis in sequential word-tag-reference explanations of stuff to a basis in life-experience and our responses to them, this distinction becomes eminently critical. To the point, the nature of Truth itself is shifting from a rational/logical-sequential propositional-base to an individual-experience one. Truth is moving from an exclusively *propositional* position to one that is far more *personal,* far more *individualistic*. NOT, as some would have us believe, a personal, individualistic rendition of reality; but, rather, a position reflective of one's *personality* and *preferences*. Lost yet? This is important, so stay with me.

One of the definers of humanity is, according to the Bible, the way in which we hold the Truth within us. Romans 1 describes our attachment to the Truth best when it says—

> *For the wrath of God is revealed from*
> *heaven against all ungodliness and*
> *unrighteousness of men, who suppress the*
> *truth in unrighteousness, because what may be*
> *known of God is manifest (obvious) in them,*
> *for God has shown it to them.[lxiii]*

The word translated here as *suppress* is made up of two Greek words (κατ–εχοντων) that come together to mean "holding-down with-myself." Postmodern people embrace the Truth of God within, but then push it down deep, suppress it, in their consciousness. The point is that the Truth must first be within them (God made it known to them) for them to suppress it. Though people suppress it, it is still there. So although postmoderns may not acknowledge the Truth within, we can count on people having some connection to internal Truth that God built into them all along.[lxiv]

Before I go on it must be stated that no thinking Christian can concede that Truth is created (versus discovered), as Rorty would have us believe. That would make Truth truths and each individual an author of their own truths, irrespective of others. Actually, Truth/truth resides both inside and outside the realm of human creation. Discoveries throughout history have "created" new truths— the earth is actually round, not flat, the earth is not the center of universe with everything revolving around it, the speed of light (186,000 mps) is not the fastest thing out there, women can multitask much better than men, etc. More precisely, even these truths have not been created after all: they've been discovered. In the same way, humans need to *discover* the rest of the truths God has set in operation to keep the universe from falling apart. Some of those truths are not so easily discoverable. They remain hidden in the depths of our oceans and in the far reaches of our universe. In time, we may uncover them. But they are the discoverable truths. There is another kind of Truth not found within the created, discoverable realm. These truths God has clarified in the life experiences, stories, poetry, history, correspondence, and prophesies found in the Christian Scriptures— the Bible. Yet they also need to be discovered, and applied to life for it to work correctly, smoothly; for human life to function properly within the context of discoverable truth, the earth, and the universe.

With this perspective in mind we can now move to the main point of this chapter— namely, that the essential nature of Truth is not primarily *propositional*, but *personal*; and, it is also quite *powerful*. To find support for this audacious assertion please grab a Bible and read the words of Jesus Himself.

> [1] *"Let not your heart be troubled; you believe in God, believe also in Me.* [2]*In My Father's house are many mansions; if it were not so, I would have told you. I go to prepare a place for you.* [3]*And if I go and prepare a place for you, I will come again and receive*

*you to Myself; that where I am, there you may
be also. ⁴And where I go you know, and the
way you know."*

*⁵Thomas said to Him, "Lord, we do
not know where You are going, and how can
we know the way?"*

*⁶Jesus said to him, "I am the way, the
truth, and the life. No one comes to the Father
except through Me.*

*⁷ "If you had known Me, you would
have known My Father also; and from now on
you know Him and have seen Him."*

*⁸Philip said to Him, "Lord, show us
the Father, and it is sufficient for us."*

*⁹Jesus said to him, "Have I been with
you so long, and yet you have not known Me,
Philip? He who has seen Me has seen the
Father; so how can you say, "Show us the
Father'? ¹⁰Do you not believe that I am in the
Father, and the Father in Me? The words that
I speak to you I do not speak on My own
authority; but the Father who dwells in Me
does the works. ¹¹Believe Me that I am in the
Father and the Father in Me, or else believe
Me for the sake of the works themselves."ˡˣᵛ*

Jesus starts out with an assertion that if you believe in God,
believe also in Me. Using Modernism's logic, A=B, Jesus =

God. Belief in one is belief in the other [And people say Jesus never claimed to be God. O please!]. Or, if you will, using Postmodernism's *truth is created* principle, it seems that Jesus had just created a new Truth for His disciples— *if you have seen me you have seen the Father*. But then He continues with the most revealing revelation of all— *I am the way, the truth, and the life*. Thomas has just told Jesus that they were a bit lost; they do not know the way that He is going; they didn't know their own way, either. *"Lord, we don't know where you are going, and how can we know the way*?" Jesus' startling reply is that HE, Himself, is the way. In short, Thomas, you do not need to know the way, just follow Me. But Jesus adds two more revelations for our surprise— *I am also the truth, and the life*. So we arrive at last— the main point of this chapter: namely, that Jesus redefines Truth as primarily *personal*, and not *propositional*. Now this really *IS* new! Well, at least to us it's new.

This *new* truth should put a whole new fresh slant on *understanding* what truth is. Although it can be stated, written, or spoken, it is not primarily "understandable;" it is not primarily something to be analyzed, categorized, pigeon-holed, and systematized. This *new* Truth *is* personal; it is Jesus Christ, now, in relationship with us. Before you criticize this assumptive jump to "in relationship with us," think about this. Truth need not exist outside of the mind of man (no gender slam intended). Truth was developed for our comprehension, our convenience, our comfort, our conceptual framework. Truth exists for our minds in the form of propositions, statements about the world the way it actually is. Truth exists for our Being, for our existence as Humanity, and for our Individuality, as Persons. So if you would know the Truth (which will set you free, as I recall), then you must come to know the *Person* of Jesus, not merely the information about Him.

> **Propositional, yet personal, yet propositional—the proper positioning of Truth**— Now, if you will consent to the assertion that Truth is primarily *personal* and not primarily *propositional*, doesn't it follow, in a modernistic logical kind of way, that Truth needs to be found in relationship? [OK, Truth must be partially *propositional* because we need words to explain the reality. But the reality that the words represent is the proper possessor of Truth— Jesus Christ.] In the modern framework, people relate to one another = God relates to people = therefore, people relate to God. In the postmodern framework, truth about life can only be created in relationship with the God who created life. We will find that we actually discovered what God had created for our minds and hearts all along— to know the truth we need, indeed, to know Him Who is the Source of all Truth. Even postmoderns, who do not believe there is any meta-narrative, no ultimate story that is necessary to comprehend life, when they come to life's serious questions, life, birth, and death, even they *wonder*. Wonder...— in every sense of the word. Why? Because life cannot be explained fully from a position exclusively framed inside itself. It truly does need an external reference point. And that involves *mystery*. Modernists hated mystery. It was *pre*modern, primitive, simplistic, archaic. For the modernist all life could be explained scientifically, empirically, given time. Postmoderns hate the constant classification of life into little empirically categorized compartments— the scientific method. (Many postmoderns live dichotomized lives. On the one hand they may be scientists, professors, doctors, or involved in a

profession that utilizes the scientific method. But in their personal lives they live by a totally isolated, individually-based, postmodern set of rules.) With very little exception, both Modernists and Postmodernists hate Christianity because— 1) It reeks of mystery, of the unknown, the unexplainable, and, 2) Because it claims that Truth (True-Truth) exists outside of our human control. Worse yet, Christian Truth does not submit to the dictates of our logic. It always existed, and therefore is not created by us. It must be discovered through committed seeking and through living life to the fullest. And when it is discovered, it will not be found in any systematic compilation of theology, or in some intuitive projection of our feeling or being; no, it will be discovered that Truth resides in a Person, Jesus Christ. If this doesn't make Christianity the strangest religion on the planet then I don't know what does.

➤ **Body Parts—** One of my close friends is a massage therapist, Stacy. We met when she was a student in a school of massage therapy and I was a volunteer, well, a body-part, a guinea pig for practice. At the end of our first massage she placed one hand over my chest and the other over my forehead to *impress* her positive energy into me to ensure the effectiveness of the last one hour massage. In just under 5 seconds her hands flew off of me and she leaned down to whisper at the side of my head *"What are you?"* I responded *"You tried to infuse your positive energy into me, didn't you?" "Yes." "It wouldn't go in, would it?" "No, it wouldn't. Why? I've never had this happen before."* I told her I would tell her later; that I felt uncomfortable talking about this lying under just a bed-sheet in a room with 20 other massage therapists respective body-parts, and supervisors standing around. When we met later I explained to Stacy that I was a Christian, but that I was not one of the game players, the smiley-plastic, happy-all-the-time kind... . I was a real Christian, with access to more power than she could ever imagine. Stacy responded that she didn't believe in a personal deity as a Being and that she didn't feel that she needed an external reference point to be spiritual; her spirituality, she graciously explained, lay exclusively within herself.

In the twelve years that we have been friends, Stacy has come to believe— 1) that spirituality in fact does need an external reference point, 2) that God actually is a Being, maybe even a Person, 3) that there is some merit to Christianity and it's moral, ethical directives, and 4) she was surprised that she liked me because most Christians are judgmentalists who have lost the ability to listen and to learn anything from anyone who doesn't agree with them in the first place. I was honored.

What is interesting about this relationship with Stacy is that in that same 12 year time period she has fallen in love, married, divorced, fallen in love again, and again, and has grown tired of "the quest for truth." "*I just want to get on with my life and live it.*" But whenever Stacy and I get together, we continue to talk about trust, faith in a personal God, and how one comes to know the Truth. Never once did I impose a logical argument on her; never once did I try to convince her that I was right and that she was wrong; never once did I try to *win her* over to the Christian side. No. Instead, I let her see the person of Jesus at work in me, with all its challenges, with my failures and sins, and with my love for Jesus and her. I cared for her as a person, I the Christian, she the Hindu-Muslimatheist-Jew pragmatist; I the male, with a clean above board love; she the woman, who found in me a man she could trust, "even though I was Christian" (she was oft amazed). My job in her life, and your job in the lives of your friends who are not Christians, is the same— to be visible expressions, bodily *resemblances* of the Truth, of the Person of Jesus Christ, with His principles for living life being vitally demonstrated through us. Stacy's conversion is not my business; conversion is God's business. My business, our business, is to live open, realistic, vibrant lives and to be viable demonstrations of a God-linked person.

Not very analytical, is it? Not very satisfying, logically, in terms of defending the faith through rational argument, point and counter point; neither does it involve a systematic presentation of the gospel. (That comes later, to explain the work that God is already doing in a person's life.) What it does involve is—

a. a sensitivity to the person
b. a sensitivity to the Spirit of God at work (or not yet at work) in them

and

c. a trusting patience that God will perform His miracles of grace in them in His own sweet time.

You see, the communication of our faith is not so much about the transference of information in *propositional form* as it is about reflecting the living *presence* of a Person through *living form*. I know we would all say this, but very few of us actually practice it. We are much more comfortable with nailed down versions of Truth that are logical, simple, and reasonable. So instead, we fall back on gospel outlines to explain the propositions of belief, when more often than not, what the person wants to see is evidence of the effect that the Person of Jesus Christ has on our daily lives. Postmoderns have *rethought thinking* and decided that Christianity doesn't bear much thinking about. Thinking, for them, is the *reflection* on life experience that lays the foundation for making sense of what comes next. In a very real sense, it is *truth being created in process*. What a surprise it will be later in life when they find out it was actually *Truth being discovered* all along.

➤ **"I have the POWER!"**— When our son Joshua was very young he enjoyed watching a TV cartoon called HE-Man™, a hulky warrior type who fought to rid the universe of evil. He did so by cooperating with the ultimate source of power in the universe, taking it into himself through his really cool warrior's sword. To gain access to this power, He-Man would stand on some high pinnacle and cry aloud "I have the power!" and a bolt of lightning would surge out of the air into his body through his up-stretched sword. Then he would go off to banish the world of its invaders. Our son Josh would mimic He-Man's behavior by lifting his modern wooden-plank sword into the air while shouting "I have the power."

Not incongruously, the Bible also compares the Word of God to a sword— a two edged sword capable of dividing soul and spirit.

> *For the word of God is living and*
> *active. Sharper than any double-edged sword,*
> *it penetrates even to dividing soul and spirit,*

> *joints and marrow; it judges the thoughts and*
> *attitudes of the heart.*[lxvi]

But is it the Word of God, the Bible, or is it the Word of God, Jesus Christ to which this passage refers? Is it even important we know? The point is that the Word of God, propositional or personal, has power to clarify reality; it/He has the right to weigh our thoughts, our actions, and to exact judgment upon us all.

But what if an individual doesn't accept the Bible as the Word of God? What if the Bible's assumptions about reality are not his/hers? Can the words of the Bible have impact on that person? That's where the other side of Truth comes in— its *personal* side. It is the Person of Jesus Christ who brings life to an individual, not the Bible; it is the Person of Jesus Christ who empowers a person to turn to Him for life, not the Bible. Yet one influence cannot have sufficient affect without the other— Christ, the Word of God, empowers: the Bible, the Word of God, clarifies what has just taken place. If anything, the Christian life is about being empowered by God to live a life that is in keeping with the principles *for* life God has set down for us— the Bible.

So which came first, the chicken or the egg? No matter— have eggs for breakfast, chicken wings for dinner. You need both. (Personally, I like a little salsa with my eggs. Life needs a little spicing up.) And the Christian life, if not empowered by God, is reduced to mere words. Faith without spice. Religion without life. Life without spice— no way.

So on one hand we have the Bible, the propositional explanations of what God is doing everywhere. [Note— The

Bible was written in stories, songs (Psalms), historical documents (Pentateuch, Prophets, Gospels), poetry, personal correspondence (Epistles), & summaries.] On the other hand we have Jesus Christ, the embodiment of the Godhead here on earth; the Word becoming flesh, taking on human form. The two together can empower people to embrace intelligent, meaningful lives, contributing to the needs of the saints and healing the heartaches and pain of the world. We dare not merely distribute Bibles as if they will magically empower people to live God-honoring lives: we cannot subjectively will someone to *experience* the presence of Christ without some explanation as to what is going on inside them. We need both. But whereas *faith without works is dead* (doesn't work) neither do explanations of Truth empower a person without the power and presence of the Person of Christ in their life. In the end, Truth is primarily embodied in the Person of Jesus Christ. But without the Bible shedding light on this reality the Truth cannot be known.

But there is yet one more ingredient to consider in our mix of Truth with life— Passion! Read on.

Fun Stuff—

1. Try to think, "I am a Christian." without using words. "Image" it.

2. If you just read this section in summer, try to feel the first snow-flake of winter on your tongue. If it's winter, try to imagine basking in the warm sun on a beach or out in the desert.

3. If you are Christian explain your faith to someone without using any Christianeze words. If you are not Christian try explaining Christianity to someone who has no understanding of it. [Note- The person cannot be another Christian.]

4. Kiss someone. Explain the kiss. Kiss them again. Explain the kiss in other ways than using words. Kiss them again. Okay, again. Enough already. Savor.

5. Try thinking of a portrait (Renaissance, preferably), an emotion, in color, with smells.

6. Project yourself back in time, to a memory. Experience as much of the memory as you can— place, temperature, surroundings, scent, emotion.

Further Fun Stuff (for group-games)

Distinguish between philosophy and religion. Under religion, separate out written precept, personal rightness with God (satisfaction of requirements) and the ritual expression of that religion. Ritual can either represent personal rightness or replace it.

Discuss how Christian Truth is imbued with POWER in the Person of Jesus, unlike any other religion. Take a risk and say that the Bible is the Word of God, propositionally; yet it is only that which explains (puts feet on) the TRUTH that is Jesus (yes, it is mystical, vs. empirical). People want mystical relationships today, especially with a god…; how about our God, Jesus?

Other re-definings of Truth by various beliefs and religions:

FYI—

Buddhism—

Four Noble Truths:

1. All of life is marked by suffering.

2. Suffering is caused by desire and attachment.

3. Suffering can be eliminated.

4. Suffering is eliminated by following the Noble Eightfold Path.

Noble Eightfold Path:

1. Right beliefs

2. Right aspirations

3. Right speech

4. Right conduct

5. Right livelihood

6. Right effort

7. Right mindfulness

8. Right meditational attainment

¿CLUELESS CHRISTIANITY?

Redefining Spirituality.

Questions—

1. To what extent is spiritually defined by visible, external practices?

2. How can one be "monk-like" and move smoothly through a postmodern, postChristian society?

3. Given the Creation/Fall/Redemption/Fulfillment rubric, are there more than 4 points necessary to a "gospel" presentation? Or less? Or, maybe something totally different?

4. What will it take to move the Christian community in North America out of the mental stranglehold that Modernist-thinking seems to hold over them?

*"Nothing worthwhile is ever accomplished
without passion."*

— fortune cookie: Panda East, Amherst, MA

Chapter 5: Of Passion & Propositions:
growing a non-balanced faith.

When I was in the final stages of producing my doctoral dissertation I ate out a lot. Escapism, most likely. During one such luncheon at Panda East, a fine Chinese restaurant in Amherst, MA, I opened a fortune cookie which read— *Nothing worthwhile is ever accomplished without <u>passion</u>*. I thought of some of the great names throughout history for whom this proverb has proven true— Hammurabi, Moses, Alexander the Great, Jesus, Christopher Columbus, John Harrison, Albert Einstein, Orville and Wilbur Wright, Vladimir Ilyich Lenin, Thomas Edison, Mother Teresa, Ronald Reagan, Osama bin Ladin, even Barrack Obama— all were driven by passion and tenacity to accomplish something beyond themselves. Yet, the church in North America seems driven by balance— balance in life, in our families, in faith, in our behavior— moderation in all things, no rocking the boat, no swimming against the current. Straight-forward, rational explanations of life should suffice to renew the mind and focus our resolve. It is almost as if being out of balance, off-center, or slightly extreme in any way is viewed as the real threat to the church and to the stability of our individual faith.

But if Truth is *primarily* personal (though certainly not exclusively), found in the Person of Jesus Christ, there are some very critical implications for us that impact our Christian lives, balanced or otherwise, and how we demonstrate our faith to others. If point and counter-point propositional arguments no longer dominate the apologetic of our faith, or even sustain the curiosity of the normal Western cultural person, then maybe it's time to express our faith in ways not so idealistic or rational..., or not even so balanced.

As you continue reading you will detect a couple shifts. The first shift is one of approach. We move from the historical analysis of the previous chapters to a thoughtful consideration of our present day dilemmas; from the BIG strokes throughout history, to a specific manifestation of *one* era, one geographic location, one time, one individual—Jesus Christ. For in His life we can find the bridge between the preModern, Modern, and postModern perspectives on what it means to live *in context* within a specific culture. What I hope to do is to persuade you of the importance of living your Christian life as Jesus lived His— in the context of whatever world you find yourself in. Right up front I want to admit that this chapter (okay, the whole book) is a polemic for us to grow a non-balanced faith, a passionate faith, an exuberant faith that is in love with Jesus Christ and with the people around us. The *personality* of our faith must outshine its propositions to give its Truth a proper *context*.

The second shift you will experience is simply one of writing style. The first chapters were data-weighted, historical, linear/sequential, and logical (A=B, B=C, therefore A=C, remember?). They were analytical; they stated a problem, built a case, substantiated an argument. Most of us feel safest in the world of rational thought and logical argument. Most Christians feel safer in a world where rational argument, logic and words prevail. Why? Because the Western articulation of our faith was formulated not in the preModern Era that had an understanding of the spirit, of mystery and the heart, but in the Modern era, where logical consistency, scientific verification, and systematic cohesiveness prevailed. But modernism's presuppositional perceptions do not ring as true within this postmodern era; nor do modernism's assumed stances of the Bible as *primarily* a *systematic* presentation of Truth (excluding, of course, the incredible logic/debate style of the Apostle Paul). The language of the Bible, predominantly, is one of story, of history, of pictures and images; they each work together to paint us a grand portrait— they declare a passion for God and of a passion for life. They lay down laws for the functioning of a society. They raise real-life problems that required real-life solutions. They burst forth in song in praise of God Almighty. They give us a glimpse of the struggles of the early Christian movement through the Gospels, through circulated correspondence, and individual epistles. Far too long have we limited the expression of our faith to the logical/sequential analysis of the Euro-western hemisphere of theological constructs. We have raised the Truth of the Bible above its context-in-life. A saying I come across constantly is— *"right beliefs produce right actions."* Have you heard it, read it? Sounds right on, doesn't it? But in real-life it doesn't quite work out that way. You and I know many individuals who claim the name of Christ, who believe the right stuff (or at least say they do), and whose lives reflect little of Christian character, compassion, or concern for the Truth.

Contrarily, there is the opposite, popular belief— *you can't trust your emotions*. As if emotions are less reliable than logical/sequential thinking. The assumption is that emotions are fickle, not as locked down as logical, rational thought process. The logical thought process *can* be locked down more than emotion. Emotions, by definition, shift more readily than belief systems. But what good is one without the other!? It would be comparable to releasing a chemical analysis of *kissing*. So now you understand the complexity of kissing better; and this is helpful..., how!?! Where do we come up with this stuff— for a need for cohesiveness, control over minutia, consistency, for a need to believe that people always act on their convictions? [Sociologists have tested it – we don't. Even in church attendance.] I don't..., always, do you? Remember, we all *sin*; we are all, at best, consistently inconsistent. Did this idea come from some male-ego approach that emotions are exclusively feminine and can't be trusted? Men supposedly are the "logical thinkers." Somehow this makes us more stable, more consistent. O please, spare me the stereotypes. Let's face it, men are afraid to be out of control; and it is easier to be in control of *thought* than it is our *emotions*. Who *is* the weaker sex?

This will probably flip me from the frying pan into the fire, but it is time we examined these two positions in light of Scripture. After a great deal of scrutiny, I must admit that I do not find a lot of *only believe-ism* in the Bible. We are far too syncretistic (def.- the merging of contrary beliefs or divergent philosophies) a species for anything that simplistic. But there isn't a lot of touchy-feeling stuff either. There is, however, a significant amount of blending of emotion and understanding, of heart and mind in Scripture. The Modern Era Church— it emphasized the mind over the emotions. In past centuries we have somehow equated *belief* in Christ with follow-through in life. A fair assumption I suppose. In the Bible, Hebrews 11 does say that our actions will validate our faith. [Simple observation will find many people living by Christian actions, which may or may not be representative of inner faith.]. Yet the dichotomy remains; over the past 75 years it has plunged the church in North America into a lot of trouble. People who have prayed "the sinners prayer," or come forward to an altar or to the front at a Billy Graham Crusade and confessed their sins and said in some form *"I believe in Jesus Christ as my personal savior"* are told they are Christians and that they should attend a church somewhere. You and I have met people who believe they are Christians because they have, at some time in their life, complied with one of these. But not everyone comes to faith in Christ in the same way. In my own church, as in many churches I would presume, there is a large banner running the length of the back of the sanctuary— TO KNOW CHRIST AND TO MAKE HIM KNOWN. Now hear me out on this one. I find no fault with this banner. But I do find it curious that it seems to be all about the knowing. It is assumed that everything else will flow out of that, even the *"making him known"* part. There are many churches that excel in fulfilling the first part of that equation: teaching their members to know a great deal *about* their faith. But I find very few exerting any effort whatsoever in training their members to fulfill the second part: making Him known (to those *outside* the church). Most sorrowfully, our interface with those outside the church has become solely an effort to pass on the information about Christ, rather than any genuine immersion of ourselves within the evil culture.

¿CLUELESS CHRISTIANITY?

A cursory reading of any church history will bring to the fore the dangers of an overly-emotional religious expression. There were extremes in the early church, in parts of the Sacred Heart of Jesus Movement in Southern France, in early Pentecostalism, in some of the Sawdust Trail practices, and in the Jesus Movement of the early 1970s. In contrast, the emotions were deemed as an integral part of conversion and Christian expression by men like Jonathan Edwards (1703-1758) and George Whitfield (1714-1770), during the American Great Awakening in New England, 1740-42, and later by Charles Grandison Finney (1792-1875) as he drew many to Christ in large assemblies in mid-nineteenth century New York State. Nonetheless, neither emotion nor belief stand thus separated from one another in the Bible. The separation of thought/emotion and the subsequent mistrust of emotion was the gift of Western Culture's Modern Era. There remains almost a fear of emotion within many Christian belief circles..., except, of course, during worship music, or if you're Pentecostal, then you've always been this way.

➤**Control Issues—** *re-basing the basics*. This may sound funny, but I've often wondered if this propensity to want things nailed down theologically (beliefs), and the commiserate fear of emotion was more a reflection of many men's desires to preserve *control* over life's myriad situations. Not control, in an exclusively bad sense, but control for its own sake, for some men's personal sense of safety and identity. Often, as I enter into conversation with a pastor or someone I have just met, I find myself in a kind of out-of-body experience where I look down on the conversation from above and try to find the answer to a question— *"Where does this person feel safe?"* If you really want to get to know a person, try to discern where they feel safe. If you examine the last 400 or so years of Western Christendom you will find that there was an intense desire to nail down as much as possible theologically. Some distinguishing marks were definitely needed as the Church had become almost indistinguishable from the world around it. But after 400 years, the nailing seems to have become an obsession. *The Roman Catholic Church is the one true church; the Church of Christ is the one true church, the Jehovah's Witnesses are the one true church, the Mormons are the one true church.* Why is it we have this drive to claim that we <u>alone</u> are right? *Calvinism is the only complete theological construct: Dispensational theology has the corner on the End-times and the expanse of human history.* Why is it that we have come to believe that our theological construct, our theological position on baptism, the Second Coming, or church government must be the most right one!? Could it be that these are issues of control? It may well be more than that; maybe it's control for the sake of a personal, positional sense of safety. Most of us do have a keen sense of self-preservation built into us. When it comes to the church, maybe it is some men's need for personal/positional safety that underlies the need to be in command. Controlling belief, which is quantifiable, and thus measurable, is easier to manage than human emotion. But fear of emotion because it is an unreliable reflector of an inner reality is as crazy as believing that making a statement about one's beliefs is *more* reliable. In reality, it is the combination of our heart and mind that explicate this Christian condition within an individual. But there is one ingredient more— action.

When I was in the midst of my teens I remember my mother saying to me *"What you do speaks so loudly I can't hear what you are saying.*" I know she was probably quoting her mother, but her point was obvious. In the office where I work we have all kinds of little witticisms that remind us of what we are trying to accomplish. One of these quips is— *Talk's cheap: action's everything.* In many churches I find that is exactly what we do … we talk a lot. Remember THE DECADE OF EVANGELISM? 1990-2000. Of course you don't. Why? What happened in 1990? We argued whether the last decade of the century really began in 1990 or 1991. And what happened in 1991? 1992? 1993? Very little. The Decade of Evangelism just faded away. All talk, not much action.

To this writer there seems to be a tremendous emphasis in the church on understanding what you need to believe and very little emphasis on DOING anything with it. This is an imbalance; but it is *not* the kind of non-balanced faith I am talking about. If anything, Christians are a long way down the road in clarifying, refining, honing, and re-clarifying what it is we believe. It just has not seemed to translate into very much action. Especially any that has any positive influence on the lives of those around us— those who are unaware that we are followers of Christ, those who have never seen a Bible (let alone opened one), and never darkened the door of a church. It's time we revisited Jesus and read the stories about how He lived, where He spent His time, and how He related to those with whom He came into contact. Consider Jesus in two situations— one where He is teaching, and another as He faces one of life's typical conundrums— the conflict between completing a task…, and being side-tracked along the way. First, an example of Jesus' teaching.

¹ And seeing the multitudes, He went up on a mountain, and when He was seated His disciples came to Him. ²Then He opened His mouth and taught them, saying:

³"Blessed are the poor in spirit, for theirs is the kingdom of heaven.

⁴Blessed are those who mourn, for they shall be comforted.

⁵Blessed are the meek, for they shall inherit the earth.

⁶Blessed are those who hunger and thirst for righteousness, for they shall be filled.

⁷Blessed are the merciful, for they shall obtain mercy.

⁸Blessed are the pure in heart, for they shall see God.

⁹Blessed are the peacemakers, for they shall be called sons of God.

¹⁰Blessed are those who are persecuted for righteousness' sake, for theirs is the kingdom of heaven.

¹¹"Blessed are you when they revile and persecute you, and say all kinds of evil against you falsely for My sake. ¹² Rejoice and be exceedingly glad, for great is your reward in heaven, for so they persecuted the prophets who were before you.

> *[13] "You are the salt of the earth; but if the salt loses its flavor, how shall it be seasoned? It is then good for nothing but to be thrown out and trampled underfoot by men. [14] "You are the light of the world. A city that is set on a hill cannot be hidden. [15] Nor do they light a lamp and put it under a basket, but on a lampstand, and it gives light to all who are in the house. [16] Let your light so shine before men, that they may see your good works and glorify your Father in heaven.*

~ Matthew 5: 1-16

Look at the setting in this passage of Scripture. It is outside, on top of a mountain, or at least on its slopes. It was probably warm, scenic, serene. Now look at Jesus' style. It was not a "lecture hall." Jesus was not debating or setting forth an argument. He was with those who trusted Him and would listen to what He had to say. And what did He do? He spoke to them where they were in life— *poor in spirit, sorrowful, timid about life, hungry for God, in need of mercy,* and so on. He was addressing the weak and painting a picture for them of what it would be like to make a difference in the lives of their friends and in their society. He gave them hope, He gave them a challenge to be the *light of the world*. To be bold— *to shine*!

The next scene is quite different. Jesus had just crossed a lake when He was approached by Jairus, a trusted leader of the people. It went like this—

> *[21] Now when Jesus had crossed over again by boat to the other side, a great*

122

multitude gathered to Him; and He was by the sea. [22] And behold, one of the rulers of the synagogue came, Jairus by name. And when he saw Him, he fell at His feet [23] and begged Him earnestly, saying, "My little daughter lies at the point of death. Come and lay Your hands on her, that she may be healed, and she will live." [24] So Jesus went with him, and a great multitude followed Him and thronged Him.

[25] Now a certain woman had a flow of blood for twelve years, [26] and had suffered many things from many physicians. She had spent all that she had and was no better, but rather grew worse. [27] When she heard about Jesus, she came behind Him in the crowd and touched His garment. [28] For she said, "If only I may touch His clothes, I shall be made well."

[29] Immediately the fountain of her blood was dried up, and she felt in her body that she was healed of the affliction. [30] And Jesus, immediately knowing in Himself that power had gone out of Him, turned around in the crowd and said, "Who touched My clothes?"

[31] But His disciples said to Him, "You see the multitude thronging You, and You say, "Who touched Me?"'

[32] And He looked around to see her who had done this thing. [33] But the woman,

fearing and trembling, knowing what had happened to her, came and fell down before Him and told Him the whole truth. [34] *And He said to her, "Daughter, your faith has made you well. Go in peace, and be healed of your affliction."*

[35] *While He was still speaking, some came from the ruler of the synagogue's house who said, "Your daughter is dead. Why trouble the Teacher any further?"*

[36] *As soon as Jesus heard the word that was spoken, He said to the ruler of the synagogue, "Do not be afraid; only believe."* [37] *And He permitted no one to follow Him except Peter, James, and John the brother of James.* [38] *Then He came to the house of the ruler of the synagogue, and saw a tumult and those who wept and wailed loudly.* [39] *When He came in, He said to them, "Why make this commotion and weep? The child is not dead, but sleeping."*

[40] *And they ridiculed Him. But when He had put them all outside, He took the father and the mother of the child, and those who were with Him, and entered where the child was lying.* [41] *Then He took the child by the hand, and said to her, "Talitha, cumi," which is translated, "Little girl, I say to you, arise."* [42] *Immediately the girl arose and walked, for she was twelve years of age. And*

they were overcome with great amazement.
⁴³But He commanded them strictly that no one
should know it, and said that something
should be given her to eat.

~ Mark 5:21-43.

Jesus had set his course toward the house of Jairus. Yet this ostensible interruption by an insignificant woman gives us more to consider than the simple completion of a task. [I've often wondered…, was this planned? Hummm.]

I'll not attempt extensive analysis of these passages, but taken together, they bring to light two seeming extremes in Jesus' way of communicating. The Matthew passage contains the opening lines of Jesus' SERMON ON THE MOUNT. In this passage Jesus is *teaching*. He is reviewing some of the life-principles that God has designed to give people hope when things no longer make sense. Remember, Judea was suffering under Roman occupation during the time of Jesus' life. There were many Jews who were imprisoned and executed, so the cultural mood was somber, frustrating, fraught with anger and despair. Jesus' message offered hope of the most compassionate kind. At the end of the Matthew section, Jesus uses three images to remind His followers what they should be like— the salt of the earth, a light on a lamp-stand, and a city built on a hill. If you would allow me to amplify— those who are *genuine* followers of Jesus Christ are to be salt to preserve life and add flavor to it; we are to be light, to clarify the way to God; and we are to be like a city built on a hill that cannot be hidden, so as to provide a haven for hope and a goal to be reached. How did Jesus envision that others would see these things in us? Through the sense of safety and stability that grows in us when we accept what God offers us—

- Are you poor in spirit, discouraged—you will come alive in heaven.

- Do you mourn at the loss of loved ones—you will know God's comfort.

- Are you timid, afraid—the earth is yours.

- Do you hunger for righteousness within—it is yours!

- If you've shown mercy—it will be granted to you as well.

- Are you pure in heart—seeing God is your great gift.

- Do you bring peace between warring peoples—you will be seen as my sons, says the Lord.

- Are you being persecuted for Christ's sake—great is your reward.

Do these words bring you hope, today, as you read them? Then you can understand some of what Jesus' first followers felt as they heard them. There was hope, Jairus' daughter might live again: we can have hope. Jesus' teaching made sense, even though it meant being merciful to those who had raped your daughter or executed your father. How else are people going to see that followers of Christ are different other than through our lives and in the ways we wrestle with life's common hardships? My wife and I have two wonderful neighbors, Midge and Dave. They are a generation up from us but we have gotten along fabulously for the past 30+ years. It was about five years ago that they responded to our annual

¿CLUELESS CHRISTIANITY?

Christmas letter, which everybody and their grandmother receives, with a simple Christmas card containing this note—

> *Dear Gary & Starr,*
>
> *Great Christmas newsletter. What's even greater is that we have watched you two live out your Christian lives next door to us for the past 25 years. Maybe we should talk about it sometime.*
>
> *Love,*
>
> *Dave & Midge*

Now, you need to know that both Dave & Midge had horrible experiences with Christianity growing up. They had very little use for anyone who called themselves "Christian." But over the years they both had come to respect and admire our Christian faith because of the lives they saw Starr and me leading. Any new explanation of this Christian faith for them needed the foundation of years of observation and relationship to establish credibility. The explanation follows observation and relationship. Their Christmas note to us was one of the most humbling notes I had ever received.

Do not fail to understand this. If you are a Christian, not simply a nice person, but one with genuine faith in Jesus Christ as the Lord God Creator of all that there is, you *are* being observed, scrutinized, studied by people who want to know if your so-called faith in Christ really makes any difference in your daily living. If it seems not, your words are merely religious dribble.

Jesus' words called for life change. Whenever He spoke He called people to be different than those around them. Using the simple formula— Jesus' Words= Life-change, we are not supposed to fill our minds with more words, like a new ammo-clip in a gun. Rather, we are to live the changed lives called for by the words. I once delivered a lectureship at Columbia University Graduate School on the Integration of Ethics and Faith. At the close of the meetings one grad student came up to me and said, "*This has been good for us to hear. You need to come back and tell us more.*" He had missed the point entirely; he did not need to hear more explanation. He needed to DO something with what he had just heard. Jesus' expects the same of us— Words for Life's sake…, not words for more words sake.

The Mark passage also teaches us something, quite different than the Matthew passage. Mark depicts two intertwined events; a throng-clogged walk to witness the healing of the daughter of a synagogue official named Jairus, and a spur-of-the-moment interruption along the way by a middle-aged, outcast woman with internal bleeding. I'll not re-describe the order of events, but rather delineate how Jesus dealt with each situation differently.

Jesus and the Hemorrhaging Woman	Jesus and Jairus' Daughter
• He stopped the crowd & drew attention to her.	• He put everyone out of the room except the family and his disciples.
• The woman thought "*If I*	• Jairus' daughter was

just touch his clothes I will be healed."	already dead when Jesus arrived at the house.
• Everyone around saw the woman healed.	• Jesus told them to tell no one about this.
• Power goes out from Jesus.	• Power goes out from Jesus.
• Jesus told the woman, "*Your faith has healed you… .*"	• Jairus' daughter, being dead, did nothing to believe or move. Jesus simply spoke, "*Little girl I say to you, 'Get up!'*"
• The woman went away a whole person.	• The little girl was alive again.

Now, some questions for you to tackle.

- What is it that the crowd learned?
- What did the disciples learn?
- What was the mood of the crowd on the way to Jairus' house?
- What did the crowd expect Jesus to do there?
- What did they think of this socially unacceptable, sick woman approaching Jesus?
- How do you suppose Jairus felt when his servants came to inform him that his daughter had died?
- What might have been the disciples' attitude about this?

- Could Jairus have believed Jesus after hearing this news?

- After all was said and done, and Jesus had left Jairus' house with his disciples, in the big scheme of things, what did the disciples pick up?

- Do you think the healed woman believed in Jesus? Do you think Jairus and his family believed in Jesus?

In either of these passages, where is "the gospel?" In these two situations, where do you find a delineated, rational, logical presentation of the Christian faith? Nowhere! Where is there a cognitive, propositional explanation of what happened— of who Jesus was and why He came here? Nowhere! Where was an understanding of the effects of sin on the human condition presented? Nowhere to be read! Where did the recipients of Christ's grace and mercy have it explained to them? Not here, at least. Who was directly *asked* to "repent and believe?" Ouyveh, enough already! You get the point. Very often in the gospels there was no need for the rational explanations or arguments we seem to find so critical to impart today. The Jewish people of Jesus' day were not Modern. They didn't need logical explanation. They needed life evidence, life-proof; they needed a model of hope. If anything, the Mark passage points to a gospel that is beyond explanation, beyond words. It is the gospel of presence, of power, and of peace. There was no need to explain anything or even to call anyone to repentance; both were intrinsically present. Each scenario presented the gospel in a way most appropriate to the situation at hand. The words of the Gospel played in the background to Jesus' presence and power.

Far too much of our *witness* to the world around us is about staying in control. We have to be in control of the conversation, we have to present our content, we have to take control of the outcome. Yet Jesus seemed to let go of control, relinquishing it to His Father. Maybe He understood something about the connection between empowerment and explanation we need to learn (again).

➢**Letting Go—** Where is a non-balanced faith to be found in all this? For the past 400 years or so North American Christians have grown attached to a *shape* of faith that is primarily linear/sequential. That is, a faith where understanding is couched in a systematic progression of information leading to an inescapable conclusion. "To know," in our banner, was equated with comprehension, belief, theological purity, and implementation. This was a quantum shift from the previous period. Formerly Christian faith was either exclusively mystical or quite proactive in converting the infidel on his own turf, if you get my drift (Crusades). With the Protestant Reformation came a primary emphasis on the Word of God in the Bible, as opposed to the traditions and misappropriations of the Roman Church. Martin Luther's emphasis on "Sola Scriptura" defined the battle. This was a reemphasis, a revolution that was long overdue. The Word of Truth had been supplanted by a usurper— the church itself. Religious leaders were so corrupt that their positions in the church became more important to them than the Lord of the Church; position had replaced purpose— a true bureaucracy.

By the mid-seventeenth century, many Christians had fled persecution in Europe for the Americas. The faith they brought with them went through yet another adaptation. This one occurred because of the new continent and the new cultural context. Just the fact that America was not as densely populated allowed for more diversity in faith than in Europe. In Europe if you publically disagreed with the theological emphasis of a region, you were executed (or martyred, depending on your point of view); in the Americas you simply moved further west. Geography alone accounted for a wide variety of developments in the shape faith. Virtually all new churches founded in America, developed a distinctly American flavor, but always with an emphasis on the Bible as the final rule of authority. Over the past 250 years within more conservative, evangelical traditions, the faith that emerged came to stress an almost fanatical bent for adherence to propositional truth above all else. If anything would typify the evangelical tradition over the years it would be this— that belief in a *system of truth* was first and foremost in demonstrating one's personal faith in Jesus. If anything could be called *imbalanced*, it is this insistence. The twentieth century epitomized the extremes of what could follow an imbalanced faith. One extreme emphasized adherence to propositional Truth exclusively, and held theological compliance at its sole rule. It expelled any recognition for relational, emotional or passionate aspects of faith. The second extreme developed mid-century and into the next.

The early twenty-first century now finds North American Christians in a new cultural climate; a climate in which precise, correct belief is not viewed as quite as significant by those who have no Christian-faith context. What *is* important for them is <u>life</u>. They look at Christians and ask if our faith helps us with the everyday issues of life? Does it provide us with a platform to deal with establishing our self-esteem? Does it offer practical guidance in inter-personal relationships? Does it provide perimeters of proper behavior in society? Does it help us deal with weight gain or loss, financial gain or loss, broken relationships, unfulfilled expectations, and mid-life crisis? Does it make us happier, more fulfilled, or leave us with a sense of accomplishment at the end of a day? Does it allow us individual creativity and foster it? People who are not involved in the Christian world are not, generally speaking, on a quest for the meaning of life. They are seeking their own personal comfort and safety, regardless of its effect on others. They are *not* seeking truth. [They believe they create it as they go along, remember?] They are not asking questions like "Is there a god?" "What is the truth?" "What is my purpose in life?" or "What must I do to be saved?" [And they are most assuredly not asking *"What would Jesus drive?"*] Most don't even know they are lost— or even care. The immediacy of the moment has replaced the quest for answers to ultimate questions. Their questions are more practical and need to be addressed *without delay,* in order to deal with life's constant stream of crises. *I've been out of work for 99 weeks. In this economic crisis, where can I find work? I am constantly afraid of commitment. Why can't I trust anyone? Our daughter is 15 and pregnant. What do we do? My stress level is out of control. Help me! Does anybody care about me at all?*

➤**Going Non-balanced— *scary faith indeed!*** A *different* kind of *non-balanced* faith is called for in these early decades of the twenty-first century. A faith based in Truth which is lived out in a clear, wholistic expression *in* the society which surrounds us. The emphasis today must be on living life *passionately* as a Christian, deeply immersed in our networks of relationships, our neighborhoods, and our world. We need to strive for purity of life, transparency, approachableness, and for a knack of being able to express our faith in ways appropriate to our society's formats of communication. *In the world..., not of it.* The pendulum swing we need today is toward living purely before God and just as purely in this world, with a passion for life excelling that of Christians who lived in the Modern era.

When I was growing up in Baltimore, MD, the kind of faith offered to me seemed so negative. Christians were typified more by what they did not do than what they did. "*Christians don't play cards, don't dance, don't drink, don't smoke, don't bowl* (yes, even bowling), *don't go to movies, and don't hang around people who do those things.*" I remember being so frustrated at this in my early, still-as-yet-not-Christian days. I began describing a Christian as someone who "*doesn't think, dance, drink, smoke or breathe.*" But if you "*believed on the Lord Jesus Christ with all your heart*" you would be saved. To some extent that same, simple emphasis still exists. Just say the words, pray "*the prayer,*" and that's that— you're in. For many people in North America's South and Wheat Belt this approach to becoming a Christian is still appropriate. These regions still contain remnants of the *Christian consciousness.* But a traditional summary-gospel, *just believe*, presentation of our faith will completely miss postmoderns who have grown up in a postChristian context. It will most likely also miss our own kids; for they, too, have grown up in a postChristian context, at least outside the home. So then, the question becomes, "*What will communicate our faith to this postmodern, postChristian mindset?*"

The answer lies in *non-balance*— in the expression of Christian passion for life surging up from within. So many Christian leaders in the west seem afraid of expressing passion. It's too much of a RISK. Yet inside closed doors, here, in our churches, is no loss of emotion; there's plenty of emotion expended in the church, in our worship services. But there is very little passion for the people outside our doors. I wonder if it doesn't go back to our propensity to be safe. Passion isn't safe. It's RISKY. It pushes us out to the edges: it screams, *"I care about this, deeply."* Passion is emotion on steroids, and that's scary. It's scary because if you feel deeply you could fall into some sin. Once you allow one passion to express itself you open the door for others to surface, and that's dangerous. Right? Of course, holding tight to correct belief will keep passion in check and prevent you from sinning more effectively than any deep fervent commitment. [Go figure that one. But many Christians sincerely believe this.] What about your relationship with Jesus Christ? Is it primarily a matter of belief, Truth, and getting your theology nailed down pat? Well then answer this: can love be devoid of passion? Of deep feeling? Of emotion? How can we hold to the propositional Truth about Jesus and yet be devoid of a deep passion for Him, for His people and for this world He has placed us in? *"Do you love me? Feed my sheep.?"*

The Gospels are full of the stories of deep faith that reflect the love God has for us. Jesus did not come to earth *only* to reveal the propositional truth about the Father to us: he came to show us God in the flesh. *"And the Word became flesh and dwelt among us, and we beheld His glory, the glory of the only begotten of the Father, full of grace and truth."* [John 1:14.] The *Word*, the Person of Jesus Christ (not the propositions *about* Him) fleshed out God for us. And the primary distinctive that became clear in the Person of Jesus was His glory; not His logic of life or persuasive argument, not His balance, or even His great miracles. Jesus did not come across as a great debater, though He certainly did not lose any. His heart was too full of glory for that. I truly wonder if He intentionally spoke in parables or mystery, not so much to muddy the waters, but to demonstrate that it was who He was and what He was doing that was more important than having a clear grasp of His teaching. His teaching merely clarified more of who He was and what He had been sent to accomplish. *"If you have seen me, you have seen the Father... ."* (John 14:9)

So I ask you, are you passionate in your love for Jesus Christ? Or do yourself find with a more reflective, cerebral faith? Are you more calculated in living your Christian life, than, say, someone who is sacrificial-to-a-fault? Is your faith characterized more by explanation or by exuberance? I am not talking about *"burning out for Jesus."* I am asking if you *feel* your love for Jesus Christ at least as much as you seek to understand it? There is probably more safety in understanding it, in keeping things intellectual, than there is in feeling a deep love for Him, or for others. But without the passion, without the depth of feeling, you are seriously missing something critical to your Christian existence. You are non-balanced, but not in the right way. You are missing the heart of God. For it was not understanding that drove Jesus to the cross, it was not purely obedience..., it was His heart, His passion, and His deep love for us. Without passion, without a deep felt love, the Christian faith would not simply seem sterile, it would <u>be</u> sterile.[lxvii]

I will admit that we need a balance between heart and head, soul and mind; but with nearly four centuries of mental clarification of our beliefs it's time we swung the pendulum over to the other side. We need to imbue some significant passion into our faith: not emotionalism, but a genuine, deeply-embedded passion. Back to my fortune cookie— *"Nothing worthwhile is ever accomplished without passion."* What would this new, non-balanced, passionate Christian look like? Would it be totally loony, all-heart-no-brains, emotions out of control? Is there no longer any room for contemplation or reasonable thought? Are we throwing out everything for the sake of expressing our faith passionately? Merely to accommodate our postmodern culture!?! Glad you asked! That's the next chapter.

Read on; inquiring minds want to know.

Play Time

1. If Truth is primarily PERSONAL not Propositional, how can Truth (capital T) be found in postmodernism's creation of truth (lower case t) within? [Hint— See Romans 1.]

2. Look at the life of Jesus. Compare his propositional teaching with his passion for people. Examine how he spent his time, where he spent his time. How POWER backed up what he said (how only our words back up our words).

3. Postulate a WHOLISTIC gospel, one with words, supported by actions; one beyond words, supported in the heart and through personal relationships between God and us.

4. How can you learn to feel love if it is difficult for you to feel anything? To what degree do you find expressing love a compromise of your need for safety?

5. Examine the bifurcated lifestyle of many North American Christians. How do Christians isolate themselves from impending "evil" culture? What practical steps can you take to overcome the barriers of fear you feel toward postModern culture?

¿CLUELESS CHRISTIANITY?

"We must become what we seek to create."
— Mohandas Karamchang Ghandi

(Oct 2, 1869 – Jan. 30, 1948
—*assassinated on his way to evening prayers.*)

Chapter 6: Being a Christian in a New Era:
a generational thing.

I just don't care! I'm not going to church this morning!

Don't speak to me in that tone of voice; and you ARE going to church.

No I'm not! Church is boring. All we do is sing songs that are really out if it and then the same sermon every week— three points, there's always three points, and then you either change or you're guilty. I'm just tired of not measuring up week after week. So I'm not going to church. You can't make me.

Well, whether you want to or not you ARE going to church and there are two good reasons why you have to go.

Two good reasons—what are they?

First, you're 32 years old and need to go to church. Second, you're the pastor.

¿CLUELESS CHRISTIANITY?

We all joke about this, but underneath we know it's a real problem. So many people come to church and find it boring, or irrelevant, or strange, or just plain confusing. If it's your church, whether you are in leadership or attend regularly, you want your worship services to mean something, to make sense, to be relevant, to truly minister to those who come. Our wellbeing and feeling good about ourselves notwithstanding, we need to praise, honor, and pursue the heart of God. But people are somewhat different today than they were ten or twenty years ago. It used to be that if you were seeking the answers to life's questions you would go to your church, schedule an appointment with the minister, or seek reading material to help you sort it through. Nowadays the BIG questions just don't seem as important to people. Life has grown so complex; even Christians find it difficult to make consistent commitments to church services or programs. Then there's this generational thing. Blended worship services, youth councils, and contemporary Christian music, always the music, seems to overshadow everything else. You start with a call to worship, worship songs, maybe a hymn from the hymnal (You remember hymnals— they came before song sheets, overhead projectors, and PowerPoint). It's as if the sermon has become secondary to the music! And we still can't keep our young people. What's going on?

The fact of the matter is that you're right— people are different now. Young people find it difficult to relate to the church's way of doing things. When family structures and society were more stable people *did* come to church to find answers, to find community, to worship God in a traditional manner. But the breakdown of our society, the dissolution of so many marriages, hippies, Vietnam, Columbine, 9/11, the

¿CLUELESS CHRISTIANITY?

2008 financial collapse, and two wars have all contributed to the fragmentation and isolation of the generations. This fragmentation has had a greater impact than we could have imagined. We set our senior citizens aside to die so we can get on with our lives; this alone constitutes a major fracture in our family cohesion. And thanks to the Baby-Boom of 1946-1964, YOUTH CULTURE (their children) *does, in fact,* dominate our world.

In the summer of '01 my wife and daughter went on a humanitarian mission to Belarus, a former Soviet "satellite nation." They were assigned to a summer camp that had formerly been a prison. Living conditions were sparse; meals, no matter what the main course, offered "kasha," a granular, crunchy, Elmer's glue-like substance (so reported our daughter). As a *fourth world* country[lxviii], they were a beleaguered nation—but at night they still danced to the music of the U.S. pop-star Brittany Spears at the discos. And, oh yes, and there was never, ever, a shortage of vodka. Never. In a country where physicians earned $300 a month, their children moved to the music of the West. Any casual observation will find the same thing happening around the world from Hong Kong to central China, from Australia to Myanmar. The music of the West, translated or not, permeates the culture. And the youth live by it. Youth culture has become a culture unto itself, nurtured and fed by older generations who want to grab some of their estimated disposable annual pocket change of close to $153 billion in the US alone. [lxix]

So when young people ages 14-25 come to church what do they find, generally?[lxx] They find a shape of Christianity virtually irrelevant to their virtual realities. They find a

141

pyramid power structure contrary to their relationally oriented internet networking. [FaceBook, a social networking website, founded by Mark Zukerberg and his college roommates at Harvard in 2004, now has more than 550 million subscribers.] They find, for the most part, the music to be somewhat archaic. One example is the SONIC PRAISE CD (by Sonic Flood) in which the worship leader tries to convince his audience that even "oldies" can have meaning if they are updated musically. I was expecting Amazing Grace or a 1950s youth hymnal chorus spiffed up a bit. The reference was to *Shine Jesus, Shine*, circa 1982. Thirty years ago, ancient history.

But has it ever been different? Well, yes and no. Youth have always found fault with the status quo. They have always wanted to move ahead a little faster than their more conservative seniors. And their parents, grandparents, teachers, and seniors in general, have always criticized their music and style of dress. If anything, with the acceleration in the rate of information exchange and the ease of international communication (Def.- Teenager = smart phone + texting + ear buds), teens & twenties not only have easier access to each other, but they can connect so much faster and in so many more ways (cell-phone, texting, Skype, Facebook, etc.) than a few years ago. This, plus their ability to be "early adapters" enables them to become more insular than any generation before them. When our daughter was in high school I joined her to watch an MTV show called *Real World*. The scenario is a gathering together of 5-8 select teens/twenty-somethings who live together, live on camera, 24/7.[lxxi] The show presents life as they experience it, with all its romantic developments, breakups and heartaches. As Bethany and I watched *Real World* it finally hit me like a jolt— if this show was about anything it was *not* the real world! It's a world with no adults, no societal guidelines, no children running around, and little personal responsibility beyond remembering to get dressed when you get out of bed in the afternoon and to brush your teeth in case you meet someone. But from this experience I learned something: there is no such thing as "western culture"; rather, there are "western cultures." The West, has in reality, multi-cultures, defined by generational differences in a big way, by geographic region, by the urban-suburban-rural context, and, of course, by economics.

If you can find a copy of James O. Gollub's THE DECADE MATRIX: *why the decade you were born into made you what you are today* (Addison Wesley Publishing, Reading, MA, 1991), currently out of print, you will learn that the title just about says it all. Gollub reviews the decades of the 20th century and delineates the common life-experiences people lived through in each decade of their lives. Gollub's point is that every generation, every ten years of births, shares common experiences that contribute heavily to the shaping of their worldview. Peer-perception, if you will. Two leading American sociologists, Neil Howe and William Strauss, have categorized our generational differences in ways that might be helpful in our understanding of those differences and in the efforts to bridge the gaps between us... and them. Keep in mind that there are many ways to classify our generational definers; this is but one among dozens.

Howe & Strauss Generational Chart [lxxii]

GENERATION	BIRTH YEARS	FAMOUS MAN	FAMOUS WOMAN
Lost	1883-1900	Harry Truman	Mae West
G.I.	1901-1924	Ronald Reagan	Ann Landers
Silent	1925-1942	Martin Luther King, Jr.	Sandra Day O'Conner
Boomer	1943-1960	George W. Bush	Hillary Clinton
Gen-X	1961-1981	Michael Jordan	Courtney Love
Millennial	1982-2002	Zac Efron	Miley Cyrus

Howe and Strauss define a *generation* as "a society-wide peer group, born over a period roughly the same length as the passage from youth to adulthood (in today's America, around twenty or twenty-one years), who collectively possess a common *persona*."[lxxiii] They point out that using birth year as a sole definer of a generation simply does not give us any useful information that deepens our understanding of a generation's profile. They say that—

> Demographers who insist on locating Boomers according to the fertility "boom" of 1946 to 1964, and then Gen Xers according to the fertility "bust" of 1965 to 1976, are not defining generations in any useful historical sense. Birth numbers are only one factor (and not always a critical factor) in locating a generation. When drawn correctly, generational birth years should indicate the boundaries for each generational *persona.*

> What is a generational *persona*? It is a distinctly human, and variable creation embodying attitudes about family life, gender roles, institutions, politics, religion, culture, lifestyle, and the future. A generation can think, feel, or do anything a person might think, feel, or do.[lxxiv]

In essence, generational characteristics must be taken into account when *any* presentation of the Christian faith is expressed. If they are not considered, both communication of the faith and comprehension levels drop into the abyss of vacuity.

Another observer of generational delineations, Mike Woodruff, offers us a demarcation that provides much more specific information. He called his chart The View from 30,000 Feet.[lxxv] [I've taken the liberty to use his original format, as well as some of his input, but have also expanded the Generational Chart to be more encompassing of the most recent reflections of the Millennial generation.]

GENERATIONS CHART

Titles	Builders	Boomers	Generation X Baby Busters	Millennials ~formerly Generation Y
Born Between	1925 – 1945	1946 – 1960	1961 – 1980	1981 - 1990
Age	85 – 65 years old	63 – 49 years old	48 – 29 years old	28 – 19 years old
Population	55 Million	76 Million	46 Million	75 Million
Expected Education	High School Diploma	College Degree	College plus some graduate education	Life-long learning, but no rush to start or finish college
Formative Experiences (first decade of life)	Rural lifestyle, strong family, church	Economic affluence The Space Race American preeminence Dr. Spock	Broken families Latchkey kids American decline The MEDIA Nuclear Threat	Economic Boom Greater division of haves & have-nots American world supremacy Daycare Hightech childhood

Adolescent Time Span	Puberty begins at 16, marriage often occurs before 20	Puberty at 14, marriage at 22	Puberty at 12, marriage at 25	Girls hit puberty before age 12. Youth remain single into their late 20s, early 30s
Formative Teenage Experiences	Great Depression No significant sexual revolution	Kent State, Civil Rights, Watergate, Inflation, Sexual Revolution, Vietnam Protests, Drugs, Hippies	Information explosion, McJobs, AIDS, Environmentalism, Trillion dollar debt, being politically correct	Internet porn, crumbling job market, global village, terrorism, acceptable alternative life-styles (sexual)
War	World War 2, Korean War	Vietnam, the Cold War	Iran Hostage Crisis, Desert Storm	Iraq, Iran, Afghanistan— LIVE on CNN
Defining Moment	Bombing of Pearl Harbor	Assassination of JFK	Explosion of Challenger Space Shuttle [13]	VA Tech Massacre, 9/11, Obama elected
Music	Big Band	Rock & Roll	Diverse mix of Rock and Rap (MTV)	Outta control— whatever goes!
Entertainment	Radio, but not TV	TV (3 channels)	TV (30 channels + video rentals), Play Station	YouTube, Streaming Video, iPods, Wii

TV Shows	(Radio only)	Father Knows Best, Leave it to Beaver, The Dick VanDyk Show, Lassie	Miami Vice, Cheers, Cosby Show, Married with Children, The Simpsons	One Tree Hill, OC, Lost, 24, American Idol
Favorite Movies	Gone with the Wind, It's a Wonderful Life, Wizard of Oz	American Graffiti, West Side Story, Jaws, The Godfather	Rocky, Rambo, Star Wars, Ferris Bueller's Day Off	Harry Potter, Twilight, Juno, Hangover, The 40 Year Old Virgin
The Nature of Dating and Sex	Dated high school sweetheart, seeking life partner	Dating around, free love, quest for pleasure and sex	Group dating, fear of one-on-one, sex as means to intimacy	Group dating, hooking-up (sex for no reason, sex with friends)
View of Authority	Honor & respect for leaders	Challenge leaders (never trust anyone over 30)	Ignore leaders and don't try to become one	Skeptical of leaders, defer to a team, be your own boss
Heroes	FDR, Churchill	John Kennedy, John Lennon	Michael Jordan, Kurt Cobain	Themselves-- & a few adults
Career Path	1 or 2 career positions, loyalty to employer	6 career positions	12 different careers	20 different careers
Technology	Mimeograph, rotary phone, slide rule	Touchtone phone, phonograph, 8 track tapes, calculator	Desktop publishing, cell phones, laptops	Cell Phones, texting, iPhones, Blackberries

Worldview	Modern-Judeo-Christian	Modern, Judeo-Christian	Modern with movement toward postmodern-ity, political correctness	Increasingly postChristian; increasingly relativistic
Saying [15]	No sweat	No problem	No fear	Whatever
Life Perception [16]	"We"	"Me"	"Us"	"Alone-together"
Major Influences	Family & church	Family & education	Media	Discretionary time, friends, cell phones (texting)
Characteristics	Loyal, hardworking, patriotic, frugal, cautious, traditional/ Biblical values	Independent, cause oriented, self-centered, opportunis-tic, live-to-work	Tentative, peer oriented, cynical, lonely, work-to-live	Technologic-ally in-touch, busy, expect a hard life, morally non-committed, tolerant

Did you find yourself looking for where you fit in? Did you find yourself saying, *"Yeah, that was it."* or *"I remember that."* I did. Still, you may have found yourself in-between generations, sharing characteristics and defining moments with more than one. But generally, we all have Defining Moments, TV Shows and certain music that is... *us.* There's no getting around it. As much as we like to think of ourselves as independent thinkers, much of who we are actually is determined by a set of common experiences that work together to determine how we perceive life. These perceptions work within a profile of an age delimited & defined people group. That's why church can be so difficult at times. Each generation of a congregation views its Christian faith in relation to the shared common experiences of *their* generation. So as a church matures, the characteristics and style of the founding generation generally remains the predominate culture of the church. This, in turn, exasperates the emerging generations, and frustrates the senior leaders who see the younger sets as rebellious. So, what do we do?

When I was in seminary preparing for a career in ministry (there, I've come out), we were taught that you never want a church within a church. That is, you never want more than one predominate culture determining the direction of a ministry. What was actually meant was "unless it's MY culture." I've learned a lot from different kinds of Christians all over the world, and now believe that what I was taught in seminary was dead wrong. Multi-cultures & multi-generations influencing direction is exactly what you DO want! You actually want as many churches and as many sub-cultures within a church as you can handle. You want to encourage each generation to develop a shape of Christian faith that works for them; a faith that is appropriate to their generation, to their region of the world, to their (sub) culture, to *their* expressions of faith. So if one set loves the old hymns of the faith (music again), you create a venue for them to sing their lungs out; if another set of people really learn from deep, analytical, methodical Bible study, you create a sphere for their growth; if another set worships God through loud, repetitive, push-rock music, then, by God, you create an atmosphere where they can kick it! In my personal life I've enjoyed all kinds of music.[lxxvi] But I have had to make a monumental decision about how I will worship God. The decision came out of a realization that worship has a bigger context; that being— **How will I** express my Christian faith in a way that is appropriate to my culture, to my generation, yet sensitive to other forms of expression, as well as to the world at-large? In the church context— how should *my* worship honor God in the Body of Christ?

Now hear me on this point. I've studied music theory and hymnody, voice and choral conducting, I've toured with a jazz band, and soloed for my meals at a Sheraton Inn; but I also love Gregorian chants. So, somewhat sadly for me, to keep my faith *upgraded*, I packed up all of my hymnals (two shelves full of them) and put them away. I did this so I would be forced to reshape the expression of my faith to fit the emerging generation of Christians. To my surprise and joy, I have found the shift quite refreshing. But every now and then I still miss my TYNDALE HYMNAL, out of England, circa 1965 (music at the top, words at the bottom— mostly Bach).

You see, sometime each of us needs to rethink the **way** we are Christians. Not that one way is better than another, but all of us tend to want our relationship with God to be comfortable. Comfortable Christian faith. Comfortable Christian faith. Do you hear the sound of that? I don't know about you but that doesn't sound exactly right: it is a contradiction in terms. If I can stretch it a bit and flip the cart on its end, a lot of us need to learn to trust God with those parts of our lives that we would rather He not touch. Personally, I find that trusting God is the one thing I find most difficult. I would much rather stay in charge and in control. That's why, I have to constantly put myself in situations where I am in over my head. Otherwise I will stay comfortable. The comfortable Christian life— yes sir, that's what I want. But that's just not going to happen. When I do trust God, I always seem to get into trouble. Not in a bad way, mind you; more in a way that stretches my faith and reminds me Who is in control in this universe. For the Christian faith in North America and in the world to move forward and regain a position of having something to say to each emerging generation we need to consciously put ourselves in over our heads. We must constantly put ourselves in a position where trusting God is the only choice that will make a difference. Where it is the only course of action that will move us out of a Christian-control-factor syndrome to a position of genuine, I-can't-do-this-on-my-own, terrifying trust in an Almighty God.

➤ EXPRESSIONS OF FAITH EVOLUTION

Trusting in God is the one thing we need to learn in order to express our faith in suitable ways as the world around us changes; but the expression of that trust between the Christian and his surrounding community may vary widely from generation to generation.

In early 2005 NEED*inc* conducted a series of interviews with genuine Christians across North America ["Genuine" being defined as a faith whose principles influenced at least 75% of their daily activities, brushing teeth, wearing ties, or displaying tattoos not considered.]. Each interviewee was drawn from a different generational grouping; each expressed answers to the interview questions in a manner with which they were comfortable. Each person was asked the following six questions—

¿CLUELESS CHRISTIANITY?

INTERVIEW QUESTIONS lxxvii

1. When did you become a Christian?

2. Why did you become a Christian?

3. How has your Christian faith evolved over the years?

4. How is God using you today versus 5-10-20 years ago?

5. What do you think of the shape of Christian faith in North America today?

6. What do you think God has in store for you next?

Two people were chosen to be interviewed as representative for each age group in North America. Of course, they could not represent their entire age group, but their expressions of faith carry a common, generational thread. Key excerpts from the interviews can be found in the Appendix.

What we learned from the interviews surprised us a little.

1. Some saw church as central to their Christian worship while others did not. A common frustration and disappointment in the state of the church crossed all generational lines.

2. Though all were genuine believers and held a rich faith in Christ, they expressed that faith through worship, music, and societal involvement in different ways and to different extents. This observation followed generational lines and complied with their peer group expressions.

3. Though younger generations held a respect for their elder's expressions of faith, it was not reciprocated.

Older believers had no clue about the formats and subtleties of *twenty-something* expressions of faith. They thought the younger generation's faith too emotion-based, too relational, and not grounded enough in a Biblical, comprehensive worldview.

4. Everyone was willing to consider the other person's faith expression…, in theory. In practice, well, that didn't work out so well. "Getting together" at all was the first hurdle to overcome.

5. ALL considered themselves *in process*; that is, they understood they were each at different places in their spiritual journey and had much growing yet to come.

➢ **REFLECTION**

How might you answer these six questions? Could you imagine older/younger Christians (whom you know) responding? How might they respond? What *commonalities* have you observed between different generations of Christians? What about their generational *differences*? What issues do you believe still exist between diverse generations? What issues might they share in common? How might different generations of genuine Christians teach each other about the individual expressions of their own faith?

Each of the individuals interviewed grew up in a different faith expression. Each found meaning and joy in the music and thought of their faith history. Yet each had to come to a place where they realized they had to go through an *upgrade* of their faith, despite the fact that their current faith expression was rich, deep and meaningful. Like that new computer, which works so beautifully the first couple of years, then slows to a crawl, forcing you to upgrade. Our faith also needs a periodic upgrade, not simply to be relevant, but to work and be alive in us at all. If we do not upgrade our faith but decide we are comfortable with the one we've got, we cease to be able communicate it to those around us, and, eventually, like our computers, we will crash. Why? Because we refused to upgrade our faith and take the risk to meet the challenge of learning a new way of being a Christian.

I grew up in inner city Baltimore (the part of Baltimore they now call a ghetto; to me, back then, it was just home). In my home church there was a man who gave the same faith testimony, word for word, every week. I hoped, even though not truly a Christian yet, that one day I would have such a rock solid faith. Now as an adult, I look back and feel sorry for that man. As far as I could tell he had not grown in the expression of his faith because he articulated it in the same rote, mechanical manner for 40 years. *O God, may that never be me*, I thought. We need to constantly upgrade our faith in order for it to *fit* each successive stage of our life, and also, so that it will be understandable to those around us.

We need to learn *how* to become new kinds of Christians. We need to express our faith in ways that our peers can understand and then adapt its expressions to each person we meet in different generations, in different regions of the country (or world), or in cultures significantly different from our own.

➤ HOW WILL WE HAVE TO CHANGE?

With all the innumerable differences between generations there are some traits which every generation of Christians share. There have to be. The question then becomes, *How will we have to change to fit the changes that are taking place all around us? What will we need to look like so we will be identifiable as genuine followers of Jesus Christ as our culture understands less and less about true, Biblical Christian faith?* Here's my list of some of the key identifiers of genuine Christians in this next era.

1. **A Rich Faith in Christ-** No matter what our generation or culture, our emphasis on having a quality faith must remain constant— a deep trust in Jesus Christ that works its way through our everyday decisions and practices. We must insist on a belief that He is who He said He was, and that He accomplished what He set out to do. Surface faith is a mere religion without power or purpose; it is play acting; it will go by the way and die. There is no room for a superficial faith that puts on a pious façade and a smiley face.

2. **A Generationally Specific Character-** One of the constant complaints of teenagers is that their parents are always trying to force them to express their faith in the same way that they (the parents) do (or did). How much better would it be if parents helped their teenagers develop a faith that reflected *their* own generational formats of expression? Many 50 year-old+ Christians hold propositional truth and understanding the Bible to be the underpinning of their faith. People 30 and under, generally, think in music. They've developed a way of *imaging* life. Many may be engineers by profession but they play-out their faith with a beat. Thus, they *image* their faith in God as a

set of experiences, and find in the Bible a context to explain their realities.

3. **A Generationally Sensitive Interface-** There are a lot of TV shows (One Tree Hill, The OC; certainly NOT the Country Music Channel Bull-Riding competitions) that picture a generation of mostly young people living in a place seemingly devoid of anyone older or younger; no older adults, no grandparents, no children or babies. Where is this place? I haven't found it. We live in a world of juxtapositions— of diversity, if you will, where different philosophies, penchants and personalities coexist side by side, spanning the generations. We need to learn to live with each other on a daily basis; but the ability to love something or someone different from yourself is no small task. The best way I know of learning to relate to someone older, someone younger, or someone different is to make a conscious commitment of time to be with them. I learned this from some older Christians who tolerated my youth and spent time with me (Dick Grey, Jack Miller, Jim & Velma Keifer). I learned this from my mother (Florence Andersen Davis) who modeled a non-judgmental love and clarity of thought that is matchless in my experience to this day. I learned this from an 8 year old boy (Dean Cromack) and a 14 year girl (Julie Evans) in a Sunday School class—they brought the voice of God to me in a way I was not used to. And, yes, I was most surprised. It drew me to think about the different ways that God might direct all of us. The first, of course, is through the Bible. In all of God's Creation, this is the only

revelation that is binding on all of us. For in the Bible we find the precepts He sets forth for us to live honorably in this world, and the guidance we seek to live peacefully in the next. Second, God might communicate to us through other people, or through reading a book. We've all experienced that odd sensation that what someone just said to us in passing was more than an off-handed comment. It sounded suspiciously like the voice of God speaking to us individually. Enough said. Then, thirdly, God communicates to us through His Spirit within us. This is a quite subjective thing; it's that little voice in the back of your head that gives you a sense of what is right and what is wrong. But of course, it may be someone else; someone we know we should not be listening to—God's adversary, and ours. Test the waters cautiously before you act upon this last form of communication.

4. **Ageless-** Obviously, as long as we have the aging process and breathe, agelessness is impossible. But outside of the aging process, if any inter-generational connection is to be forged, it is necessary for Christians of every age to adapt to the relational and communication patterns of those outside their own age/experience group. This *new kind of Christian* will have to be intergenerational, adaptable, able to express their faith in more forms than just their own. Two personal inspirations to me are Alan & Diane Galbraith, life-long friends now in their 70s. Their zest for life still finds them on Navajo mission trips every summer; and they are richly involved in their Jackson

Hole (WY) secular community. They are wild about God, people, and life—and love all three! Go figure? I think it's great. If the older generations can turn up the volume (or turn it down, as the case may be) and listen to the younger generations, if millennial can turn down their car stereos, or pop the ear-buds and listen to the older generations, what might it produce in the church, or, for that matter, in our country?

One of the ongoing revelations of my life is that I still have so much to learn. Every now and then I am surprised at the insight and wisdom that comes out of a teenager's mouth. My wife, Starr, recently told me that a 10th grader walked up to her, spun to face her, looked intently into her eyes, and spoke like a prophet of old. In my own life I have found that my friendship with one amazing man from Greece— Euclid Djefaris, who died at age 88, to be one of the most educational experiences I have known. What is the point? Just this— that we need to learn to cross the generational thresholds and mix with those both older and younger. If we do this, unforeseen insights could be gained into the meaning of our life together. If we do not do this, we are doomed to repeat our mistakes over and over again, oblivious to the solutions learned by those who have gone before.

5. **A Culturally Adaptable Faith Expression**- Pluralism has attuned us to be sensitive to dissimilar cultural value-expressions other than those of our personal heritage. Style of dress, dance, music, food, and the language mix have turned North America into a multi-

culture with life expressions galore. People are used to dining out in whatever culinary culture they fancy—Chinese, Indian, Mexican, Greek, Italian, Polish, Thai, Hungarian, etc. Just punch through any radio display and you will hear as many music styles as there are languages. So also should the new kind of Christian be able to adjust the expression of his/her faith to fit the surrounding culture, inside and outside of the church. Because I grew up in the inner city, crossing the white/black cultural line was easy for me when I started in ministry. But over the past 30 years that line has widened more than diminished. I dare say I would need to learn a whole new language today. Soon after the founding of NEED*inc* (1985), of which I serve as president, we were asked to develop an evangelism strategy by our local Episcopalian diocese. At that time I was a Baptist, with fairly evangelical expressions to my Christian faith. But to work effectively with the Episcopal Church I had to learn new ways of expressing my Christian faith, ways that were unfamiliar to me. At one point a particular priest approached me and commented, "I *just don't know how you can pray so earnestly without reading it!*" [from the Prayer Book]. So I learned how to pray the Book of Common Prayer, in earnest. It deepened my faith and gave me yet another way of praising God I had never before considered.

When it comes to expressing our faith outside the church we take our stand alongside any missionary who has crossed an ocean or cultural barrier. It used to be that *evangelism* was what went on inside your own culture and *mission* meant going (overseas) to another culture. Not anymore. North American culture has moved far away from any understanding of the gospel of Christ. Most people are totally ignorant of who He is, why He came to earth, and what He did for us. When our son Josh was just out of high school, he had one of his friends over to the house who never goes to church. *"Actually, I think I've been three times to weddings. I just never think about religion."* I asked her who Jesus Christ was. *"I don't know..., God? Is that the right answer?"* She fit the profile of people I describe as *Clueless for Christ*. The old model of *evangelism/mission* is gone. Today, evangelism is what goes on *inside* the church; *mission* is what you enter into when you step outside the church into the community. So it is paramount for new kinds of Christians to adapt their faith both to the variety of expressions within the church as well as to be able to express it to people (versus *explain* it) outside the Christian mindset, of whom, believe me, there is a plethora!

6. **A Musically Acclimated Faith**- Music is such a powerful expression of every culture of the West that it deserves special attention. The reason for this is, again, a paradigm shift from modernism's logical/sequential approach to life to postmodernism's visual-imaging and experiential basis of approaching life. Whereas the last 500 years produced great insights, understanding and an analytical approach to life, in this emerging era people value experiences of faith more than they value explanations without the

experience. One key expression is that younger millennials *think* in music. They do not bifurcate or separate words from music, even though in the making of music the two are kept separate at first, then blended. On the receiving end it is all blended together as one whole. Add to the words/music mix the MTV image presentations and you have an audio-visual words/music/image amalgamation that creates, controls, and implants a sensory assault within a person. "*It's not about the music*," a teenager in Starbucks explained, "*it's about the experience.*" Music, like life beliefs gleaned through experience instead of logic, becomes a new alloy in the hands of the millennial generation. And they forge it to express their realities in forms that excel far beyond the communicational impact of mere words.

New kinds of Christians will have to learn to express their faith and their beliefs musically. And in different genres of music— from rap to country, hip-hop to soft jazz, classical to well, something that's probably just going pop up while you're reading this sentence. But it's not just music expressing faith and belief that must come of age. The structuring of theology itself needs to go through an overhaul and be upgraded, just like our computers.[lxxviii] And whatever it is that emerges will be something worth dancing to! Maybe it is time we stopped analyzing so much and started dancing. Turn up the volume!

Go out for ice cream with someone who is not of your generation. Ask them about their life. What is important to them? What do they enjoy doing?

> ## ➤ GENERATIONAL TRANSITIONS—
> ### *the laundry is still in the dryer*

But remember, the laundry isn't done yet. It's still spinning around in the dryer. This early part of the twenty-first century has seen only the first 25-30 years of the paradigm shift from modernism to postmodernism. We don't even know what to call the next phase of North American cultural reality yet; it's just post-something, post-modernism, right now. Or, if we keep going in the same direction, postChristian. So we wait; all the definitions, perspectives and styles of the kinds of Christians we will need to be are not yet in. They're still spinning 'round 'n 'round. We have to wait to see what comes out in a size that still, hopefully, fits. We have the privilege of writing the new rulebook, of designing the new church, of expressing our Christian faith in a way that is tied to its past in the Church history and in our Lord Jesus Christ; but we also have the privilege of writing the script for the new Broadway play of faith for all the world to see. Who will be the new Christians? What will they be like? Surely not just the young. Maybe not even those yet born. And probably some of us old timers will actually lead the way. Surprise, surprise! Wanna boogy? Gotcha!

What will Christians in this new century do to shape their societies, their cultures, their political and business arenas? Whatever they do, Christians in this era must carry a clear message of hope to be found in living a life that honors God, both in belief and action. Their lives must reflect a true personal godliness *over against* a merely factual, systematic, and correct theology. They must be sensitive to those around them and seek to communicate their faith in a manner that considers the other's point of view or even their ignorance of the Christian faith. They must learn to live among the peoples of this era *as they are*, with no delusions about what they know about the Christian faith. Above all they must learn love as the first expression of faith. The music, words, and images of faith come later.

Time to Play

1. What music people of different generations like? What songs, specifically? Ask them to play them for you. Enter into their world, on their turf, and learn to learn from them.

2. Try the interview on some of your friends who are your age. How did they answer the questions? Now try the interview on some believers who are older, now younger. Learning anything?

3. Go to a church that is not of your tradition. If you're Baptist, try Episcopal; if you're Catholic, try any Protestant church (not Episcopal, too close). If you're Pentecostal, try Lutheran. Can you worship there? How does it feel to you? What are the differences/similarities from your tradition?

4. Buy some music you would NEVER buy! Play it more than once on your record player, tape player,

Walkman, CD Player, MP3. Oh, forget it— just download it online. Get my point? [I guess I should download some RAP, huh? Oh the sacrifices! Hey, if I gotta make 'em, so do you!]

* * * * * * * * * *

FURTHER STUDY & PONDERENCES—

Utilize William James VARIETIES OF RELIGIOUS EXPERIENCE.

Utilize Gollub's THE GENERATION MATRIX: HOW THE DECADE YOU WERE BORN IN DETERMINES WHO YOU ARE.

Delineate the faith expressions of American Christianity by era, start with the Great Awakening (1736, Edwards, Whitfield, through Finney 1950s) Or Strauss & Howe- GENERATIONS: 1654-2069?

¿CLUELESS CHRISTIANITY?

"To prophesy is very difficult,
especially in regards to the future."
— Bob Fryling, IVPress (quoting a Chinese Proverb)

"The best way to predict the future is to create it."
— Peter Drucker

Chapter 7: Upgrading Your Faith:
reformatting the expressions of faith.

STORY— ZOOM, ZOOM

Tom Hawkes, founder of Christ Covenant Uptown Church, a PCA church plant in downtown (called "uptown") Charlotte, NC, related this story of one of their first worship services. One of the church elders, a man in his early 30s, had the duty one Sunday to give the call to worship. According to Tom it went something like this—

> *Good morning..., and welcome to*
> *Christ Covenant Uptown Church. How was*
> *your week? Mine <u>sucked</u>; how about your*
> *week? Well, we're in God's house now, so let*
> *us put our week aside and come together to*
> *worship the Lord.*

Then the elder led the congregation in singing the opening hymn. Tom said he just sat there and wondered— *"Sucked?!*

166

¿CLUELESS CHRISTIANITY?

Did he just say that? Well, so much for words retaining their original meanings." Tom told me he would have to learn to adapt more quickly to the rate of change overtaking younger generations.

It had taken the word *awful* almost 300 years to move from its original meaning: *awe-full* of the glory of God, full of awe, to its converse— terrible, horrible, etc. It took the word *suck* just over 5 years to move from its original meaning of simple sucking, as a baby on a bottle, to connote something quite sexual, or, conversely, something unpleasant. It is now part of our vernacular, a commonly acceptable speech pattern. [Though it still makes the 50+ crowd a tad uneasy.]

Innovations in inventions & language are changing at a rate that has accelerated beyond being measurable. I recently ordered a Motorola Droid for my wife. Within two months Verizon released the HTC Droid Incredible, a major upgrade. Now it's the Droid X. Apple Computer sold 300,000 iPads on launch day- April 3, 2010. In the next 80 days that figure rose to 3,000,000.[lxxix] iPad2 is soon on the way. Go figure. You *cannot* keep up.

➢ EARLY ADAPTATIONS

The same is true in the exchange between the church and the world. When James Hudson Taylor (1832-1905) went to China in 1854, he had much to learn about the mission to which God had called him. As with most foreign missionaries of that era (or in any era) he first had to learn the language. Through careful observation he continued to learn about cultural mores, kinship relationships, and of the subtleties of cultural protocol and nuance. He learned how to dress

¿CLUELESS CHRISTIANITY?

appropriately so he would be more approachable, in Chinese regalia, the clothing of his host culture. He had to learn *how* to communicate the Christian faith to the Chinese culture within a Chinese framework. But the biggest shift Taylor had to make was that of expressing his own faith in a Chinese format. This meant he had to change, or sacrifice, some of his cherished expressions of faith— western hymns, common wording (*thee* and *thou*, in that era), familiar forms of worship, and an understanding of family relationships as they related to the larger family, the Body of Christ, the Church.

When Bill Hybels wanted to plant a church in South Barrington, IL, (in Palatines Willow Creek Theater, Oct. 1975) he had to upgrade some of the ways he thought about Christian faith expressions based on what he learned from personal surveys of the community wherein he sought to plant a church. His strategy for ministry came from going door to door, asking a very basic question—"*If you were ever to come to church, what would it have to offer you?*" His question was really about the interface between the church and the world, between the individual and his access to God; it was a question about understanding and about very basic, very human felt-needs. Another way it could have been expressed would be "*What is it that you need to find an access to God?*" or, inversely "*What is it you would want God to do for you if you came to Him?*" These interrogatives convey a very different deportment than a question like "*What is truth?*" or "*Why is Christianity true?*" How? They define the *subjective* quest for meaning within, more than they seek an identification of an external definition of truth. Bill Hybels understood this. He understood that the pace and consumerism of western culture had taken over people's lives, ruling and running their time with everything

168

from soccer to working late, to Whole Foods™ take-out dinners. Even then we were utterly out of time! He knew that the questions people were asking in the mid-70s were different than those being asked in 1945 (end of WW2), or in 1963 (President Kennedy assassinated), or later, in 1980 (John Lennon assassinated), or in 2001 (Terrorists attacks on the World Trade Center, the Pentagon, & other intended points in Washington, D.C.).

The quest for God (purpose, meaning) exists in every generation in every culture, worldwide. In some generations it is more external, in other generations it seems to be more internal. We in North America are dealing with a shift in the way Truth is understood, perceived, and grasped. We are witnesses to a shift in everyday society from a cognitively grasped truth to an experientially based truth. As pointed out earlier, people today see truth more as something to be created than something to be discovered. Truth (capital T) is seen by many as virtually irrelevant and non-existent— it is an antiquated remnant left over from the Modern Era. True postmoderns believe there is no absolute, supreme, transcendent model of truth which supersedes and imprints itself upon all others. This shift in the view of truth, and the rejection of the very idea of an external, objective Truth, places pressure on the Christian community to accommodate. The pressure to realign its expression of Truth (yes, upper case) with those outside the Christian circle *so that* it can be understood is immense. This demands a change in us— to *deny* any absolute Truth, which I am sure, the secular world would relish. Of course, we cannot deny Truth— that we are created, fallen, redeemed by Christ our Lord, and will be fulfilled in Him when He returns for us at the end of the age.

¿CLUELESS CHRISTIANITY?

At the very least this requires Christian expressions of Truth become more accessible to those who assume the Christian faith irrelevant to their existence; which, of course, it is not.

These pages will address some of the intricacies of reformatting the Christian faith, both in approach and application that are pivotal. They are pivotal if our faith is to make any sense to the world outside Christian culture in the West. But it is just as important that our faith make sense to **us**, seriously. So we need to upgrade our faith expression for the sake of our children. We dare not hold tight to our *comfortable Christianity* at the cost of losing our children. The emerging Millennial Generation (George Barna calls them Millennials,[lxxx] a more appropriate term might be ***Mosaics***— a tapestry of styles of life and belief) finds it very difficult to identify with the Boomer-Buster/genX approach to the Christian faith. Boomers/genXers are seen as having ruined the foundation for the future. And Christian Boomer/genXers feel out of it, both in their need for a cohesive "world and life view," and their expressions of faith— *"way too archaic,"* they say. Older types may feel comfortable with *their* Christian faith but their kids don't. This generational confrontation has created the foundation for a major renovation of the Christian faith in North America. What follows are some foundational premises and consequent actions. These should be considered and acted upon..., quickly. Gradual change is no longer an option— not with the velocity of change increasing exponentially. Our world is ramping up— the church, on the surface at least, is lagging behind significantly.[lxxxi]

¿CLUELESS CHRISTIANITY?

> ### CHRISTIAN FAITH FOR THE EARLY 21ST CENTURY— NORTH AMERICAN EDITION

The early 21st century finds us in a time where Christian leaders need to reexamine the premises of our faith. This is not a challenge to the Bible or questioning its authority: it is reassessing, a repositioning, if you will, of how we approach the Bible as our founding source. It is how it is perceived by emerging believers and their contiguous culture. The theological constructs of the past had no need to deal with the new definitions of life prevalent in North American society today. Former approaches to the Bible were couched in concerns for the issues of *their* day; but the issues of this era are more complex than those of an earlier time. The issues of our day are different: the world has truly changed. The Church in North America needs to address our present culture's felt needs, pluralities, diversities, and philosophical fancies, and then implement a new kind of Christianity appropriate to the expressions and approaches to life of *our* time.

I've been attending an international evangelistic program known as ALPHA. It is highly successful in communicating the basics of the Christian faith worldwide. It's a great experience, and really a lot of fun, where great food and growing friendships abound. I have enjoyed it immensely! I was talking with a youth worker who was also in attendance, and was not surprised when I was told, *"This is great, but I cannot use it with my kids."* Why? I asked. *"Because it answers questions that are totally foreign to their thinking."* This, I thought to myself, is a real problem! Someone has to address the issues facing the emerging generations of North America. Oh (I thought next), that might be you.

¿CLUELESS CHRISTIANITY?

What are the **foundational premises** we need to establish for a vibrant Christian faith to flourish in our generation? They are the non-negotiables in the next wave of Christian life and expression in western society.

FIVE FOUNDATIONAL PREMISES

1. The nature, purpose, and *rubric of Christian theology* need to be reformatted to fit this present cultural, generational, western society. I am sure you are aware that in any era, ALL theology happens through the interplay between the church, the culture, and the Bible. Note Figure 1—

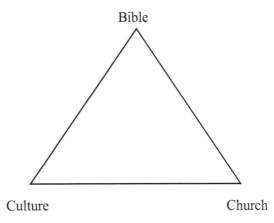

[Of course, individual personalities, personal positioning and church power politics are also a great part of the mix.]

The last *major* theological construct in western society was **Reformed Theology**, circa 1517/1520.

This theology grew out of a sense of injustice in the way clergy represented the faith to the people of Western Europe. Martin Luther's cry was *"The just shall live by faith!"* and nothing else. Though that is still very true, the issues of North America in this 21st century are much more multifaceted. Time for an upgrade? What do you think? My own premonition is that we will move (yea, must move) away from a *global* systematic theology to one that adapts to the *ways-of-perceiving* of each specific culture, not only in North America, but worldwide. It will most likely be a people group, generationally specific form of theology..., which wouldn't be all that bad. Think of it..., a culturally sensitive, Biblically based and attuned, generational/regional/kinship theology. Boggles the mind! (Note-missionaries already do this.)

2.   The Christian community and individual believers alike need to start living their lives as if they were truly **forgiven by God**. In the winter of 2003 Johanna, at that time NEED's CHINA Consultant, attended an Emergent Convention in San Diego. Upon her return I asked her opinion of the conference. To my surprise she said she was confronted with her own reticence to accept Christ's forgiveness for her sins and to stop feeding her guilt. She never believed that she was truly forgiven. Today, she is a different person with far more freedom in her life, and a freedom to fail before God, again..., and to be forgiven, again.

For whatever reason, so much of the Christian faith is about **doing** more to assuage your guilt and/or to prove yourself to God as worthy [i.e., being moral]. Please, people, it's time we trust in God and stop this nonsense. *"Christ has died, Christ is risen, Christ is coming again."* Is this true? Isn't this enough!? Isn't this what is proclaimed every time we celebrate Holy Communion? CELEBRATION!? Everything that is necessary for us to be reinstated into a relationship with the God who made us has been accomplished by Jesus Christ on the cross of Calvary. We *are* forgiven. This is foundational to the Christian life; without forgiveness there is only fruitless effort and a sense of never being able to measure up. And that is precisely the point. Our foundation of faith IS forgiveness. We can NOT measure up. That's why Christ came in the first place. If we don't make the shift to proclaiming thorough forgiveness and cease from reminding people that they are still sinners (like I need to be reminded) then we will never be able to get on with being the Christians God intends us to be. Accept the forgiveness, deal with future sin and rebellion as it comes up, and then return to being proactive Christians in an antagonistic/apathetic world.

3. Building on a new sense of genuine forgiveness, we must move to the ***holiness*** granted us by God. God declares us to be HOLY. Therefore, holiness too, becomes for the genuine Christian, foundational. I've often wondered if holiness isn't more of a *platform* for launching the Christian life than a goal to be striven toward. In my own life I have carried on a conversation with God that runs something like this—

> *"Now come on God, how can you declare me holy. You know my life. I know my life. There is just no way I am a holy person. So how can you declare that I am holy?"* And the Lord God of the Universe would reply, *"Listen to me, my son. I have declared you holy. Now live like it."* End of scenario.

He has declared us holy…, live with it. We are still to seek after God and personal holiness; but we must always remember that He has already declared us holy…, as odd as that may sound. Therefore, living *as if* we hold within us a **clean spirit** is essential to any new foundation of the Christian life.

4. The Body of Christ must truly become the Body of Christ. Commitment to *Christian community* is foundational to twenty-first century faith. Yet so many of us live in isolation, with little commitment to a church or even to a small group of believers. We need to be more a part of each other's lives in a society where there is so much pain and fragmentation. Any profile of the Millennial/Mosaic generation reinforces the need for genuine Christian community.[lxxxii] And that community might not be defined in terms of your immediate geography. Thanks to the marvels of our postmodern, technological society, our "community" can be pin-boarded on a worldwide map. Though I have many dear friends where I live in Amherst, MA, my personal community also extends to places around the world. I have deep friendships with Christians in

every part of the world— Lima, Peru; Changsha, China; outside Hyderabad, India; Vancouver, British Columbia; Adelaide, Australia; St Petersburg, Russia; and just across "the pond" in London, England. Our world has shrunk!

In mid-2003, when I was in Macau, China, Kirsten Britcher, at the time an administrator for *INTERNATIONAL CHINA* CONCERN, asked me if I had talked with my wife since I had been there. *"Well, no."* She threw her mobile phone to me and said, simply, *"Well, call her*!" I knew my wife would be at work at our church back in Northampton, MA, USA. I punched in (note- PC punched..., *not* dialed) our country code, city code, local exchange and got through to her. A church secretary picked up. *"Good morning, this is the College Church; how may I help you?"* I told her I was calling my wife, Starr. She asked *"But I thought you were in China!" "I am." "Well, where are you, specifically?"* I knew my reply might stun her a tad. *"Well, to be quite honest, I am sitting by the pool at the Hyatt Regency Hotel in Macau, talking on a friend's cell phone."* Total disbelief at the other end! *"I'll get Starr,"* ended our brief encounter. That's just the way our world functions now, and has for quite some time. Get used to it.

We have no option but to be part of a Christian community, broadly or locally, if we are to flourish in a world that holds less and less sympathy for Christian Truth. You know the mantra *think globally, act locally*? Well, it's changed—*think locally, think globally* now *act locally, act globally too*. We are now part of a much larger…, and smaller world. We are all part of something bigger than we could ever have imagined 25 years ago. Our rugged American individualism must give way to mutual dependence. We must make a conscious decision, and effort, to mingle among the strong, and gentle, with a sense of determined empowerment for the weaker brother.[lxxxiii] And we must do this on a global scale. The answer to the question, *"Who is my neighbor?"* has grown exponentially.

5. Finally, the last foundational premise is the ***power of God,*** which is able to draw unbelievers into relationship with their Creator, nothing else. He alone is the author and designer of life: he alone has the power to bring people into a relationship with himself. I want to be careful here: the fact is we often act as if it is *belief in the Bible* that brings people to life. *"Only believe!"* We hear it all the time; but the New Testament context contains more assumptions and cultural nuances than our culture can imagine. How so? The Bible, when you honestly consider it, is the only source we have on earth to know about Jesus Christ. It is inspired by the Father, transmitted to us through human hand, and kept accurate and true-to-the-fact by the Holy Spirit. But as necessary as it is to the Christian faith, it still stands behind the work of God in the redemptive of a person's life. Remember, God's Word, though foundational for all we believe, is still purely a *historical recounting* of the descriptions

of the works of God on earth. God's *work* is so much more than the historical descriptions of it. It is not simply that Truth brings people to life— it is the Author of Truth Himself who does. Any new foundation for emerging generations of believers must be founded, not on Truth alone, but on real life ***encounters with God***, on the God of the Bible who stands behind the Bible. We *all* must learn to trust in our experience of God as much as we do in our belief about God (the Bible); one is validated by the other. Still, if someone's experience of God is questionable, and is not addressed directly in Scripture, there is always the larger body of Christian believers to challenge, guide, correct or affirm. This past year an Amherst teenager came to me with a question. *"What is a Christian?"* A somewhat odd question from a liberal-based youth culture. So I responded with questions— *What is your interest in Christian faith? Why do you want to know? What happened to you?* It was then that he launched into monologue about dreams and experiences he had gone through recently. He called them *encounters*— encounters with God. I described the context for Christian faith in creation, the context for Christ's death to fulfill the requirements of Jewish law, the mark of His deity verified in His resurrection, His call to repentance and trust. [Not using those words, of course.] In essence I was explaining the Christian faith as the context for his experiences. He responded, *"Oh, that's it..., that's what happened to me! This is great! I'm a Christian aren't I!?"* And so he was. For postmodern, experience-based individuals will not believe in Truth alone. This is *their* way to come to faith; until they see it working its way out in people's lives, Truth is no more than *descriptive words*. But when they see Christian life lived, and the power of God demonstrated in other peoples' lives, and subsequently experience it in their own lives, then, our Biblical explanations have a context— they make sense. Frankly, I find this amazingly wholistic.

These Foundational Premises lay the groundwork for a new kind of freedom wherein Christians can grow and flourish with less spiritual baggage, less ecclesiastical classification, and less theological fuss. If implemented, these premises create a framework for us to explore new and different avenues of Christian life and thought. Each Foundational Premise, in turn, evokes an ensuing response that must be joined with its principle, and implemented. Do you think you've got that? Sorry to be so obtuse; this form of thinking doesn't exactly proceed along linear/sequential lines.

IMPLICATIONS-TO-BE-IMPLEMENTED

1. Any new construct of theology must be visibly reflected in real *LIFE*. Taking a saying from the modern-era church , if *correct belief produces correct action*, then all the more so in a reformatted theology. *"Faith without works is dead."* says James. Or, as we say around our office—*Talk's cheap: action's everything*. Theological belief as a foundation, *per se*, will have to be reflected in the lives of people changed by the power of God. It cannot stand alone. A systematic or Biblical theology will never become

irrelevant to forming the Christian life, but it will acquiesce to the **demonstrated work of Christ** within the believer. LIFE will replicate Truth.

When Starr and I were first married, a young woman dropped by our home and asked if she could talk with us. I had met this young woman at Amherst College, where I served as chaplain with InterVarsity. She had had a couple of talks with Starr, but from what I could tell, nothing pivotal. In our fire-room (so named for the woodstove), she opened the conversation with a quite surprising statement— *"I want to become a Christian."* This was a shock, to say the least. When we asked her why, her reply was just as straightforward— *"I have been watching you. I like the way you love each other. I want that kind of love in my life: I want to become a Christian."* We went on to explain what it meant to be a Christian; she responded, *"Yes, that's it. That's what I want."* No further explanation, no coercing, no challenging. Fini, done! A new sister in Christ was born. How? Solely by the work of God's Holy Spirit. Because she was watching us. So, do you think your actions speak louder than words?!

2. Building on the previous platform, living with forgiveness will require that we learn to grasp **guiltless living**. So many of my friends, who are far from Christian, comment that *"You Christians may claim to be freed by the power of Christ, but you still come across as motivated, even driven, by guilt. At least I don't live my life riddled with guilt."* Therefore, they

don't see any advantage to becoming a Christian. They have a point. Unless we shift our "encouragement" from constantly reminding each other that we can never be good enough for God to one of being truly FREE, then we can never even begin to believe that our guilt is taken away. (Nor can they.) It's time we started to live like God intends us— guiltless before Him, truly forgiven, new creations, through the eyes of Christ.

3. Once you've cleaned out your soul, cleared your spirit of so much stuff, a funny thing happens— *you can see things more clearly.* In other words, having a clear view to God, and allowing Him to have a go at cleaning out your life, opens a window for you to gain a **clear perception** of things around you; like people, problems, life's normal situations, and the effects of sin on life. But this can happen *only* if you accept the forgiveness Christ obtained when He gave His life for you. So much of our present way of being a Christian demands we live up to Biblical standards of behavior and a set of systematized beliefs. This has been true of the Christian way of life ever since Christ came. For some, it is a place of certainty, of safety: for others it is a constant chore, a duty. But at times, this kind of living seems as if we're boxed in, trapped, and manipulated into a behavioral form of Christian practice. In contrast, if our spirits are clean before God, if we have accepted the forgiveness and freedom Jesus purchased for us on the cross, we can see His point of view and understand His way more clearly. Living the Christian life then ceases to be a chore or a

duty and becomes more like a great challenge or an adventure. I truly wonder if our lack of accepting Christ's forgiveness blinds or fuzzes our perception, forcing us into a deeper legalism or cerebral faith. In John 8, a woman caught in the act of adultery is thrown at Jesus feet. The law said she should be stoned. Jesus takes the situation in hand by admonishing those calling for her stoning: "*Let the one who is without sin cast the first stone.*" After everyone has faded away, Jesus asked the woman where her accusers are. "*There are none, Lord.*" she replies. Jesus simply says "*Neither do I condemn you. Go and sin no more.*" Those who sought to stone her couldn't see through Jesus' eyes: Jesus saw things from another vantage point— he saw the forgiveness he would purchase on the cross and bestowed some of it on her... early. Do we see people who don't understand, whose lives are driven by guilt, who think they can never measure up to the standards of God, do we see them like Jesus did? I wonder. We need to develop that same clear perception our Lord manifested if we are to live in the new realities of North America's *post*Modern, *post*Christian culture.

4. A fourth characteristic of this new reality for the Christian is the need to be **immersed in the surrounding society**. But first a warning. To genuinely immerse yourself in your surrounding society, you need first to be a committed member of a Christian community. You need the emotional and spiritual support of like-minded believers who know the importance of being a clean, genuine Christian. It

is imperative if you are going to be immersed in a hostile (though somewhat passive-aggressive) society. And make no mistake, North America is adapting a more contrarian position to the Christian one on almost everything. There are so many preconceived assumptions about Christianity (judgmental, bigoted, racist, anti-environment, anti-abortion, pro-war, to name a few) that, at least in the valley where I live, to answer the question *Are you a Christian?* in the positive could bring an extremely negative reaction. Before I answer it, I ask "Well, *what do you mean by 'Christian?' That can be a somewhat pejorative word.*" In your community, what would be an appropriate answer to the question— *Are you a Christian?* What would the reaction most likely be? Most of us never find out. Why? Because for many of us, our lives come across as so marginally Christian that no one would think to ask. Still other Christians are so weird, out of it, dork-like even, that normal people in our society don't want to know. We've already confirmed their suspicions.

So we Christians have developed a society within a society; a subgroup just slightly to the right of center; okay, maybe far more than slightly to the right. More Christians are *cocooning*, to use Faith Popcorn's term, inside their families, their churches, and their Christian subcultures. Commitment to Christ has morphed into Cocooning in Christ— moving away from the culture and into the Christian cave. Nevertheless, the purpose of commitment to a Christian community remains the same— to equip and enable believers to immerse themselves in the society which surrounds them, gaining a position of influence for its stabilization and flourishing for the glory of Christ. Make no mistake; we are *all* called to be vessels of light in the darkness. And the darker, the more ignorant the society is of Christ's principles, the more necessary it will be for His followers to take their place in the darkness. Got a light?

5. Oddly the last ingredient of faith in this new reality brings us full circle. If people will not believe in a Truth they cannot see, then there must be some explanation provided for what they do see. In short, we need **Christian explanations** for the behavior of people who claim the name of Christ. This returns the Christian to become once again the *student of the Bible and of the world* in which he dwells. For any Christian explanation of a Biblical principle must be set forth in a manner which can be understood by the seeker. I said earlier that *Talk's cheap: action's everything.* That's where belief hits reality. But action needs both context and explanation. We do not want postModerns thinking Christians are *good people* just to be good. The *Motivation* to act must also be understood as well. It's the *why* of life that gives our actions meaning and context. And for anyone who has had an experience with God (and many I have met have) it is absolutely tantamount that they understand their experience through the filter of Christian faith and Christian Truth. Their experience can only be validated through filtration and reflection in the Bible. To validate it through any other source would be to

invalidate it as a genuine experience of God. So we Christians had better know what we are talking about when it comes to explaining our faith. We had better spend the kind of time in the Bible, studying it, pondering its original contexts and learning how to apply it, so that we can "handle the Word of God aright." For if we do not understand the basic message of Scripture of God's creation of life, of our rejection of His claim on us, and of all the subsequent efforts God made to draw us back to Himself, then we truly will not be able to express our faith in ways that make sense to anyone.

These **Five Foundational Premises** and **Subsequent Implications-to-Be-Implemented** must not stand in isolation to each other, or be "worked on" in sequence. They exist as a spiritual/personal/cultural **matrix**, woven and connected at multiple overlapping levels to strengthen and stabilize life. None is more important than the other; each is necessary to produce in the believer the kind of faith that can cope with today's postmodern cultural challenges. Diagrammatically, it might look something like this—

¿CLUELESS CHRISTIANITY?

JUGGLING AN ACTION BASED FAITH

(PRODUCES = NEEDS)

Biblical Truth =
Life Demonstrated
Actions

Commitment to Christ =
Immersion in Surrounding
Society

Living with Forgiveness =
Guiltness Living

Life Encounters with God =
Biblical Explanations of
Experiences

Clean Spirit =
Clear
Perception

In essence, Biblical Truth *produces* Life Demonstrated Actions: conversely, Life Demonstrated Actions *need* Biblical Truth to explain their root. Living with Forgiveness *produces* Guiltless Living; conversely, Guiltless Living *needs* to Live with the Forgiveness granted us through Jesus Christ's work on the Cross; and so on. One without the other is a mere shell of the Christian life, whether unfounded in Scripture and lost in the mind, or not exhibited in the life of the follower of Jesus.

If we still lived in a culture based on a Modernist view of reality (belief in scientific verification, rational thought, discoverable truth, etc.), then all you would need to live the Christian life would be an agreement with Biblical Truths and some form of Life Demonstration (going forward at an alter in church, praying the *sinners prayer*, ceasing our cursing and smoking, and attending church weekly). But so much more is demanded of the Christian in postModern times. He/she must actually *live* their Christian life consistently, openly, and transparently before the world, and *in* the world. Anything less will bring ridicule and rejection of the whole *Christian idea*.

On a more practical level, older Christians with children must live out their faith transparently in the home. Warts, flares of anger, family difficulties, teenage rebellions, interaction with neighbors, job produced stress, marital failure and more are ALL up-close-and-personal before our seeking (or rebellious) children on a daily basis. Our children seek to know a Christ who makes a difference in their parents' lives. Our children seek to know if God's forgiveness translates itself into everyday living, especially in regard to their idiosyncrasies and fowl-ups. Our children want parents who do not put on a front of Mr. Nice-Guy-Joe-Christian for the world and then treat them badly in private. And our children want Christian parents who can admit when they are wrong and when they have failed. NOTHING sustains their trust and love more than truthful transparency.

Truly, it is time for an upgrade to our faith. It is time for a reformatting of *how* we believe. Postmodernism's myths have forced us into it. BUT, and this is a BIG BUT, how do we do it? How do we express our faith in the language, idioms, and formats of our culture and still present our faith in Christ as the only legitimate way to God? Well, that's the next chapter. Read on if you dare. I mean that. For the next chapter will stretch you about how you perceive and present your life of faith to others. And it all starts inside your soul. Is all this feeling a little unnerving for you yet? Good.

Play Time

1. Ask someone at work (or school) what they believe are your Foundational Principles about life. Then do the same thing in your home.

2. How is your faith *appropriate* to your culture? How might you relate what you believe in a better way to those who are clueless4Christ?

3. I've listed Five Foundational Principles and Five Implications to be Implemented. Are there others? I could have missed some. Write me and tell me what they are.

4. To what extent does the way you came to Christ influence how you introduce others to Him?

5. After reading this chapter, what do you think of the idea— *Belonging before Believing?*

¿CLUELESS CHRISTIANITY?

*This modern age [circa 1900] is characterized by a
sadness that calls for a new kind of prophet, not like prophets
of old who reminded people that they were going to die, but
someone who would remind them that they are not dead yet.*
-G. K. Chesterton

No matter where you go, that's where you are.
-Will Rogers
(quoted by Buckaroo Banzai)

Chapter 8: Getting from Here to There:
what to do, what to do...?

In many ways this chapter is what you're really
looking for in this book. Please don't feel jilted that you have
read this far to get to the meat. For those interested in the shift
from a Modern worldview to a *post*Modern/*post*Christian
worldview you are well aware that we have analyzed this shift
to death. Between George Barna and George Gallup we have
enough statistics to fill a barn.[lxxxiv] But **understanding** is not
the issue. It's what to **DO** about the shift that is the real
problem. That is what this chapter will address. What follows
are some simple things you can do to change, adjust, adapt,
cope, whatever— first, on an individual level, and then
corporately as a church. They are much needed to deal with
this strange, frightening paradigm shift in which we all find
ourselves, whether we want to be there or not. But please, as
you read, DO NOT give in to *BUT WE'VE NEVER DONE IT
THAT WAY BEFORE* (Thank you Ralph Neighbors). That,

would warrant your death. On the one hand, *"There is nothing new under the sun."* (Ecclesiastes 1:9)[lxxxv] and on the other hand, we have entered into a new phase in history. An entire generation has been born in the West with no Christian history, no Christian memory or experience whatsoever. Any semblance of "Western Christian culture" is fading into oblivion as a forgotten archeological relic.

➤ **Paradigm Pioneers Get Shot First:**
don't be too quick to sign up!

BUT first, a warning! You need to understand that as someone who is concerned, frustrated, or even angry at the church's seeming inability to adjust to a new set of cultural rules, you will not be a popular person, especially with the powers that be. True Christian leadership within this Postmodern mentality is what is desperately needed. We've all seen those SUCCESS sections in Flight magazines— you know, the ones with motivational posters to put up in your office. You can find another series at the website www.despair.com that offers a truly different slant on motivational posters. The one I find most germane to being a paradigm pioneer depicts an eye-level bright green lawn, with one blade of grass standing taller than all the rest. The caption reads— *Remember..., it's the tallest blade of grass that gets cut first.* Get the picture? Ask yourself a question— *"Are you more interested in a position of authority, where you are respected within the Christian matrix, or are you convinced that you want to lead the way in reshaping our faith in this emerging postmodern/postChristian world?"* If you find yourself in the latter position (which I am assuming you might, since you've read so far in this book), then you must adjust your self-perception to a new reality— you are a target. To be sure, ALL Christians are targets…, it's just that some are more selected targets than others; *they* are the tallest blades of grass; *they* are the ones who are the greatest threat to the kingdom of the dark lord. They are the ones who are on the front lines of the battle, who are the most visible to our enemy. Are you sure you want to be this kind of B-I-G, visible target? If you are sure, then rest assured you will take the first shots. You will most likely be wounded first in battle. The sad thing is that the shot is more likely to come from the back— not from up front, from enemy lines. Christians across North America have long valued their own comfort and safety over frontline battle. Don't expect a lot of support or followers. If you do find any comrades-in-arms you will probably find many of them on the fringes of faith. Few tend to rise to central leadership, though many more are desperately needed there. Outfielders …, without whom the ball game would be lost.

But every new wave of the Spirit of God always starts with committed, called, set-apart men and women of vision…, and courage…, and risk. In short, any changes or ideas to be implemented in the Christian community must be initiated by people like you. Don't wait for someone else to take up the flag and lead. We don't have that long. It's up to you. I've designed a translucent cube, a paper-weight-type-thingy for my desk. Six sides, with different phrases that reflect and define who I am and want to be— *"imagine," "The fear of the Lord…," "think outside,"* etc. But the side I will always want to describe me the most is *"the buck stops here."* It must also describe you. Are you up to the task? If so, you will not find yourself alone, but you will find yourself scarce, in the minority. And you will need to learn to duck a lot; moving targets are harder to hit. Such are the postmodern/postchristian prophets— you..., a Christian paradigm-pioneer. You will be the first one to take the shot. If this sounds like fun to you, keep reading.

Another preemptive move must be addressed before we tackle the practical stuff. To re-gear your faith, start with a spiritual check-in. How would you describe your relationship with God? Close, cautious, committed? What? When you pray (you do pray, don't you?) do you expect answers? Are you able to hear those answers in whatever form God chooses to send them? Do you act, immediately, on what you know God is directing you to do? Or, do you wait 'till things seem safer, when you have the support of others? Your spiritual health and your spiritual perception are the foremost armor you will need to do battle in a postChristian context. Do not even attempt to pioneer anything without a firm grounding in personal cleanness and righteousness before the Lord God. You need His support too much to show up in dirty clothes to the banquet.

Leadership in postChristian times is always a matter of sticking your neck out, of starting first and not waiting to see what others think. This has been true in all eras. Think of it as a kind of *first* faith; like the clothing line known as *STARTER*— the illustration from sports, summoning images of *up front on the team, first on the line, in the first squad to the front*. If you are a *STARTER* there are some things you will have to re-gear on your own before you begin to inspire others. Modeling is everything.

1. **Express your faith through life experiences**. Realign your faith to balance *experiencing God* with *understanding God*. Western Christianity in the Modern era swung the pendulum of understanding to the extreme. Faith was about belief and theology more than it was about life. But faith is really more akin to *trust* and *risk* than it is related to *understanding*. Remember, TRUTH is first personal, in the person of Jesus Christ, then propositional, explaining the life of faith. Like Jesus, we need to learn to think of our faith as stories, metaphors, and experiences of the *ah-ha!* Faith is a *journey*, not an outline. Make sure your beliefs are in line with the teachings of Holy Scripture, but do not get bogged down with getting every aspect of a theological system locked down and in place. Spend even more time in solitude, in prayer, in union with God, and then immersed within a world that doesn't know Him, to gain a visible faith *in word and deed.*

2. **Learn to speak one language, the language of the culture**. Every subculture has its own language pattern. Football has its nickel defense, fullbacks and wishbones; computer geeks talk about Clouds, Wi-Fi, TCPIPs, i3s, i5s, i7s, even i9s, and smart devices. We Christians have our pre-mills, post-tribs, and supralapsarians. Get the point? Notwithstanding, we need to learn the language of our surrounding culture (we may already know it..., but *awareness* is an utterly different thing). We need to learn to express our faith *within* the church, *within* our families, and *within* our daily conversations with Christians and normal people, in a language pattern that anyone can understand. They may not agree with what

it represents, but we need to express it so they can comprehend it. In order for communication to take place, a common language must be understood by both sender and receiver (Communication Theory 101). And don't you dare assume that all Christians understand one another. Remember, Christian expressions of faith are generationally delimited with little crossover to younger generations. Just ask your Christian teen to translate "*the Lordship of Christ*" into their generational mindset. You'll see. It's an embedded language pattern from a former era.

3. **Let go of your sin**. There are many blockades to the Christian life in postChristian America. Communication is definitely a big blockade. But the one that has the greatest effect on Christians living out their faith is our own sinfulness. Not that we need to be rid of *all* sin in our life to be Christians in the postmodern matrix. Until Christ comes back our sin will be ever with us. If you don't believe that please pay more attention in church. We sit painfully on the bull's horns of a dilemma regarding our sin. On the one hand, many churches constantly remind us that we are sinners. Not that we don't know it already, but some pastors believe it their duty to constantly point it out. That is part of their job— to call us to account. On the other side of the bull is a duality. On one hand we are forgiven through the work of Christ; on the other hand, we still find ourselves wallowing in the guilt of confessed, even forgiven sin. This is in no way a healthy dilemma. We need a genuine trust in Christ, sins forgiven, new beginning in progress, a done deal! Then we need to get on with life *as if* our

sins are actually forgiven. The reality is that they actually ARE! If the world around us is ever to be drawn to our Lord Jesus Christ they must see a difference in us. They need to see genuine, real, Christians. They do not need to see perfection— they see enough fake faith in seemingly *perfect* Christians already. But they do need to see Christians living forgiven lives in spite of their continuing sin. They need to see them pressing on, striving to please the one we love, Jesus Christ. So cease and desist living like a guilty Christian and start living like a forgiven sinner! So it is written; so it is done!

4. **Learn to love**. If letting go of sin frees the Christian for living in a *post*Christian era *as if* those sins were actually forgiven (duh, again) then *learning to love* makes that life visible to others. This may sound quite simple for virtually any Christian, but it is not. Loving has become difficult in the church in North America, nestled in a conservative, pluralistic, gender-terrified, harassment-screeching culture. All of us have become quite cautious and guarded in our love lives; so much so, that we generally withhold love because it's simply safer that way. And so the greatest of Christian virtues becomes the greatest matter of concern and risk. But isn't that what the Christian life is about anyway? Risk! I cannot imagine any other model for Christ's love for the world than for it to be exhibited through us. That was a risk. Loving people in this era is also a risky business (especially of the opposite sex). But love is a definitive corollary of safety. More than anything else, *post*Christians crave safety— safe places, safe people, safe activities. When a person feels safe, and actually *is*

safe, then taking risks becomes more of a possibility. And I know of no greater place of safety than sensing that you are loved by another person.

But coming to a place of loving, or of being loved, is no small matter. Accepting love is just as risky as offering love. Nonetheless, the central character of *genuine* Christians that people need most in a *post*Christian culture is their proactive ability to love with abandon. Is this a risk— yes, absolutely! Is it necessary— absolutely so! Note: you cannot start loving people with abandon from the get-go. But you have to start somewhere. So find someone who is not a Christian, who does not attend church anywhere, a neighbor, a workmate, a fellow student, and take them for coffee, ice cream, or whatever. Start by caring— listening to them talk about their life, their daily ups & downs, their existence: you will find an increasing sense of underlying love for them growing inside you. You will find yourself praying for them, calling them, wanting to be with them, loving them, just like Jesus did. Jesus learned to love the people of His time by being with them on an almost daily basis— so also must we.

5. **Lose the intensity [you don't need to win].** A lot of western Christianity in the modern era became pretty intense. Intense about theology, intense about denominationalism, intense about appearances, intense about proper relationships, etc. I don't know about you but it wore me down. I was always worried about what someone else thought about what I did, who I spent time with, and whether or not I had my theology straight

according to their stamp of endorsement. People who aren't Christians saw it and concluded that Christianity wasn't for them— too intense, too judgmental, and too narrow. This intensity, too, is a corollary of our ability to love and to risk. We Christians seem to feel safest when we have as much as possible nailed down in its proper place, quantifiable and definable. So we then strive for meticulous exactitude in as much of life and theology as is humanly possible. This takes an awful lot of effort and energy. I wonder if God intended us to spend more effort defining our faith than in exercising it, in living it out among those who truly needed to see Him in us? Where should the emphasis be? Some things can only be learned, realized, and grasped through *living* it, not through cerebral comprehension. In short, we need to lose some of our intensity over life, guilt, and failure. Lose the obsessive-compulsive drive, and learn to trust in our God a bit more. We don't need to win— He has. He does. Let Him.

6. **Don't do everything - Give God some room to work**. If any attribute characterizes everybody in early years of the twenty-first century it is **busyness**. Most of us are over-worked, over-booked, over-committed, out-of-time, frantic fanatics about squeezing as much into life each day as is in-humanly possible. When our kids entered Middle School they had to take a course on *TIME MANAGEMENT AND SETTING PRIORITIES: or, how to use your Day-Timer*. You're probably reading this book curled up in bed too tired to retain much of what you are reading. Why? Not because you think it's the best stuff on growing a *post*Christian faith you have ever read, but

because this is the only time you have to squeeze in any reading whatsoever. And, you are t-i-r-e-d! Bone tired. If you must put in an appearance at one more political rally, one more church meeting, one more pressurized late night at work, one more PTA meeting; you just don't know how you can fit it in. And you feel like you have no choice about it whatsoever. One foot in front of the other— just keep it going.

Or, is there another way? Try not doing so much. Breathe more. Slow down your life, cut some commitments (even for your kids), and take a walk. Throughout all life there are growth-plateaus where our bodies and minds must rest. I remember a story about Dr. Helen Rosevere when she was just starting out as a missionary in 1953. Upon hearing that her assigned mission station was 44 miles into the interior of the Congo (now Republic of Congo), she packed her belongings on the 15 or so porters she had hired to transport her there. Usually the trek took 3-4 days, depending on conditions, season, and density of forestation. The first day the caravan made 22 miles. Dr. Rosevere thought, *"Why, at this rate we'll be there by tomorrow, dinner!"* She was thrilled. So the next morning she arose bright and early and ordered her porters to load up! They just sat there. When Dr. Rosevere asked the #1 porter *why,* he explained, *"Oh, Dr. Rosevere, we are so sorry, but you must understand. We moved so fast yesterday that now we must wait for our spirits to catch up to our bodies.* Are you moving so fast that you must slow down to even hear God? If you are involved in a ministry of some kind, full time or volunteer, are you trying to do everything? Please, for Jesus' sake, STOP! Let your spirit catch up to your body. Give God some room to work. Pressurized postmoderns need to see that kind of tranquility, that kind of s-l-o-w-n-e-s-s, and that kind of trust in our God being exercised daily in our lives— and so do our kids. When was the last time you moved slow enough for them to talk to you about their lives? We all need to incorporate some peace into our life's pace.

7. **Open a channel to God— keep it open**. There are probably many more qualities that we Christians need to exhibit to make sense to *post*Christian people, but I'll end with this one. *Open a channel to God— and keep it open.* It sounds so simple, yet, in a compartmentalized society we tend to pigeonhole even our relationship with God. We go *to* church, rather than being the church. We have times of prayer, but then manage our life as if God has little to do with it. Instead, let me propose to you that we learn to *pray without ceasing*, in a sense. If you've ever noticed people about to go to prayer in a small group, there is a funny little ritual they go through. First the glasses come off, then they rub their eyes, then there is a l-o-n-g silence before any praying actually begins. This forced me to wonder... why? *O, well we need to prepare ourselves to come into the presence of God. But aren't we always in His presence?* If God is all powerful and all knowing (a.k.a.- omnipotent and omniscient, old words) why do we believe we need to prepare ourselves to come into his presence? Why not just assume His constant presence, always there, always on? Why not merely shift the direction of your

conversation from horizontal, with whomever, to vertical, with God? This pre-positioning of God in our midst makes much more sense to me than *getting ready to come into His presence.* [I admit that coming into His presence is nothing to be taken lightly. Nonetheless, we are, in actuality, *never* out of His presence. Ever!]

Curiously, at the same time, I'm never quite ready to come into His presence. Never. Still, I come; I come often, and at times I even know that I am invited to come. That is one scary aspect of prayer— that He wants us to talk to Him. He knows us clear through…, and He still loves us. Remember the little poem—

> *Isn't it odd,*
> *That a Being like God,*
> *Who sees the façade,*
> *Still loves the clod*
> *He made out of sod;*
> *Now isn't that odd?*

He who knows all still loves us and wants to hear our voices. I actually wonder if God didn't create prayer solely for our benefit, for our sense of connection, communication, and closeness to Him? However, two things constantly trouble me about prayer—

1) When God remains silent and doesn't seem to answer my prayer. His silence feels deafening. and,

2) When He does answer my prayers, often detailing exactly what it is He

wants me to do. Dictation, direct command, not just a "feeling." A communication bummer, a specific command to obey, with a blessing attached..., if I follow through.

I am convinced that unless we are in touch with our God on a moment by moment basis we stand in danger of creating a truth with which *we* are comfortable, which does not come from Him. We all want to feel safe; but, as said often, safety for the Christian is only found in the presence of the Lord. You've been here; you've heard God admonish you, direct you, call you to a task well beyond your ability; you've cringed when He has asked/told you to do something you did not want to do. That's the danger of keeping the channel open; you can always hear the voice of God in the back of your head saying, *Okay, now you need to get up off your..., er, you know, and put into action what you say you know you must do.* Think of God not so much as a DSL or ISDN connection, or even a T1 or T2. You have a constantly open, wireless access to the Throne Room of God. Of course, reciprocally, He always has access to you too. Ah, the thrills of spiritual awareness!

> **Let's Reinvent the Church:**
> *yes, I know, it's nuts, ..., but necessary.*

So where are we in process? I have laid out what we as individual Christians need to do if we are to grow a faith that is appropriate and accessible in this postmodern, *post*Christian era. In many ways the list is not all that different from lists of other eras; but *post*Christian perceptions make its working out significantly different.

Now about the corporate expression of our faith—within the church: it is not enough to live your Christian life in isolation— the Lone Ranger Christian, going it alone in the evil world. Christ called us to be a body of believers…, His Body. We stand or fall together. But if individual Christians re-gear their faith and the church does not, then we will have what sociologists call a *paradigm conundrum*. Individual Christians will be expressing their faith in one mode while the church still expresses its beliefs in another, older format— one that was appropriate when developed (1654 or 1945, take your pick) but has since lost its significance to the *post*Christian heart. Like offering the gospel of Christ to people, it's not the Truth that changes, but the *context* for the Truth. In the same way, the *context for the church* in every generation changes. Sometimes that change is not insignificantly one of *style*. This occurs within western society at large about every 3-5 years; paradigm shifts in a culture come about every 15-20 years, historically.[lxxxvi] I'm sure we can expect the same degree of acceleration in paradigm shifting within the church as we have seen in the velocity of technological change.

What follows are suggestions that the church-at-large needs to consider if it is to make sense— both to twenty-first century Christians and to the rising tide of millennials/mosaics.

1. The church will have to **rethink the *nature* of theology** itself. Please do not take this as a rejection of any or all theological constructions of the past 500 - 1,600 years. It is not. But the last *major* rubric of theology was constructed at the time of the Protestant Reformation in 1517, when priest Martin Luther posted his *Ninety-five Theses,* a critique of many of the practices of the Roman

Catholic Church, on the door of the Castle Church in Wittenberg (Mecklenburg, Western Pomerania, Germany). In a similar way we will need to construct a theology based on a new examination of Scripture rather than simply another polishing of a theology based on a previous structure. Polishing American Colonial Period furniture doesn't make it Danish modern. Re-systematizing systematic theology does not upgrade it, bring it up to date, or even make it a better system. We must return to the Bible, not in an arrogant, oh-no-one-has-ever-seen-it-this-way-before way, but as students with new eyes; eyes that, though they have read the texts many times, view it now through new glasses. Glasses that filter Scripture through today's culture, a *postChristian* culture, and not the culture of the Modern era.

Do not imagine this an easy task. To read the Bible through *post*Christian eyes is not to be addressed simplistically. It is akin to being a Roman in a Jewish culture, 2,000 years ago, trying to comprehend their festival celebrations, rituals and traditions, Pharisees and Sadducees. Now add 2,000 years, shift continents, and enter a culture that, at the time of the writing of Scripture, did not exist.

The rubric of the Bible is a tapestry woven over 2,000 years. Its cohesiveness and consistency attest to its veracity, as do numerous archeological findings. The Bible just plain works. The life of Christ and His redemptive work on the cross are our model for living the Christian life, today, throughout history, and across cultural variances. The Gospels and New Testament Epistles corroborate the threads of redemption that run throughout the Old Testament. The context for Christ's death on the cross is found in the Old Testament. Church theologians will have to take Biblical Theology, with its answers to the issues inherent in each culture, century, era and generation, and reissue their responses with new references to this postChristian era. Their response must take into account a thorough ignorance of any Christian beliefs or concepts. My guess is that this new Biblical Theology will arise in a people-group-specific, image-based format, and somewhat generationally-considerate. What will that look like in reality? Hey, I'm just writing the suggestion. I'll leave the development of a *post*Christian theology to the experts.

2. **Redesigned corporate spirituality**— The church will need to try on a new suit of clothes, spiritually speaking. It will need to try to express the Christian faith in *multiple formats*. What has been accepted as *traditional* will have to make room for newer forms of expression, previously foreign to our Christian traditions. And it will have to embrace these new expressions even if it feels terribly risky to do so. Remember, though, that we are in *transition* (versus a *phase*), in a time of *paradigm shift*; things are in flux. The Truth will remain constant while its expressions can vary with mood, disposition, generation, region of the world, and culture. What you can do to prepare yourself: if you are Baptist, try expressing your faith from your heart, through liturgy, in an Episcopal/Anglican manner. If you are high church (Catholic, Lutheran, etc.) try free church expression for a

time (Baptist, Pentecostal, Willow Creek, etc.). Or journey to another culture and enter into their forms of worship. Christian worship services in Kenya are something else!

But please take note of this— we will have to allow for multiple forms of expression within the same local church as well, even within the same congregation. Decide to learn from those who express their faith in manners different from your own. Extend your comfort level to embrace expressions that call you to God in new ways. Our society isn't what it used to be. Church isn't what it used to be either. We will need churches within churches, if you will (something we were warned of in seminary); one building (or tent), multiple expressions; even multiple campuses of the same "gathering." New wine; new wine-skins..., and old ones.

3. **Immersion vs. isolation..., not an option**— One aspect of being a church is that we will no longer have a choice of opting out of our culture or its societal issues. The church of Jesus Christ must take a lead in healing our society's sicknesses, from media to medical treatments, to definitions of life, death, and what it means to be a healthy human being. We have too long held back for fear of rejection or recrimination; it is time we took a stand. One thing we must not do is supplant our Savior's role as Judge. That is not our place. Our place is to come along side of our fellow sinners and serve as their guide to freedom and life! The church in the first century understood this; so also must we. Jesus immersed himself in the lives of those around him, making little

distinction between his followers and those who needed him. He served both: He loved both: He saved both.

My wife, Starr, and I live in the beautiful New England town of Amherst, Massachusetts. I love it here. I love our house, our neighbors, our friends. About 2% of Amherst's population attends church. The rest, on Sunday morning..., rest. [Hey, they could have something here.] Yet it is not a godless town— just a non-Christian kind of town. People hold deep seated beliefs about life, faith, sexuality, politics (we have a bumper sticker that reads *Welcome to Amherst, you'll like our foreign policy*), and what it means to be PC— *politically correct*. It is quite easy to engage just about anyone in conversation about their beliefs, life, god, whatever. But being a Christian, I always assume that I have one mark against me. I am also Danish/Welsh, blonde, and a white male, which means I've been peculiar for quite some time. Maybe that's another reason I love it here. I have often wondered if Jesus ever reflected upon the odd time and place the Father ordained for Him to complete His work of the redemption of humanity. Judea was every bit as hostile as Amherst, I'm sure. Actually, more so. Romans slaughtered Jews by the hundreds in Jesus' time. Amherst hasn't killed any Christians..., that I know of. So, I still love it here. My kind of place. Immersion, with no capitulation nor compromise in what I, and we, are called to, wherever we live.

Will the church be accepted readily upon first re-entry back into the society? Not likely. Trust in any relationship is something that must be first gained, then if lost, regained with great commitment and agony. The church has a lot of negative history to overcome that the world remembers with a vengeance. But we have no choice. We can no longer afford the luxury of isolation, of feeling good about ourselves as long as we don't have anything to do with the world outside. That, if anything, is true blasphemy. Jesus did not go to the cross so we could go to church.

4. **Cooperative**— Remember that classic movie, **_Miracle on 34th Street_**? Kris Kringle was encouraging people at Macy's to look for what they needed that Christmas at Gimbals', across the street. Management, as first, was enraged; then they saw the light: customers were surprised and delighted to see this new cooperation-over-competition between the two stores. Since the Reformation the church in the West has been more about separation than about cooperation. It's akin to twentieth century coal miners being forced to shop at the company store with little freedom to go elsewhere. The modern era saw western denominations first forming and then defining themselves in *juxtaposition* to one another. The *post*Modern/*post*Christian era, or whatever it becomes, will not see all churches coming together under one organizational banner. But we must cooperate across denominational lines, despite different worship styles and theological preferences. Labels like *liberal* and *conservative* need to go away. They must move aside for a new nomenclature— genuinely Biblical, Christ centered, locally missional, accepting, alive to life, "makes sense," deep, meaningful, and even "now that

was worship as it should be!" It is not that theological positions are of no minor consequence; they are. It is a reality that some churches have *lost their first love* and become little more than social-networking centers, where cultural mores are given a nod but no Christian practice permeates its members' lives. These churches have not only lost their first love, they have completely lost Christ as their center and have turned to *another gospel*. But must we so viciously oppose one another?! Before a watching, critical world, the church must learn to work together again, united behind one goal— to see our world, our society, our friends and neighbors, be restored in a relationship with the God who made them, who loves them. We can scarcely call ourselves *the Body of Christ* if we cannot even talk with one another outside of opposing each other.

5.   **Sacrificial Servants**— One of the things that has always bothered me in the Old Testament is how Israel wanted to be like all the other Kingdoms around them. The Church in the modern era built a similar Kingdom for itself with newer castles— called cathedrals. They were meant to stand as permanent reminders of the power and presence of God in the world— if not as a political presence as well. Their success at this kind of influence was, at best, questionable. Now most of these great cathedrals are little more than exquisite edifices, *object d'art,* or mausoleums, and homes of past saints and relics. During the last half of the twentieth century the church in North America grew in wealth beyond belief. Not that wealth is wrong in itself, but, like Israel, the American church seemed to want to be just like the

society that surrounded it— consumer driven. *Being in society* is one thing: remaining part of a pretentious *charade* is quite another.

For the church in North America to truly have an impact on its culture it must shift its mentality and present itself as a sacrificial servant of the society, not as a judge of its illnesses. When people are sick, they need a doctor, not a critic. We must learn to give graciously to our world— much more graciously than we give to build for ourselves modern cathedrals of comfort. We must learn to *give up* rather than to calculate next year's pledge units. This is difficult and complicated. We must also provide places where the normal people of our society can find solace, safety, feel at ease, and see Jesus Christ embodied in those who go by His name. Another Gordian Knot to be cut.

6. **One Lord, one Faith, one *Language*...**— In the same way that individual Christians need to learn to express their faith in the common everyday language, so also does the church need to learn to use the metaphors, idioms, and common expressions of the day to express historical Biblical Truths. Oddly, the stories of the Bible can stand on their own with little amplification about their context. This is akin to becoming *seeker sensitive*, but not entirely. It is more a reflection of becoming *culture sensitive*. The only place most of us use *Christianeze* is *in* church or when trying to explain our faith to someone else (a.k.a. evangelism). But more and more the language of the faith has become the property of Christian professionals. Not even the people in the

pews use it (there's an example right there— pew.). Many years ago comedians Lou Abbot and Budd Costello performed a baseball Vaudeville dialog titled *Who's on First?*[lxxxvii] It was a classic example of miscommunication due to a misunderstanding of the use and definition of words. *"Who's on First? What's on Second. I-don't-know's on Third."* Their dialogue was funny: the Christian miscommunication block to a confused world is not funny. We dare not have an *in-house* language which only Christians can understand, vs. a *normal* language that we use to talk with the world around us. Besides being crazy, it creates a lot of extra work for us. How much easier would it be if we had one language pattern that everybody could understand? Think of it, you could talk about your faith in church the way you would naturally talk about it in the rest of your life; no stomach knots, no translating, no shifting language/emotional gears. *Just breathe.*

7. **We need Leaders who will go out on a limb**. One of my favorite quotes comes from Mark Twain— *"Why not go out on a limb!? That's where the fruit is."* The last shift that the church in *post*Christian society will have to make is one of leadership. Our leaders will actually need to *LEAD*! Too many Christian leaders have become conciliatory politicians, mediating their way to church peace or to a better position with more prestige and/or money. Others have become theological authoritarians, sweeping their will and interpretation of Scripture over their congregations. Why? Because theology is safe…, you can nail-down just about everything. And being "the pastor" carries authority and power with it. [Authority

and power are both appropriate and normal to leadership, but we must fight the tendency to misuse it.] Leadership isn't quite as safe as it once was. I'm not merely talking about leadership in the church, but leadership in our society as well. The world around us longs for visible, risk-taking leaders; not leaders who pretend to have it all together or who know everything, but leaders who make a few mistakes along the way..., admit they were wrong, and change.

The late-Modern Christian world had to adjust to a Christianity which gave us such individuals— Billy Graham, Thomas Merton, Bishop Desmond Tutu, Mother Teresa, Kathy Ireland, Charles Colson and a handful of others. These were seen as the exception. Well, there are frankly more than a handful, but the world's perception is that there are very few. I have met many people, mostly under the age of 20, who have never heard of Billy Graham. They have virtually no conception of what it means to be a Christian. *"Jesus Christ? Isn't he supposed to be god or something?"* Believe it. But whether they have heard of men like Graham or Teresa or not, The Church of Jesus Christ could do so much for this *post*Christian world if we could just produce leaders who lead, who make sense to these emerging *post*Christians, whose lives carry an aroma of Truthfulness, of a faith that makes a difference in our world, of integrity, of honor, of Jesus Christ.

But a problem that has arisen in strong church leadership is that we expect our leaders to lead **us**— just us. I remember one church in New England that actually asked me to speak with their pastor about all the time he was spending *in* their community. Duh!? He was meeting with gas station attendants, high school students, town council members, restaurant owners, and farmers who were experiencing hard times. What was wrong with this picture? Then I saw it— it was all about control. If a pastor is spending time with those who aren't Christians, or who are not members of "our" church, it's harder to monitor his use of time. But the number of people he met who turned to God in time of crisis, and then to the church, and then to Christ, grew steadily over the years. Sadly, the church leaders still sought to control him.

Genuine leadership, as opposed to *positional* leadership, is a risk. It goes with the territory. Just get used to it. There was an ad from a brokerage firm in NYC that used to read— *The only real risk in life is not taking one.*[lxxxviii] May Christian leaders in North America become just such a risky bunch.

So, where do we go from here? To the trenches of life, to the committee meetings and shopping malls, to the overtime days and family gatherings with ol' lip-sticked Aunt Maude who always kisses her grandchildren on the cheek? We go back to living. But, now, having read this far, I pray you go back with a new feeling of energy and empowerment; I pray you go back with a clearer perspective and hope in who you need to be to make sense to this world. Along the way, I hope you'll make more sense to yourself too. I cannot convince you of the exuberance that comes when you start to morph your life, your church, and/or your family to a postChristian faith.

¿CLUELESS CHRISTIANITY?

It's quite a ride! Risky, with the outcome yet to be written. Write it well; honor God, serve this world, and make a difference.

Play Time

1. How might you become a *paradigm pioneer?*

2. From your own life experiences, try expressing your faith to someone who has never been to church, using his/her language. Buy the coffee.

3. What sins seem to hang on in your life? How do they affect your soul?

4. What do you need to do to become more openly loving?

5. How can you grow to trust God for the lives of those around you and still remain *intentional* in your relationship with them?

6. What words might describe your times of prayer? How does your prayer life need to change?

7. How might the church in the West need to be reinvented?

8. What kinds of theological rubrics do we need for a reformatted church?

9. What distinguishes *Christian spirituality* from other spiritualities in this postChristian era?

10. What are some ways that the true Church of Jesus Christ can immerse itself in Western society while remaining *in the world..., but not of the world*?

11. What would it take for Catholics and Protestants, Baptists and Presbyterians, Reformed theologians and Only-believe-Christians, old line Liberals and Conservatives, to finally unite around one goal of Salvation through faith alone in Jesus Christ, for both the individual and for society?

12. What would it mean for the church in North America to genuinely adopt the heart of a Sacrificial Servant?

13. If you are a church leader, in any capacity, what risks of faith is God calling you to take that you've been shying away from? Isn't it time to take up your cross and follow Jesus?

> *[15] But in your hearts set apart Christ as Lord. Always be prepared to give an answer to everyone who asks you to give the reason for the hope that you have. But do this with gentleness and respect, [16] keeping a clear conscience, so that those who speak maliciously against your good behavior in Christ may be ashamed of their slander.*

~ 1 Peter 3:15-16.

Chapter 9: A Christian Message to a postChristian Heart: *"it's not that easy bein' green".*

Sarah had come to faith in Christ through the Navigators. After two years in the campus group she showed up in our home out of frustration. She was visibly distraught. Her staff worker had told her she *"just needed to trust Jesus."* *"That,"* she said, *"just was too simplistic."* She was aggravated, angry, and very near the detonation point. As we sat that evening in front of our wood stove she collected herself to tell me a story I could hardly believe.

Sarah[lxxxix] had grown up in a proper family in a rural New York State community; mother, father, two sisters and one brother, older. On the surface everything appeared to be status quo. But just below the surface, Sarah revealed to me, lay insidious evil. Sarah's older brother had been raping her every day of her life since she was eleven years old. One of her sisters found her in tears one day after one of her brother's assaults. In the process of trying to shield her brother, Sarah's sister Jennifer[xc] guessed what had been going on and told Sarah that she, too, was also being raped every day. When they confronted their brother he threatened to commit suicide. Sarah and Jennifer told Bob[xci] that he had to tell their parents within the week or they were going to the police.

The two sisters were resolute in their determination and insisted that Bob follow through and tell their parents what he had done to them. Instead, to their shock, Bob committed suicide two days later. He left a suicide note for his parents blaming Sarah for everything (leaving out any mention of Jennifer completely). Sarah began to sob, scream, curse, and go completely out of control as she told me that her parents believed what her brother had written in his farewell letter. They told her that she would just have to admit her complicity in the ongoing, five year "affair" she had had with her older brother. After Bob's funeral, Sarah's and Jennifer's older sister told them that she too had been raped by him, repeatedly; but she did not want their parents to know about it, ever.

It was now close to midnight and I was having trouble staying awake. As I put another log in the wood stove, Sarah cried to me, *"How can I ever 'just trust in Jesus!?!' He suffered and died for my sins once and for all..., and it was done with. I died every day of my life for five years. He has no idea what I went through."*

Sarah's story is not the only one of its kind. In my role as a counselor I have heard similar stories more times than I would have imagined. There is truly a lot of pain out there, isn't there? Not that the pain in our era is any greater or more severe than at any time in history. Each epoch inflicts its own form of tribulation and torture on its populace. Wars, genocides, rapes, wholesale slaughter of entire peoples and other gruesome agonies have found their way into our history books. They remain glibly reported events of a distant past. But for those who lived through them, who suffered war or rape, or witnessed genocide, the actuality was excruciatingly devastating and left lifelong scars. Life was lost to an evil enemy from whom there was no escape, and there seemed no end to suffering. But people always held out hope— hope of rescue, hope of survival, hope in their God. Hope that, in the end, things could be worked out.

Until now.

As we have shifted into this postChristian era any spiritual basis for hope has been totally supplanted. It has been supplanted by forms of pragmatism, hedonism, self-absorbed isolationism, or a simple denial of the harshness of personal tragedy. People are also disappointed in a god who is *not there*. Hope has become a contrived notion of a cynical society, held out like a carrot on a stick. Hope in a god, any god, is perceived as a naïve pretense couched in the spiritual jargon of religion. Empty words.

> *So how can the message of hope that is offered by Jesus Christ be heard, understood, and believed in such a truth-weary culture?*

This is the question that we will now seek to answer. And the answer will cross many lines of safety, many given definers of the gospel and how to present the truth claims of the faith.

¿CLUELESS CHRISTIANITY?

➤**Summarizing the Gospel:**
  the gospel-made-simple, since 1949.

Historically, the Christian message has always contained at least four ingredients—

1. There is a God in the heavens who has created us and loves us; He wants us to worship Him.
2. We (humans) have rejected God's love for us as well as His call for us to worship Him; this rejection we know as **sin**.
3. Jesus Christ, God's Son, was sent to earth, *voluntarily*, to pay the penalty for our sin and rebellion against our Creator.
4. Belief in Jesus Christ, coupled with repentance, will result in our forgiveness and salvation from certain punishment for our sin and rebellion. And we get to go to heaven.

Or, more popularly—

1. You have a problem—you are a sinner.
2. We have a solution to your problem—Jesus Christ
3. Consent to agree with our solution to your problem— Believe in Jesus Christ as your *personal* Savior (as opposed to being just a church member).
4. Your problem will be solved—Then you will be saved from eternal damnation in hell. And you get to go to heaven.

The difficulty *post*Christian people have with either of these formulations is that they no longer hold a presuppositional platform in their thinking process. These historical Christian

¿CLUELESS CHRISTIANITY?

Truths rest on certain assumptions once widely understood in both Modern and *pre*Modern times. They are now lost to the *post*Christian mind. These assumptions are—

1. There is a God who created everything.
2. Mankind owes allegiance and thanks to their Creator for what He has given them.
3. But people are primarily evil, not prone to honor their Creator or one another.
4. People need a Savior to come to their rescue from outside the influences of sin. That Savior is Jesus Christ.
5. Belief in Jesus Christ as the Lord God, Creator-Savior demands a change in a person's life-values and practices.

Furthermore, these assumptions take for granted that people also believe in the veracity of the Bible. To question that the Bible was anything other than the divinely inspired Word of God in *pre*Modern or Modern times was tantamount to blasphemy. It was further assumed that the Church was God's Body on earth. As such it was responsible for maintaining purity in belief and practice, as well as propagating the faith through evangelism *of* the heathen through the immersion of Christians *within* a culture.

These were the assumptions and presuppositions of the vast majority of Christians worldwide, but especially of those in the Second and Third Worlds— Europe, colonized Africa/India, and the West, North America. These assumptions, the *core values* of the Christian faith, are now obliterated amidst the milieu of skeptical pluralism in *post*Modern/*post*Christian societies. Let's give our attention to the *post*Modern mindset in more detail.

➢**The Gospel in Limbo:** *the loss of a Christian conscience*

The assumptions of postModern/postChristian philosophy are no simple matter to collect due to their very nature. For if you start with the assumption *The only absolute truth is that there is no absolute truth* (Paul Feyerabend, 1924-1994), which postmodern philosophers posit, it becomes somewhat impossible to state *what is* and *what is not* in describing it. Nonetheless, with special thanks to Mathematical Physicist Dr. Milo Wolff, the assumptions of postmodernism might be as follows—

> *The current Postmodern belief is that a correct description of Reality is impossible. This extreme skepticism, of which Friedrich Nietzsche, Ludwig Wittgenstein, Karl Popper and Thomas Kuhn are particularly famous, assumes that;*
>
> *a) All truth is limited, approximate, and is constantly evolving (Nietzsche, Kuhn, Popper).*
>
> *b) No theory can ever be proved true - we can only show that a theory is false (Popper).*
>
> *c) No theory can ever explain all things consistently (Godel's incompleteness theorem).*
>
> *d) There is always a separation between our mind & ideas of things and the thing in itself (Kant).*
>
> *e) Physical reality is not deterministic (Copenhagen interpretation of quantum physics, Bohr).*

f) Scientific concepts are mental constructs (logical positivism, Mach, Carnap).

g) Metaphysics is empty of content.

h) Thus absolute and certain truth that explains all things is unobtainable.[xcii]

To put it another way, the assumptions of postmodernism in regards to Christianity might be—

1. There is no single theory, be it scientific, philosophic, or religious, that can explain everything. (Read-Christianity does not have the corner on Truth.)
2. All accepted assumptions about our values, philosophies, religious beliefs, or scientific discoveries must be reexamined and challenged.
3. Religion, though once important to explain mystery, is of no further use.
4. Karma— payback is sweet. What you give out is what you will receive.
5. Individual, pragmatic values are more important than group systems.
6. The tenets of the Christian faith are, at best, mythical, relying on unreliable and unverifiable historic documents.
7. Personal *Christian* experience is most likely a projection of wishful thinking, culturally delimited by experience and religious exposure.
8. Individual beliefs are not binding on anyone else.

No matter how you slice it, the assumptions of postModern thought cut across and thoroughly reject the historical formulations of the Christian faith. They leave, literally, no room for any reformulation of Christian Truth in their "*mindset.*" Truly, we are two ships passing in the night.

But postmodernism, as disheartening, critical, and empty a value (*non*)system as it was(is), has been drawn to its own natural conclusion— the loss of meaning in all realities, with no hope of ever constructing a belief system based on anything but personal projection and fanciful hope.

> *Post-modernism is arguably the most depressing philosophy ever to spring from the western mind. It is difficult to talk about post-modernism because nobody really understands it. It's allusive to the point of being impossible to articulate. But what this philosophy basically says is that we've reached an endpoint in human history. That the modernist tradition of progress and ceaseless extension of the frontiers of innovation are now dead. Originality is dead. The avant-garde artistic tradition is dead. All religions and utopian visions are dead and resistance to the status quo is impossible because revolution too is now dead. Like it or not, we humans are stuck in a permanent crisis of meaning, a dark room from which we can never escape.* (Kalle Lasn & Bruce Grierson, <u>A Malignant Sadness</u>) [xciii]

Thus say the critical commentators of the *post*Modern mood. The reality, as it is worked out in peoples' lives, is often just as stark. Anti-depressant consumption in the U.S. has risen to an all-time high; more SSRIs are prescribed than any other kind of medication.[xciv] So many tranquilizers were taken in the second half of the 20th century that it was known as the Age of Anxiety. Lawsuits, in a legal system not allowed to pass "value judgments" are now filed like popcorn.[xcv] Hypochondria, the sickness that convinces people they are really sick even though they are not, is also on the rise.[xcvi] And considering the widespread closings of Catholic Churches across America, it also appears that the vast majority of Americans seek little solace or guidance through their faith.[xcvii] Protestant Churches, in contrast, struggle with consistently turning out *"fake Christians,"* people who use the lingo of the faith, but who adapt it to fit their lifestyle and personal preferences, regardless of Biblical mores or principles. [xcviii] Not that these symptoms can all be *directly* correlated with a shift to *post*Modern thinking, but the loss of meaning and connectivity in *post*Modern thought does leave us with a brooding sense of skepticism and aloneness in the universe.

Because of these shifts in attitude, beliefs, and ethical compromises, North America's *post*Moderns have truly lost any sense of a *Christian conscience.* The ships are not in fact even passing in the night; they sail in completely different oceans. The assumptions of *post*Modernism (*The only absolute truth is that there is no absolute truth)* preclude any common ground whatsoever with any Christian precepts; the world and life views (*weltanschauung*) of genuine followers of Christ would hardly allow them admittance into the public or private forums of a postModern discussion. This does not put genuine Christians on the defensive, as you might think; it keeps us completely out of the conversation. *How then shall they hear....*

¿CLUELESS CHRISTIANITY?

Borrowing a phrase from Verizon Wireless' mobile marketing strategy, the Christian communication strategy is no longer simply *Can you hear me now!?!*, but more precisely, *HOW can you hear me now?* or, *What might the Gospel of Jesus Christ look like to a postModern/ postChristian heart?*

➤**Framing a postChristian Gospel:** *opening Pandora's box*

For the past 60-75 years Christians, especially evangelical Christians in North America, have adhered to a formulation of the Christian message known as a *Summary Gospel*. [See above.] This formulation came into being for thoroughly pragmatic purposes— to get the gospel out to as many people as possible as quickly as possible. It was considered the "core" of the gospel; it was the least amount of information that an individual needed to know to make a decision about turning their life over to God. Over time it grew to be known as "the gospel". Whether intentional or not, this simple, usually four point summary, came to be understood as the WHOLE GOSPEL.

It is not.

Not coincidentally, it followed the typical *problem solving/sales model* of the post-World War II era (1949), popularized by companies like Fuller Brush and Hoover Vacuums.

- *You have a problem.*
- *We have a product that will solve your problem.*
- *Buy our product.*
- *Your problem will be solved.*

This formulation worked quite well, quite *pragmatically*, as long as people retained a sense of their own rebellion and sinfulness before a Holy God. They understood the problem, their need of salvation, even if most rejected the *product, Jesus Christ*, as the solution to their sinfulness. But we now live in a society that no longer accepts the presuppositional basis for the Christian faith, nor understands its own need for salvation. *Truly, then, HOW shall they hear?* What has been lost in our society, in a very real sense, is the *context* for the Christian message. It no longer has anything to say to *post*Modern man, woman, child, anybody. We have no sense of God's love for us, we have no sense of our own rebellion against Him, or of our own sinfulness before God. And we certainly see no need for a personal Savior. It is this loss of *context* that is at the heart of the shift from a modernist-mindset to a *post*modern-mindset.

Moreover, in this *post*Modern era, it is not only the *postmodern mind* that needs to hear a new shape of our message. It is also the *postmodern heart* that needs to grasp the greatness of Christ's work on the cross. If I might play devil's advocate for a bit, allow me to address the loss of a Christian perspective in our culture through a rhetorical dialog.

Mental Discussion #1

> *Why become a Christian?*
> *To have your sins forgiven.*
> *Why do I want my sins forgiven?*
> *To go to heaven?*
> *Why do I want to do that?*
> *So you don't go to hell.*

¿CLUELESS CHRISTIANITY?

Sound familiar? In one form or another, this is the gist of how many genuine Christians view their work in evangelism— saving people from hell. To say it feels somewhat condemnatory explains why so few Christians have the heart to engage their non-Christian friends in Christian conversation. That is, if they even have any non-Christian friends. We see ourselves as people trying to save people from hell, eternal damnation, and the pit of fire. [Sadly, many Christians aren't even sure there is such a place any more. Good luck with that.]

Mental Discussion #2

Let's try another approach that is more holistic, more in-tune with the deepest heartbeat and mindset of our *post*Modern/*post*Christian culture.

Why become a Christian?

To fulfill your humanity.

What are you talking about!?! You don't think I can be fulfilled unless I am a Christian?

Well, actually, no.

That's arrogant.

Not really. If God created us to live in harmony with Him how can we be fulfilled as human beings, as His creation, unless we are in tune with the God Who made us?

Keep going.

¿CLUELESS CHRISTIANITY?

To fulfill our humanity we need to be in a healthy relationship with the world around us that promotes peace, propagates our race, nurtures and develops the natural resources God has given us, and protects those who are weaker from evil.

That's Christianity? I'm already doing a lot of those things.

BUT..., we also need to enter into a healthy relationship with the God who made us— Jesus Christ, the Creator and Sustainer of life. We need both a vertical relationship with the God who made us and a horizontal relationship with the world around us. BOTH need to be governed by the Life Principles found in the Christian Bible.

What about sin?

As Creator, God set up safeguards for us to keep us from hurting ourselves and destroying His creation. These are His "Perimeters-of-Protection," so to speak, that keep us in His safe-keeping. When we step outside those perimeters of protection we put our lives at risk, literally. So sin is more precisely described as not only breaking God's Laws (Life Principles) but also stepping outside His perimeters-of-protection for us. It is a very foolish, life threatening rebellion at the least. Not smart.

So becoming a Christian involves a reentry into God's Perimeter-of-Protection. So sin is taking matters into my own hand and ignoring God in my life.

You got it.

The second scenario is incomplete, of course, because every conversation proceeds just a little differently from the last one. The point is that present-day Christians have forgotten the PURPOSE of the Gospel; namely, to bring men and women back into a relationship with the God who made them, not just so they can have their sins forgiven, not just so they can avoid hell (punishment) and enter into heaven (reward); but so that they live in harmony with the Creator of all things, in harmony with the earth, the universe, other people, and even relatives. Christ came NOT merely to pay the penalty for our sin: He came to set everything back on track; He came to initiate a *course* correction throughout the entire process of our relationship with this world and with His Father, the God who made us. There is a sentence in the Book of Proverbs, (ESV Bible), that clarifies our dilemma the best— Proverbs 14:12.

> *There is a way which seems right to a man, but its end is the way to death.*

Couple this with something philosopher Jean Jacques *Rousseau* (28 June 1712 – 2 July 1778) once said and we gain deeper insight to the problem.

> **"God created man in his own image. And man, being a gentleman, returned the favor."**

We want a god with whom we are *comfortable*; a god who resembles us, who has human qualities, but not divine ones. We want a god of our own design, not one who tells us who He is and what the rules are; we want a god who plays by our rules. We do not want a God like the Christian God who sets up the parameters of how we are to relate to Him and His world. Even so, this is the God that postModern people need to see for who He truly is; not a watered-down version of Him, nor a *Christianized-sweet-Jesus* version of Him. They need to see the God of Glory, the Creator-Sustainer God who desires to love us and enable us to fulfill what He intended for us from the foundation of the universe. And that can only happen in reestablishing a connection with Him in and through Jesus Christ. Confessing our sin, seeking His forgiveness for our rebellion and finding fulfillment are all mixed together for *post*Christians as they try to understand our strange faith in this God/Man, Jesus. Any other formulation of a relationship with God will lead to death, literally. We do not tell the Creator of all that we know what is best.

[Note to Reader— Now you see why this section deals with *"Opening Pandora's Box."* Please understand that it took a lot of courage to write this last sub-section. I do not want to be deemed heretical in my view of God, of Holy Scripture, and especially of the Gospel of our Lord. But it is well past time when the Problem Solving/Sales Model gospel presentation needs to be laid to rest. Even those who live in enclaves of evangelical America are so familiar with the content of these formulations that the words have lost their definition and import. Summary outlines, though helpful for us to remember the "main points" of the message, lack an authentic depth and life-context. It is time for genuine followers of Christ to build rich relationships with those who don't have a clue as to what our faith is about. The Gospel is much more than a 4-5 simple points summary. It is time we put flesh on the Words of Scripture; it is time we started *reading* our Bibles and not simply quoting from them. It rests upon us to learn the *heartbeat* of the Scriptures and the *language* of our surrounding society. We need to frame our faith and message in formats that can be comprehended, felt, seen, and lived out in our individual and corporate lives together.]

➤**Framing a *post*Christian Gospel: *a heart to heart thing***

Besides being able to couch our message in the mindset of our host culture, we also find it rests upon us not only to learn their language (Missiology 101), but one thing more— we need to learn to love them. *Love them?!? Love people who are different from us!?! That's easier said than done.* Quite true. We can hardly love the differences among ourselves. Jesus understood how diverse a people His Church would become; that is why He said, *"By this will all men know that you are my disciples, if you have love for one another."* (John 13:35) We MUST learn to genuinely love one another (also read- *forgive too*) if we are ever to love "the world!?!"

Yes, precisely.

Any communication to people who have no Christian understanding whatsoever, true postChristians, must be couched in *their* language, *their* experience-set, and *their* precepts. To do so involves expanding our own understanding of the very substance of the Christian message. The gospel is *not* simply about solving the sin problem. It is so much more. It is about pulling the entirety of human history back in line with the principles that God our Creator set down for us to live by. The greatness of our Christian message reaches far beyond simple conversion; it calls for relief for those who are poor, justice in our courts, freedom for the oppressed, and healing for those in need. Jesus knew this when he read—

> "*The Spirit of the Lord is upon me; he*
> *has anointed me to tell the good news to the*
> *poor. He has sent me to announce release to*
> *the prisoners and recovery of sight to the*
> *blind, to set oppressed people free.*" (Luke
> 4:18 ISV)

The gospel in a postChristian era has more far reaching effects and implications than individual justification: it involves challenges for the whole person, the whole culture, the whole world.

The Question— *So then, what should the Christian message (heart & mind) in a postChristian society look like?*

First, it must be exhibited in the lives of those who call themselves *Christians*. Genuine Christians will act differently within a postChristian society. For one, we will not withdraw from the society and seal ourselves within our Christian peer groups, small groups, or large churches. We will be immersed in the matrix of our culture, from politics to pubs, from businesses to the broken hearted, from philosophical forums to the Supreme Court, from single parenting to the sexual conundrum and all its complications. In short, true *postChristian Christians* will be active members in our communities, both locally and globally. And we will be involved, openly & matter-of-factly as Christians, with little apology for our faith. For our faith will in no way resemble the narrow-minded, withdrawn hibernation of the last era of western Christendom; that era is dead and gone. All that remains is its façade— edifices of theatre, actors and stage hands still putting on weekly performances. Instead, a *post*Christian faith will speak of the greatness of our God and how important it is to live by the principles He has set down for His creation. It will have to exhibit a kind of Christianity that encourages people to flourish and grow. Christians in this new era will be a positive contributing force for Christ, working alongside those of other faiths, even *post*modern atheists, for the glory of God and the enrichment of the peoples of this earth.[xcix] True evangelism takes place when it becomes the unconscious expression of new life in Christ. It makes a difference in peoples' lives through the kind of life lived out, publically, by Jesus' followers. The gospel will be communicated *heart to heart* through commitment, caring, and a cohesive Christ-honoring presence in peoples' lives.

Second, the WORDS of the gospel will become secondary to the LIFE of the gospel exhibited in the lives of Christ's followers. *PREACH THE GOSPEL AT ALL TIMES; WHEN NECESSARY, USE WORDS* was how Saint Francis put it. Remember, the WORDS of the gospel merely explain what the God of glory has done to bring the human race back into a relationship with Him through Jesus Christ's work on the cross…, and subsequently, through His Holy Spirit living within us. As necessary as they are, the WORDS of our message are empty without a practical demonstration of their Truth through the way we live. [Do not misconstrue this to mean simply— *live morally*. It is more than that. It is a summons to *live Godly,* based on the precepts set down in the New Testament by Jesus Christ.] The WORDS of the gospel will take the *post*Christian perspective back to the reason d'etre for the Christian message— namely, that this human race, and each of us individually, should live in harmony with the God who created us. This is the nature of our Salvation, to be rooted in the fulfillment of Christ's work at Creation through His sacrifice on the Cross. Repentance and forgiveness have no context outside the restoration and fulfillment in Jesus' work at Calvary.

Thirdly, the core of the Christian message must abound with LOVE. Simple enough!? Not really. This is a problem. Why? Because we often say we love people (normal people), but in reality we hardly know them at all. We have social contact with people who never go to church but rarely are we involved in their lives enough that we can say we truly love them. Love grows in relationships when people become open and honest with one another about their inner lives; when agreements are adhered to; when trust is constant and never betrayed. It might be helpful if we morph the idea of *loving another* into the romantic mode— *falling in love with them*. The language of romance holds far more concrete images than does the idea of loving another person in a platonic, spiritual, evangelistic kind of way. It engages our emotions as well as verbal communication and spiritual concern. It ignites our passion and deep desire to be with the other person. It encourages our heart desire to give everything to the other person for the sake of Jesus Christ. You know what being in love does to you. It makes you alive again!

Maybe our problem is that we don't allow Jesus to love us passionately; therefore, we cannot love another passionately. It is questionable whether a genuine follower of Jesus Christ who will not allow God to love him fully would ever be able to love anyone else, Christian or otherwise. This is an issue which our *post*Christian church in the West must yet grapple. We still speak of love more than we exercise it.

➤**Framing a postChristian Gospel:**
   talk's cheap…, action's everything

It is tantamount to include action in the *post*Christian gospel. The apostle James *writes,*

> [14]*What good is it, my brothers, if a man claims to have faith but has no deeds? Can such faith save him?* [15]*Suppose a brother or sister is without clothes and daily food.* [16]*If one of you says to him, "Go, I wish you well; keep warm and well fed," but does nothing about his physical needs, what good is it?* [17]*In the same way, faith by itself, if it is not accompanied by action, is dead.*
>
> [18]*But someone will say, "You have faith; I have deeds."*
>
> *Show me your faith without deeds, and I will show you my faith by what I do.*

–James 2:14-18

Given the present-day imbalance between Western wealth, emerging Chinese wealth, and the poverty of First World countries this writer must insist that our *post*Christian Gospel, our "good news" include a definitive Christian presence and immersion (as so often already stated) in the midst of our world's tough situations. These run the gamut from local poverty and homelessness to national insurrections, global inequities and human indignities. Unless individual Christians and the Body of Christ in the West, in all her various forms (churches, parachurch organizations, missions, social services, home groups, etc.) are willing to take their place alongside of other non-Christian agencies, in concerted, cooperative enterprises to care for our world's impoverished, ill-treated, and subjugated masses, the "good news" of Christ's salvation will seem *all talk, no action*. Nowhere in our Scriptures are we called to withdraw from our world, except for times of fasting and prayer. Instead, we are commanded to be involved in our world as active participants in its daily endeavors. To this end Jesus prayed to the Father on our behalf in John 17—

> *17:1 When Jesus had spoken these words, he lifted up his eyes to heaven, and said, "Father, the hour has come; glorify your Son that the Son may glorify you, 2 since you have given him authority over all flesh, to give eternal life to all whom you have given him. 3 And this is eternal life, that they know you the only true God, and Jesus Christ whom you have sent. 4 I glorified you on earth, having accomplished the work that you gave me to do. 5 And now, Father, glorify me in your own presence with the glory that I had with you before the world existed.*

> *6 "I have manifested your name to the people whom you gave me out of the world. Yours they were, and you gave them to me, and they have kept your word. 7 Now they know that*

everything that you have given me is from you. 8 For I have given them the words that you gave me, and they have received them and have come to know in truth that I came from you; and they have believed that you sent me. 9 I am praying for them. I am not praying for the world but for those whom you have given me, for they are yours. 10 All mine are yours, and yours are mine, and I am glorified in them. 11 And I am no longer in the world, but they are in the world, and I am coming to you. Holy Father, keep them in your name, which you have given me, that they may be one, even as we are one. 12 While I was with them, I kept them in your name, which you have given me. I have guarded them, and not one of them has been lost except the son of destruction, that the Scripture might be fulfilled. 13 But now I am coming to you, and these things I speak in the world, that they may have my joy fulfilled in themselves. 14 I have given them your word, and the world has hated them because they are not of the world, just as I am not of the world. 15 I do not ask that you take them out of the world, but that you keep them from the evil one. 16 They are not of the world, just as I am not of the world. 17 Sanctify them in the truth; your word is truth. 18 As you sent me into the world, so I have sent them into the world. 19 And for their sake I consecrate myself, that they also may be sanctified in truth.

20 "I do not ask for these only, but also for those who will believe in me through their word, 21 that they may all be one, just as you, Father, are in me, and I in you, that they also may be in us, so that the world may believe that you have sent me. 22 The glory that you have given me I have given to them, that they may be one even as we are one, 23 I in them and you in me, that they may become perfectly one, so that the world may know that you sent me and loved them even as you loved me. 24 Father, I desire that they also, whom you have given me, may be with me where I am, to see my glory that you have given me because you loved me before the foundation of the world. 25 O righteous Father, even though the world does not know you, I know you, and these know that you have sent me. 26 I made known to them your name, and I will continue to make it known, that the love with which you have loved me may be in them, and I in them."[x]

Christ wants us embedded within our communities as a way of displaying who He is to those around us. This is the context for our verbal message—our lives demonstrating the character of Jesus Christ and His principles for living in front of our families, neighbors, and work associates. Then investing ourselves in national and international efforts to bring justice and financial assistance (wells, grain, cattle, etc.) to those in need.

> *"Is not this the fast that I choose: to*
> *lose the bonds of injustice, to undo the thongs*
> *of the yoke, to let the oppressed go free, and to*
> *break every yoke? Is it not to share your bread*
> *with the hungry, and bring the homeless poor*
> *into your house; when you see the naked, to*
> *cover them, and not to hide yourself from your*
> *own kin?"* (Isaiah 58:6-7)

If our *post*modern/*post*Christian world is ever to grasp the import of our "good news" its context must be the holy lives of Jesus' followers lived out in community, both inside and outside the church. Truly, we who claim the Name of Jesus Christ as our own do not have the option to withdraw from this present society, except for prayer, rest, and rejuvenation in His Holy Spirit.

Not of this world…, absolutely! But definitely *in the world.*

➤A Christian Message for a postChristian heart:
"it's not that easy bein' green."

If you've been challenged by this call to develop a *postChristian Gospel*, please know that it has been something I have struggled with for quite some time. Remaining true to the Biblical/historical constructs of our faith, and to the Church, while trying to adapt our message to yet another cultural context is no easy matter. Wycliffe Bible Translators face this challenge with every new language group they encounter, as did early Christian missionaries during the European and American Colonial eras (Western Christian constructs introduced to Asian, Oriental, and African cultures). Our difficulty is in recognizing that our *post*Christian era has developed its own *language* group, based on its basic premise that there are no absolute truths; there is no *meta-narrative* to explain all of reality; there is no one singular system of belief that can encompass the grand diversity of human experience. At this point, of course, genuine Christians must disengage with the prevailing opinion.

It is thus, at this point of division, that we must still follow our Lord into this world's various cultures, adapting His time-tested message to be understood within the grand diversity of human experiences. This is not a task to be taken on lightly, let alone naively. Our message can neither be too complex to be grasped by the simple, nor can it be so simple that its matrix, woven throughout human history and into both ends of eternity, be lost in "the simple gospel," with no context outside of the Creation/Fall/Redemption/Fulfillment rubric. That is why we must end our consideration of a *post*Christian Gospel with a reference to BEING GREEN.

Being green, surprisingly, refers to more than environmental/ecological responsibility. The framework to which I refer comes from a 1969 musical piece sung by Kermit the Frog, Ring-master of Jim Henderson's MUPPETS.

I encourage you to watch it; go to—

http://www.youtube.com/watch?v=hpiIWMWWVco&feature= related, to view our hero sing it in his own croaks.]

¿CLUELESS CHRISTIANITY?

"It's Not Easy Bein' Green" (lyrics by Joe Rapposo)

It's not that easy bein' green;
Having to spend each day the color of the leaves.
When I think it could be nicer being red, or yellow or gold-
or something much more colorful like that.

It's not easy bein' green.
It seems you blend in with so many other ordinary things.
And people tend to pass you over 'cause you're not standing
out like flashy sparkles in the water- or stars in the sky.

But green's the color of Spring.
And green can be cool and friendly-like.
And green can be big like an ocean, or important like a
mountain, or tall like a tree.

When green is all there is to be
It could make you wonder why, but why wonder why? Wonder,
I am green and it'll do fine, it's beautiful!
And I think it's what I want to be.

Kermit's point is this— that he may not like the way he is, blending in, often passed over, ordinary; but this is the way he is and that's that. He *is* the color of Spring; he is cool & friendly-like. And though as a frog he is small, he can be big, like an ocean, or important, like a mountain. He is green, and that's just fine. Engaging the *post*Christian heart is a lot like being green. We may not be too good at it, we certainly don't fit into our culture's predominant mindset, but we have to remain true to who we are, to what we believe, and to be what Christ has designed us to be in the grand scheme of things. We are each called upon and designed to play our part in the daily activities of the Lilly Pond. Some days we just sit around and zap flies with our tongues; other days we may meet up with some other cute little froggy who captures our fancy; and some days we run into those postmodern Bull Frogs that beat up on us and take away our pad, trying to push us out of the operations of the Pond entirely. Nonetheless, God has plopped many of us in the middle of the *post*Christian Pond and expects us to live up to our responsibilities as a vital part of this society's nurturing and development. We are here to bring Christ's peace, forgiveness, and new life to the rest of the Pond. We may not like the taste of fresh fly on our tongue…, but we'd better get used to it if we're going to make a difference.

There remains yet one more thing to consider— merely practical suggestions on how to be who you are, within your own personality, family, church, and society as you endeavor to translate the Christian message into *post*Christian-speak. Thus, the next chapter comes clean as— AFTER*THOUGHTS: my best ideas come to me in the shower.* Read on!

Play Time

1. How do you befriend a person who is in pain and angry, like Sarah?
2. To the best of your recollection, what is the Christian Gospel?

    a. Now find someone who is NOT a Christian and ask them what it is.

    b. Tell them your understanding of the Gospel. Ask them to comment.

3. Interview people, Christian and otherwise, about the statement— *The only absolute truth is there are no absolute truths.* What did you learn?

4. Ask people if they have overriding principles that govern their actions. Learn.

5. How are your overriding principles apparent in your actions?

6. Given that throughout history the Christian faith has adapted to *fit* into every people group, culture and era around the world, what do you think of the idea of a postChristian Gospel? Is it opening Pandora's Box?

7. To what extent is our message a mind-to-mind conveyance of information leading to a decision to follow Christ? To what extent is it a heart-to-heart thing leading to an encounter with Christ that can be explained later?

8. In what circumstances is a *problem-solving model* of the gospel more appropriate? In what circumstances is a *fulfillment model* more appropriate?

9. How do you determine the presuppositions and assumptions a person holds about life and the Christian interpretation of life?

10. How simple is the Gospel? How expansive does it have to be?

11. How are you doing at *being in the world, but not of it*?

12. Where do you have a tough time *bein' green*?

¿CLUELESS CHRISTIANITY?

TRUTH IS STRANGER THAN IT USED TO BE.

~J. Richardson Middleton & Brian J. Walsh
[Toronto, 1999]

TRUTH PASSES THROUGH THREE STAGES—
- First, it is ridiculed.
- Second, it is violently opposed.
- Third, it is accepted as self-evident.

~Arthur Schopenhauer (1788-1860)

Chapter 10: AFTER*thoughts*:
my best ideas come to me in the shower.

I thought the previous chapter of this book would be the last chapter. You know how it goes. You finish something, then you finish it again— similar to the "*here's my first final draft*" submission scenario of so many doctoral theses. This *really really* last chapter will set forth practical ideas to inflict guilt so you won't simply put this book aside and do nothing. First, to deal with the realities of this major cultural shift to a *post*modern/*post*Christian society, I'll suggest some personal characteristics which you will need to integrate, with some degree of wholeness, into your life and livelihood. Then I'll lay out more general observations to keep in the back of your head as you move about, surrounded by a *post*Christian/*post*-moral population. Please, as you read this chapter, know that these recommendations are only applicable if you are serious about relating to the emerging set of people we presently refer to as *post*moderns. I prefer to describe them as *post*Christian, or even as *post*-morals.

➤Personal Characteristics

First, you will need a little **patience**. It takes time to understand paradigm shifts and how they affect everything. It takes time to gain an owl's eye perspective on your own culture, community, and personal heritage. You almost need to have an out of body experience, to be able to fly over your world like an owl to truly see yourself below, in one place & time. When you step back a bit and observe, even your own self seems different; and in many ways, people today *are* different. One of the earliest indications that we were already in a paradigm shift surprised me way back in 1998. I was training a group of emerging Christian leaders from across North America and points beyond at an ARROW LEADERSHIP Conference in Vancouver, BC. During my last session I passed around a sheet of paper for anyone who wanted to stay in touch. I should have guessed what would come back— names, email addresses and mobile phone numbers ONLY, nothing else. I knew then that our world had changed into a far more connected animal kingdom. I had to bridge my generation gap yet again. Fortunately, I am an early adopter (Innovation/Adaptation Bell Curve), and had a leg up on them. But that only came after I learned to listen, to take time with people who were different from me.

We have to learn to live along side people who are increasingly different from ourselves. Don't jump to conclusions after one encounter with people outside your own social group; people have arrived where they are in life over long, hard roads; some roads, quite far from your own path. Take time to win the right to allow people to trust you with their road's story, on *their* terms, on *their* turf. The night before I first started editing this chapter I met with a group of people at an ALPHA gathering. We had met together before, but never quite like this— one Australian, two Iranian Muslims, and four Chinese students from Beijing (all in their late 20s–early 30s). Our small group fell into a discussion of the differences between being raised in a basically Christianized society (America), a basically Muslim society (Iran), and a basically atheistic society (China). The Muslims were convinced that Islam was the true religion because it was the most recent, which meant that it was the most complete, incorporating all previous religions into it. The Chinese, not-quite-atheists, were brand new to the idea of a God even existing. How could God be Jesus if Jesus came to earth? It was an exciting evening of interchange, disagreement, and friendship as each person was able to speak without fear of recrimination or evangelistic attack. No one had to win. As the only Christian in the group, I was honored to watch our Lord Jesus begin to work His miracles in these people. I just needed to be there, modeling honest, transparent Christian faith, speaking the Truth in love. It was not a time to whip out a Gospel outline and proceed to read through it; it was not a time to maneuver the conversation around to Christian things. It was rather a time for me to be still and to listen for the voice of God's Holy Spirit coming out of these curious individuals. I was amazed at the genuinely Biblical images and ideology they espoused without even knowing it. Then I just had to wait. As said earlier, God is in control; we don't have to be.

¿CLUELESS CHRISTIANITY?

New expressions of faith evolve naturally with time and generational dominance[ci]; so learn patience.

On the other hand, as Christians in a rapidly evolving society, we do not have a lot of time to adapt to our changing world. It used to be that paradigm shifts occurred about every 200-500 years. When the printing press enabled merchants to carry information (as well as their wares) across Eurasia those shifts accelerated paradigm change to about every 40-50 years. With the dissemination of communication technology that figure is accelerating even more today. What communicates our faith today will have to change or update not every 20 – 30 years, but every 5 years. George Barna, in <u>BOILING POINT: Monitoring Cultural Shifts in the 21st Century,</u>[cii] says that, at best, we have no more than 3-5 years to catch up before things shift again. Then, we need to surpass the culture in breaking ground for the next shift to follow.[ciii] *"If you can see the future coming,"* says Barna, *"it's too late."*

➤**God is full of surprises; don't trust Him. He'll throw you in over your head every time.**

Next, you will need to let go of at least a little of your calculating caution and prepare yourself for the unknown. Ready? God might want to **surprise** you. So often I have wanted everything nailed down, boxed up tight, understood logically, theologically, and rationally. It's safer that way. It is usually at one of these personal-need-for-safety points that God would throw me one of His little surprises. Have you ever experienced that? You finally have everything in your Christian life figured out; okay, almost everything. And then, WHAM! God throws you a curve ball and you need to adjust your Christian life to fit the new game-rules. Sometimes the curve ball hits hard and the adjustment takes some real effort. Other times, the surprise brings such elation and blessing that you are shocked you ever forgot that our God does some pretty amazing things for people who love Him. [Like the ALPHA group I just described.] He *is* full of surprises; you need to count on that and move on with what He has in mind for you.

A second scary corollary of surprise is **risk**. That's right, RISK. Surprised? One odd dictum I remember from my early days in church is that *"God can't direct a parked car."* Doesn't need much explaining, does it? Unless we are willing to start rolling, to stick out our necks we may not experience what it is that God has for us. New expressions of faith are always suspect, marginal, usually put forward by youth, and, in a word, RISKY. When I was a teenager and had just started driving, my mother used to tell me, *"Remember, nothing good can happen in a parked car."* Start driving. Or, as Volkswagen puts it— LIFE'S FAST; DRIVERS WANTED. *"Das auto."*

Christian Mission, too, has become a risky business. In preparation, mission candidates study for years to understand the nature of the field to which they are being sent only to find upon arrival that there is yet so much more to learn; they feel like such novices. It wasn't so much that they didn't understand the culture, or the language, or the people group— it was that, here, finally, were the actual people God had sent them to. Their kinship relationships, nuances, sub-cultural distinctives, regional and generational histories were another level of specificity that had to be mastered if they were ever to be accepted. It engaged all of their cultural discernment, intuition, innuendo and inference, and individual personality peculiarities. There was a TV commercial for a Brokerage Firm in the United States in the late 20th century that ran the tagline— *the only real risk in life is not taking one*. We all got the point.

There are other risks in life— flying, eating in Thai restaurants, drinking the water in LA, driving in Boston, having crawfish in N'Orlans, getting married, living in the Bible Belt— all risks. And ALL of them are necessary if we are to get on with life, with living in this world, to have a life that matters. What was it that Charlie Brown, the main character in Charles Schultz' cartoon strip, *PEANUTS*, used to say? *You will miss 100% of the shots you never take.* And he hit his target every time. What was his target? Earth.

So, admittedly, it is a major risk to promote a new form of expression of the Christian life to the powers that be; but do we really have any choice? On the cover of the editorial workbook designed to help me write this book I created for myself a personal reminder

> *When the values of a culture change*
> *everything changes. If the church cannot adapt the*
> *expression of its faith to the emerging culture it*
> *will, eventually, be forgotten.*

Of course, this kind of statement needs to take into account the power of God in Christ to bring about His ends. Its point was not to disclaim the power of the Christian message: its intention was that we need to be constantly aware of our surrounding society and of our tendency to lag behind in understanding the times. For we lag way behind at times; and regrettably, we are not even aware that our world has moved on. We dare not disengage from our society to the extent that we no longer understand who it is. For then they can never understand who we are.

We must also remember that taking risks does not necessarily demand that we *"throw out the old... in with the new."* Risk to move forward is always based on the foundations of the past. Without those foundations there would be no launching pad for the future. But someday the spaceship must take off. We have no choice. So what about it? Are you being called on to take some risks for God? Are you ready to be different for the sake of future generations of Christians? For the world you live in? Hummmm.

Another corollary of God's surprises is **mystery**. I don't care how old you are, when you receive a present, wrapped up in gift paper all pretty with ribbon & bow you can't help but be drawn into the mystery of what's inside. [Unless, of course, you've already snooped.] It's exciting to get gifts in wrapped packages. Trying on new forms of faith is much the same— you don't know what's inside until you unwrap it. New expressions of faith are mysterious, attractive, vague, and uncertain: they don't have all the answers in a neat, systematic package, and that's uncomfortable, albeit a little exciting. Yet, throughout history the church has had to unwrap new forms of faith everywhere it took root. Some years ago I received a cassette-tape of Indian music from a friend who lived just outside of Hyderabad, India. He had been an Indian cohort and a kindred spirit to me for a long time— still is. But I had no idea what this music was; so I wrote him. He replied via FAX (all that was available then)— *"Brother Davis, don't you realize what this is? This is the first Christian music we have that reflects our culture and not the West's."* I was humbled beyond belief. That man had gotten it! He understood the importance of living in the mystery of faith within each new generation, within one's own culture, within each emerging era. Frightening? You'd better believe it. Mysterious? Absolutely. But, again, we have no choice. There is a mystery to faith that needs to be rewrapped for every new generation and culture of Christians. You buy the wrapping paper, I'll grab the theological scissors and cultural scotch tape.

Then there's **extreme non-balance**. Somewhat oxymoronic, eh? But nonetheless a characteristic we need to cope with in this *post*modern/*post*Christian era. Throughout the modern era the Christian cultural cry was for **balance in all things**. Be reasonable. Sensible. Rational. Cautious. Tempered. The raison d'être of the era was to take the middle of the road and stay on it. That was considered safest. In fact, one caricature of western Christianity is that of a complacent, calculating, unruffled tranquility.[civ] In the American South it seems that *the* cardinal sin is to rile somebody, to offend them, to be anything but culturally middle-of-the-road. Though roughly only 43% of any southern city attends church, there is very little cross-over to the rest of the adjacent non-Christian culture. There is even less of an impact of Christians on their surrounding society. Why? Because we do not want to be perceived as extremists. We do not want to be tempted by those different from ourselves. After all…, we're not Jesus! But shouldn't we be? He mixed with sinners (normal people) daily. He was tempted, but stood firm. You say, *Yes, but I cannot be that strong.* Really!?! Then what is the use of having the God of the universe alive within?!? What is your faith if it does not define who you are and determine your actions? And what is God's salvation if He cannot protect you? Again, look

¿CLUELESS CHRISTIANITY?

at Jesus. Did they crucify him for being cautious? Inoffensive? Middle-of-the-road? Hardly. He was crucified because He spoke God's mind..., graciously, most of the time, to those who needed to hear it; but the religious establishment took offense at Him regularly. [Of course, given how He spoke of them, they had a point.] . In the same way, as new forms of faith expression arise in our society they may need to be established with some degree of excessive non-balance. They will need to be extreme to gain a hearing; they will need to be presented in an empowered yet culturally acceptable manner to be understood, and they will need to be tried. Tried not just by those on the fringes of faith, but also by those in authority within the church. Bear in mind, authority does not like to be challenged. Expect some degree of resistance as you try new ways of expressing your personal faith.

When it comes to trying on new forms of faith *corporately*, non-balance becomes an absolute necessity. For the church should function as a body, needing diversity in each individual member, yet being mutually sensitive. Problems arise when one member or group insist that their way is the only way. This is usually not due to a particular theological position, for each new form of faith expression should reflect a Biblical principle as well as a Biblical practice. More likely an insistence on being right is probably more a fear of the future, of discomfort with change (any change), or, and this is the worst, a desire for power and position that keeps things the way the dominant generation remembers them (especially if it keeps them in the driver's seat). Addressing this situation becomes, then, not a matter of truth vs. Truth, but one of cultural, ecclesiastical finesse. The encroachment of *post*Christian Christianity on the modern Christian world is

251

seen as a challenge to Truth and tradition rather than as one of a new challenge of adaptation (note- ADAPTATION..., NOT compromise). Think of how those first Jewish-Christians must have felt when they saw Greeks and Romans coming to Christ. *Hey, you have to become Jewish before you can become Christian! Right? That's not fair! How can this be?* Or what about the ministry of St. Patrick, in Ireland? Captured off the coast of Britain in the Year of Our Lord 403, he was sold as a slave to the household of *Miliue* (or *Milchu*), a Druid of the Dal Riada in what is now Antrim, Ireland. During his captivity, Patrick learned the language and customs of the land. After six years Patrick heard a voice telling him to return to his homeland, Britain. After spending some time with his family, He entered a monastery in Gaul where he studied under *St. Germain*, Bishop of Auxerre. He received his ordination and returned to Ireland in 432 to become a missionary to the Druids who inhabited the land. But he did not go in and merely start to proclaim the word of God— he en-fleshed it, he lived it..., utilizing their Pagan symbols and celebrations to paint a picture of the salvation to be found in Jesus Christ. In time, thousands turned their ancient Pagan practices into expressions of Christian faith. Patrick didn't confront or condemn the culture; rather, he utilized it to amplify their new faith in Christ. In the ancient Druid religion, worshipers always lit a fire at the entrance to any ceremony. St. Patrick integrated this into the Easter celebration by building a bonfire outside the entrance to the church for Good Friday service. No condemnation, but rather sanctification. Adaptation at its finest.

Or consider the realignment of early European Christian settlers to the American landscape. Baptists in

¿CLUELESS CHRISTIANITY?

Europe became Baptists in America. But Baptist tradition, like the Congregationalists before them, took on a distinctly "American" tenor. American Christians did not reject their European roots. They *adapted them*, and established a form of Christian faith more appropriate to the new land, with peoples coming together from divergent expressions of faith and practice. Invariably, over time, those different expressions of faith melded together to form a new shape of faith. Whenever the pendulum swings, for it to have an eventual effect on the middle-of-the-road, it must swing far to the right, or, er, left. Depends on your starting point. Anyway, just get the point.

Christians in North America are entering the second decade of a new millennium: new opportunities, new challenges, and new patterns of living are sure to emerge. [Have you checked your video-messages on your mobile sat-com *i*toy today? Oh, you forgot; you left it in your daughter's *maglev*-hybrid Honda!?!] In the same way that Christians have always had to adapt their faith to changing conditions throughout history— from Roman persecution, to Ethiopian missions, European expansion, early colonized America, Hudson Taylor in China, and the West Coast Jesus People of the 1970s, so also will North American Christians have to adapt their faith to fit the new rules of the *post*Christian playing-field of the twenty-first century. Nothing new under the sun— for the most part.

➤**General Observations for the Back of Your Head**

Now let's shift gears to some things you need to stuff into your head, just a notch above your sub-conscious, for retrieval in those moments of confusion and ah-ha.

¿CLUELESS CHRISTIANITY?

First, **not everyone in America and Canada are** *post***Christian** in their outlook on life. Actually, some of the people I've met seem more *pre***historic** than anything else; they don't think at all; they mutter guttural expletives and generally respond to whatever fad that attracts them. If you ask them about the meaning of life they will stare at you like you don't know what's going on and don't have a clue what the score of the game is. Don't even think about explaining your faith to them with *post*Christian considerations, let alone in Modern terminology. They do not think that way. What is it they need? To observe your life for 5-10 years. (Put's the pressure on, doesn't it?)

Then, you will find others to be more *pre*-**modern** in their perspective. Oddly, they seem to have much more of a sense of mystery, of the supernatural, of the existence of a divine being, of the realities of a spiritual realm. But like postmoderns they will have little tolerance for "organized religion." A postmodern expression of faith will just barely fit into their ethereal-awareness aura and add to the beauty of the universe, and to the Source, whatever he/she/it/or they, say it is. But in common with postmoderns, *pre*moderns will need to experience a divine encounter with the God who made them. A present day example of this was reported in a <u>Christianity Today</u> article regarding Muslims coming to Christ.[cv] It seems that one of the ways God uses to communicate His Truth to Muslims is through dreams & visions. All across the Middle East, Muslims are experiencing visions of Jesus, talking to them, warning them, directing them to the homes of Christians. Go figure? Not really. Even with the encroachment of Western technology and communications, much of the Arab world is mostly *pre*modern in its outlook on reality. So it makes perfect sense. Jesus Christ uses the cultural sensitivities inherent in every culture to reach the people of that culture. The same kind of thing would ring true with American spiritualists in the backwoods of Kentucky, or the tabernacles of Brooklyn, or with Native Americans in the American southwest who worship the spirits of the earth; or with the Inuit of Nunavut who identify with the spirits of the past in the frozen land above the Arctic Circle. It can also be found in the Saskatchewan housewife who has lost interest in the faith of her youth and the faithfulness of her husband, who turns to truth in more spiritual forms. She finds the God she has been seeking in a vision of Jesus Christ, totally unexpected.

Still others will fall into the **modern** (or modernist) category— logical thinkers who demand evidence and a logical/rational presentation of the Christian position before they can discuss, let alone embrace, the Christian faith. The majority of these individuals are involved in the higher Educational Academies of North America; professors, administrators, grad students, etc. But even of their number only a small percent look for *rational argument* to prove the veracity of the Christian faith. Dr. Andrew Griffis (CEO of *StrongWatch*, Inc. in Tucson, AZ) believes their number to be less than 30% of North America's schools of higher learning [most likely engineering and philosophy professors.] In reality, these modern thinkers trust in an un-admitted faith underlying their scientific investigations and philosophic presuppositions in virtually every field of study. But when it comes to finding faith in the Christian God, Jesus Christ, they demand, no longer certitude, but absolute certainty. Unfair, yes…, but that's the way it is. Christian students in these fields must be both wise and prudent in expounding upon their beliefs. They need an academic savvy to steer a clear line through the shoals of academic insecurity and professional uncertainty. Sheep among wolves; though not without our Shepherd! So, in some instances, the expression of the Christian faith must be straightforward, based on clear evidence, consistent and cohesive. It must sufficiently explain the Christian view of reality in the logic of the hearer. Presuppositions aside, well actually, they're never really aside; we must make our case for our faith in a format that is acceptable to the scientific, rational mindset of the Modern Man. But if the modern thinker cannot grant our basic premise that there is, in fact, a Creator Who wants to communicate with his creation, then, well, we're dead. We cannot win the argument. We have come to a presuppositional impasse. Too long have Christian positions and presentations lost the right to be heard in the academic or public forum. That battle must be won on another playing field. The academy is often, though not always, a harbinger of philosophic tunnel-vision and scientific denial of their own faith. The classic "debate" between the Christian apologist and the great minds of secularism is now rarely an appropriate battlefield. At the very least, Christianity does not have home court advantage. Modernism's rationalism demands a different approach.

In Amherst, Massachusetts, where we live, there is a great sports bar called The Hangar. It is there, around the tables and the bar, that the battle for the soul of the academy will be won at 1:00 a.m. in the morning— over buffalo wings and beer. Make that Coke; no, make that beer. Sorry…, minor issues should not get in the way of major ones. May I have a roll of paper towels? (Buffalo wings are messy.)

➤**NEXT, please**

Communicating our Christian faith to a *post***Christian generation** is so much simpler. *Post*Christians do not demand logical argument; they do not demand cohesiveness or consistency; they do not demand that the Christian faith explain *all* of reality before they will consider it a viable option. They do not need a person to have a completely developed world-and-life view before they will engage in a conversation over spiritual things. They merely want to see our faith being worked out in our life. Much simpler, you think, eh! Yeah, right. But, seriously, if our faith is no more than an explanation of logically consistent, sequential beliefs, where is there empowerment for living? There is none. The Christian view of life is *living life*, new life discovered (yea, verily created too) in an established relationship with the God who made us. *Post*Christian people want to see the real thing, lived out before them: *then* our explanations will have a framework, credibility and reference points in a real life context. About a month before I started revising this chapter a young man from Cambodia asked if we could talk. He said his life had recently taken a turn for the worse and he found himself floundering, not sleeping and constantly obsessing about a broken relationship. *Why me?* I asked. *Because your life seems to hold together; you make sense to me. I don't want to consider talking with anyone else.* That was it—my life seemed to hold together. Wait 'till he finds out the reason it holds together.

➤**That light at the end of the tunnel…?**
It's not New Jersey

Another thing to keep in the back of your head is that not everyone is aware of their own *generational tunnel-vision*.

257

¿CLUELESS CHRISTIANITY?

You will have to learn to listen to people in *their* mindset and from *their* perspective. On one hand this is no easy task, getting into the brain of someone from a different generation; you do not share in many of their common life experiences. On the other hand it can be quite simple and enjoyable. If I asked you to try to step outside yourself to see things from another vantage point, you would understand, wouldn't you? You would take a stab at it? It involves putting the other person first; putting yourself and your agenda aside and giving the space to them; space to wonder, think, ponder, and ponder again. Crossing generational lines is somewhat different. If I recall aright, crossing barriers and learning from one another is what the church is supposed to be— a body which needs each part to function in a healthy manner, *building up the whole body in love*. So while you're gearing up for the emerging generation of *post*modern/*post*Christians, remember that they are who they are because of the foundation built for them in your generation, or even further back, your parents or grandparents generation.

One of the biggest challenges for the Church, composed of multi-generational Christians, is to understand one another. To do that we first need to get in touch with our own cultural/generational point of view. Because we are all born into a certain kind of family, with its own patterns of behavior and beliefs, and we are all raised in a particular culture & time, which dictates a great deal of what we consider normal and acceptable. All of us come at life with engrained, preconditioned ideas of what is going on in this world. As we grow in life, these ideas become locked-down into perspectives that eventually become life philosophies, conscious or unconscious. We may not be aware of them but they're there nonetheless. We thus need first to become cognizant of our own personal-generational perspective on life before we can attempt any meaningful interface with people in another generation. The best way I know to break through our personal, generational tunnel-vision is to intentionally spend time with those in other generations. One of my best friends at our church, until he died, was an 86 year old Greek man who loved God and whom I loved deeply. Euclid Djaferis.[cvi] What he had accomplished in his life made my life look like a cheap cartoon character in a Marvel comic book. Euclid was born on September 15, 1910, in Asia Minor, now Turkey. Following the Armenian massacres[cvii] and the Greek Genocide in Turkey Euclid's family was part of the great "population exchange" between Greece and Turkey. More than one million Greeks were kicked out of their homes across Turkey. An estimated 350,000 Greeks were killed.[cviii] His family's expulsion was also due to their being evangelical believers, not Orthodox. (Of note, Euclid's grandparents and parents were rejected by their families for their conversion to evangelicalism.)

In 1927 his father, Stephan, formed the Second Evangelical Church in Athens (in the Pontus Greek language). Because of legal definitions of "church" it was referred to as merely "an association."

His father had previously held a job in Turkey with an American group, The Near East Relief Foundation, sent to care for all the orphans of the war. When they moved their work to Greece, on the Isle of Syros, Euclid and his family moved with them. The majority of the company was staffed with evangelical Christians.

¿CLUELESS CHRISTIANITY?

In 1933, his father worked in Cyprus at an American Mission High School, leaving his family in Athens. He and his father left Athens for Cyprus, then a British colony in 1934. In September, 1941, Euclid and ten others had to present themselves to the Greek Consulate on Cyprus. He was immediately conscripted into military service. (That same month, his older sister got a scholarship to study at Wellesley College, in America.) He was sent to fight the Italians in Albania. While there Euclid was deserted by his comrades on a snowy night in the mountains of Albania. He merely walked from northern Albania all the way back to Greece.

With Greece under German occupation Euclid worked secretly with the Red Cross, a cover for his work in the underground, sabotaging ship work in the harbor. When he was betrayed he and his father escaped to the island of Chios. He was smuggled out of Greece into Turkey. But because they had no passports they were imprisoned in Turkey. Through British channels, they were released into Israel, at that time still a British colony. It was during his time in Palestine that Euclid worked directly with Field Marshall Edmund Allenby (of *Lawrence of Arabia* fame). There he joined the Greek military and went to fight in the Battle of El Alamein (1942), North Africa. By the end of the war, he had also fought in the Battle of Rimini. From 1941 'till the middle of 1943 his family had no idea whether he was alive or dead. In 1943 Euclid returned to Cyprus to the surprise of his family. In 1946 he married his bride for life, Eutychia (meaning happiness).

Following WW2, Communist forces descended on Greece, battling the Greek National Forces. It was in these confrontations in Athens that Euclid was seriously wounded.

¿CLUELESS CHRISTIANITY?

In 1971 Euclid received a call from an old friend asking if he was born in Turkey. It was this way that he was allowed to immigrate to America. He was sponsored by his sister Sophia and her husband, living in Washington, DC. His first job in America was as a doorman at an apartment building. After a year, Eutychia joined. They lived in the apartment building where he had been promoted from doorman to Building Engineer.

I met Euclid just as his wife was dying, in Amherst, MA, where he had been taken to live with his son Theodore and his wife Mary. Listening to Euclid's stories of the past captivated me with the incredible wonder of God's work in his life. Euclid's life spoke to me of what I had NOT endured for my faith and pressed me to greater commitment to both my generation and the next. How his faith held firm during such troubling times amazes me to this day.

Euclid was one of the key role models from whom I learned the importance of humble service and personal holiness. I look forward to seeing you again, my friend.

Another friend I cherish is now a 23 year old married woman— Laurel Myers (Beauregard). I met Laurel when she was just a squat lil' thing— 4 years old. She had the cutest dimples! When she was 7 years old I grabbed her cheeks and squished them together and said, "*You know, some day I'm going to get a needle & thread, sew these dimples together and start calling you fish-face.*" She kicked me: then she hit me. It's got to be love. I called her fish-face up to the day she married. I figured that was a good time to stop. And yes, we're still friends. I have learned a lot about life, my faith, and the expression of my faith from these two people, and from many more like them. I have learned what it is that I need to do to be part of *their* Body of Christ, and how to make them a part of mine. So, please, get to know someone outside your generation. It's worth the investment both *in* the church, and on outside. You never lose when you walk an extra mile in the other man's moccasins. [Not sure about doing it in Prada's.]

There is one more thing you will have to keep in the back of your head to communicate to the prevailing *post*Christian mindset through your own (and my own) generational tunnel-vision that isn't all that new. In fact, it's quite old— it is the tension we always face between ***rejection and acceptance***. This tension feels somewhat amplified during this early *post*Christian period. With the elevating of *personal choice* to the position of non-negotiable godhood, people tend to build caricatures of others with little proclivity to have their own minds influenced or changed by anyone. In one of my meetings with two friends, both Iranian Muslims, they admonished me to remember that not all Muslims are terrorists. Not that I thought that— but they needed to make sure that they reminded me of it; their perception of me, as an American, bordered on a reactionary caricature as well. Good reminder. If you remember your math, there is always one more variable that you thought to be a constant.

I've found I need to be much more non-judgmental in addressing this tension between acceptance and rejection. I have come to a position where I believe, unless called upon to do so by church or court, it is not my place to judge anyone— that is the Lord God's complete prerogative. Not that I've suspended my brain or my critical faculties; but I have opened

¿CLUELESS CHRISTIANITY?

my opinion to be more accepting of *inconsequential realities*— red-red hair, body piercing, being kissed by ninety year olds (on the lips) …, not quite perfect theology, neighbors whose names I cannot pronounce, the appearance of nonchalant, seemingly defiant body posture, blue-blue hair (on the 90 yr. olds), and feeling the music-for-the-future-deaf coming from the car behind me on a $4,000 sound system. These and things like them qualify as life's little stressors; but they are not life altering conditions. In this wonderful time of pluralism and transition at its subtlest, we need to learn to lighten up and let go of the inconsequential, but to hold tenaciously to issues of importance. There are non-negotiables of faith and life that cannot be compromised. We need to know what they are, jumbled as they will be through every era, geography, and generational filter in existence.

A corollary of the *acceptance* and *rejection* factor is that of **appearances**. That punk-rocker with green/orange hair and pierced nipples may have the mind of an Einstein yearning to make sense out of God and life: and that 90 year old who just kissed you on the lips may hold life stories of evidence for the greatness and mercy of God. I've had to learn to put aside my personal stereotypes and preconceived notions of how some people present themselves and focus on their heart. Recently I met a young man, Stephen, with pierced eyebrows, lips, tongue and nose-bridge. His hair was in braids. His only clothing color— black. [Secretly I wondered if he wore black underwear; then I wondered if he wore underwear at all.] All in all, he was as different from me as I could imagine. But he turned out to be a genuine Christian with a passion to bring teens, street people, the homeless, beggars and punkers, to faith in Christ. He wanted to know if I could help him establish a "Town Center" to provide shelter, food, and faith for those he loved. He didn't even know about the idea of a *target audience*: he just loved his friends. I was ashamed of my prejudicial perspective. I learned a lot from Stephen over our lunch— not only about youthful abandon, but about myself too. Are there any Stephens in your life?

The final thing I believe you will need to file away in the back of your head is ***intuition***. As Christians we are taught to know a lot about our faith. We are trained to understand the Bible, the effects of sin on people, the meaning of the sacrificial atonement of Christ on the cross, of the cost of a maintaining a committed life; but are we taught to use our *sense of intuition*? You know, that gut feeling you have about certain situations, that *sense* that you <u>must</u> do something or telephone someone you haven't talked to in a while, or that you need to say things to someone which definitely do not originate with you. There is a strange relationship between *gut feelings* and *faith* that is hard to explain. The "leading of the Lord" or whatever it is must be considered carefully, and usually with some degree of urgency. It must be acted upon with conviction. This is no small thing to consider. Speaking *prophetically,* if you will, into another's life takes some degree of guts. It also takes a lot of soul searching, a keen sense of timing and great wisdom. But more than these, it takes a humble spirit before God and a life as devoid of corruption as possible. There is nothing like a personally clean life serving as our foundation of credibility. There is nothing like cleaning out your life and clearing the air between you and God to free your spirit within; His Spirit can be heard much more clearly when there is less crap clogging your spiritual ears. It is refreshing. AND it yields a transparency that others, Christians and normal people alike, find attractive, calming, and trustworthy. Get my point? *Intuition, spiritual intuition, discernment*, call it what you will; it comes much more easily when the barriers between God, you and others are wiped clean.

I wonder sometime if the job of the Christian, still here on earth, isn't simply one of **removing barriers**. Removing them between God and men so they can have a clearer path to God: and removing them between people, so they can become safer with each other. Maybe we need to remove the barriers between *us and them*, between normal people and our Christian sub-cultures, so that they can start a meaningful life in a relationship with the God who made them. Anchored firmly in the grace & forgiveness of God we certainly have no fear of losing our identity in Christ. We merely need to be willing to cross that line and help people find their identity in our Lord as we did.

Even so, come quickly Lord Jesus… .

Time to get out of the shower. Dang! Now, where did I put my towel? O…, one last thought to leave with you—

"Everyone is ignorant…only on different subjects."

~Will Rogers

Do not be ignorant of the tremendous paradigm shifts taking place all around us. Be diligent to develop your own *post*Christian faith for a world that so desperately needs the redemption of Jesus Christ our Lord.

¿CLUELESS CHRISTIANITY?

Play Time

1. How's your patience quotient? Do you need to sit on your explosion factor a little more? Or do you hold everybody around you to your standards?

2. When was the last time God surprised you? What might you do to put yourself in over your head so God can surprise you with one of his little miracles?

3. To what degree do you need things nailed down? How does this provide you with a safe place? Is there any room in your life for the mysterious, for the unsafe? Do you want some of life to be mysterious? Why? Why not?

4. What risks do you believe God is calling you to take? When you let go, how does that make you feel? Can you still trust in the Lord when you're not in control, or, in less control?

5. What did you think of the idea of growing an *extreme non-balance* in your life of faith? What would it mean to you to do this?

6. Identify the people in your life who are pre-historic, pre-modern, modern, postmodern. How can you relate to them as a friend, a student, and a loving Christian?

7. Any generational conflict you need to address? When was the last time you said you were sorry to your kids, or to your parents, or to someone whom you classified as below you?

8. How can you become more open to people whose appearance drives you nuts? Are there any preconceptions you need to face in your own life? How might someone different from yourself help you face them?

9. To what degree do you trust your intuition? Will you make decisions based on them? How can your intuition be supported from other senses, other points of view?

¿CLUELESS CHRISTIANITY?

APPENDIX

GENERATIONAL INTERVIEWS

[NOTE- Ages as noted were at the time of the Interview]

INTERVIEW SET #1- CHRISTIAN FAITH BUILT ON THE ROCK (80+ GROUP)

Florence Davis, 92- Retired Social Security Employee

1. When did you become a Christian?

I became a Christian when I was about 15 years old. I was in church (Christian & Missionary Alliance, The Tabernacle, in Omaha, NE). I learned it was known as an altar-call.

2. Why did you become a Christian?

I became a Christian because God was pulling me toward himself; I could not resist. I don't know how to explain it. I didn't know all that much. I didn't even know that what happened to me was called conversion. I had no knowledge of the Bible. I was illiterate of spiritual things and the Bible. I just didn't realize what happened to me. I didn't even realize I wasn't a Christian and neither did my family. I had never heard of the phrase being a Christian. I was abysmally ignorant of the fact that I wasn't a Christian. But my heart was thumping so hard that I had to get up out of my seat and go into the prayer room, not really sure of what I was getting into. When the pastor, Dr. R. R. Brown, came in I kneeled and prayed for..., I don't know. I am sure I wanted to become a child of God.

3. How has your Christian faith evolved over the years?

It has become stronger throughout my life—through tears and trials, happiness and sadness. I have never felt a time when I was not aware of the fact that Christ was in me. When the Spirit of God develops you, and you aren't even conscious that He is doing it, He forms you daily until you become what it is He wants you to be. It (Christian development) involves your disobeying him and him forgiving you all through the years.

4. How is God using you today versus 5-10-20 years go?

I don't know. I just hope my life tells people that I have this faith in Christ. If they ask me I can tell them. Earlier, I ran the Business and Professional Women's Club of Baltimore. When I started there I was terrified to talk about my faith in front of people; I was so reticent. But the Lord helped me to learn that I could say something people wanted to listen to.

I also enjoyed being a Sunday School teacher for delinquent girls in a Maryland State Institution (Prison). There were 25 of them. I taught there for 10 years and really grew from the time with them. I really loved those girls.

But, now, well, most of my friends are dead. I hope that I have influenced my grandchildren and that they see me as a strong Christian. I hope they can trust me and talk to me about their problems.

5. What do you think of the shape of Christian faith in North America today?

¿CLUELESS CHRISTIANITY?

Well, all I know is from my generation and friends. I hear about all these other kooky things going on in some churches, which weren't as prevalent when I was younger. What the church has become today is challenging for an older Christian to live through. I am so glad that my faith was well founded. The things that I see going on in the church world today (like the church sweeping some sins under the rug) offends me deeply. It's just not right.

6. What do you think God has in store for you next?

Death? (just kidding) Maybe staying here on earth until I become the person God wants me to be and my work on earth is done. I can't be more specific because I don't know what God is going to do with me. Just to be a witness. No definite orders yet.

Frank Beach, 89, Physics teacher, retired, in Coburg, NY. [Frank is still *quite* dangerous]

1. When did you become a Christian?

I had a false-start in 1938. I went on for a 40 year hiatus. When I retired to Coburg Village I considered ending it all, committing suicide. I went for a walk to think about how I would do it. When I returned to my home I came to understand that the Lord's death and resurrection were the only viable option left to me.

2. Why did you become a Christian?

Why? Because, where I was living (in West Steventown, NY), I became very concerned about everything around me and what was happening to me as well. So I picked up the Scriptures and

*read them with what felt like new eyes. And even though I fell
away for a time, the Lord did not cast me out. He never gave
up on me.*

3. How has your Christian faith evolved over the years?

*Well, I feel like I have, finally, a genuine faith now. My faith is
in what, I know, God did in Jesus Christ. I find myself more
focused and centered in the Scriptures that when I was
younger; in particular, in these days, in the book of
Revelation. Studying the history of the nation of Israel has
given me some great insights into the Scriptures as a whole, as
well as what the nature of the church should be today.*

4. How is God using you today versus 5-10-20 years go?

*I'm thinking about what Jesus said to the 7 churches. To some
He said "You're doing well, but, if you start something, make
sure you finish it. Go through the doors I open for you, and do
what I command you." I need to be doing more as God works
through me in the people around me. I pray more now than I
used to; I bought an Atlas in 2004 and I pray across the map—
starting with New England and I go right across America.
Now I pray around the whole world! I have a deep sense of
what is going on around the world and I am very committed to
prayer for all the saints.*

5. What do you think of the shape of Christian faith in
    North America today?

*Christian faith in North America is in a sorry-state of affairs.
It's like we're living in a II Timothy 3 world. We've scuttled
the Word of God. I know it's not true across the board, but*

some of the things I hear that going on inside churches is just unimaginable. Unimaginable!

6. What do you think God has in store for you next?

I only think about today. I feel badly that I can't continue to teach. So now I am back to painting my faith again. (Frank is a world-class water color artist.) *I hear a hymn or some Christian music with a video and I run home and put my brush onto canvas as fast as I can!*

INTERVIEW SET #2- BOOMER REGENERATION (40 – 60 GROUP)

Dave McDowell, 58- (pastor, COMMUNITY FELLOWSHIP CHURCH, W Chicago, IL)

1. When did you become a Christian?

Two o'clock today…, no, just kidding. I think I became a Christian, initially, when I was 5. That's when I had my first awareness of what Christ had done for me. I kneeled down by my bedside with my dad and asked Chris into my heart. That commitment became more consolidated in my life throughout my teen years. So, theologically, I don't know exactly when it happened, I just know it did.

2. Why did you become a Christian?

I think I was drawn to the love of Christ; to his sacrifice on my behalf. The fact that he loved me blew me away. Even when I was 18 I rebelled against God, I was drawn back to Him through His mercy more than His judgment.

3. How has your Christian faith evolved over the years?

¿CLUELESS CHRISTIANITY?

*Umm, I think it has evolved by gaining a greater
understanding of who God IS, and therefore a greater
perspective on who I need to be in relationship with Him. My
self-knowing has grown out of knowing Him. He is the epitome
of love and grace; the more I see myself in His presence the
more I see myself for who I am.*

4. How is God using you today versus 5-10-20 years go?

*I think that I am more believable than I used to be. The
older I get, the longer I have known God, the more credibility I
have by virtue of experience—not that I know more, just the
experience, the wisdom that comes from knowing God. I find I
see more in Scripture and understand more that is there. It's
not that I have a greater impact on people; but I have a deeper
impact on a smaller number of people.*

5. What do you think of the shape of Christian faith in
   North America today?

*I think it's culture bound. It seems shaped more by
culture than by the Scriptures. It is becoming more and more
foreign to Biblical faith. It takes the Christian message and
domesticates it to our culture rather than taking culture to our
faith. So you see a tremendous discrepancy between what
people say they believe in and how they live. American
Christians haven't suffered. Maybe we need a good dose of
suffering. We seem to have lost the ability to "think
Christianly," trying to affect our culture with our faith.*

6. What do you think God has in store for you next?

*I don't anticipate that. I think whatever is in store for
me next flows out of how faithful I am now. I really don't*

know. My ultimate destiny is with Jesus. How that will play itself out I don't know yet. For me, longevity, faithfulness in ministry is most important to me. How He is going to use me is up to him—use me further, take me home, that's up to Him. Whatever it is, I am excited about it.

Dave Rittner, 49, Department of Defense Investigator

1. When did you become a Christian?

I turned my life over to Christ in October 91, at the age of thirty seven.

2. Why did you become a Christian?

One day my daughter asked if she could start going to church with her friend Maggie. Maggie's parents, friends of my wife and me, had offered to pick her up on Sunday mornings and drop her off after church. This sounded like a great idea since that gave my wife and I Sunday mornings to ourselves, free baby-sitting too. Gotta love that old time religion!

After telling Kathy that it was fine with me, I started thinking that maybe I should at least ask the people of the church if they minded having to be responsible for my daughter each week. I contacted the pastor of the church, Doug Vinez, about discussing the matter. I knew Doug a little because his wife worked with my wife and we had socialized on a couple of occasions.

Doug and I met for lunch and he made it clear that they would love to have Kathy with them each Sunday and no one would think badly of us. In fact people would probably even think favorably about us for encouraging our eight year old daughter to explore her spiritual curiosities.

Doug and I then discussed my feelings about religion and why I had a negative feeling about the whole thing. After politely listening and asking a few questions Doug simply looked me in the eye and told me that my problem was that I was ignorant of the Bible. At the time I understood ignorant to mean stupid and was at first somewhat offended. Doug suggested that if I was interested in seeing what Kathy would be hearing, or just explore what was in the Bible, I could go to church myself, sit in the back and listen.

This wasn't going at all like I expected. My Sunday morning secular Sabbath was quickly evaporating. I was put on the spot and being too cowardly to just answer no, and too slow of mind to make up any reasonable excuse, I replied as to how he was right and that would be the appropriate action for a caring father to take.

So for the next few Sundays I headed off to church with great anxiety. But Doug is a very gifted preacher and teacher and his messages made a lot of sense. So much so that I started to enjoy what I was hearing. I had opened that door that Jesus was knocking on and He burst through!

The miracle of this, beyond the unfathomable reason Jesus loves us so, is that at the time, unbeknownst to me, my life was in crisis. My wife had a private medical practice and the demands of running it were causing her to work sixty to eighty hours each week. She seemed to be at work more than at home and when she was home her work often came home with her. She faced great pressures, had little time for Kathy and I, though she tried hard to make time, and was often in a less than happy state of mind.

I had reached the point where I was tired of the whole situation and had pretty much decided to leave her. I felt that I was losing out on the many joys I had hoped married, and family, life would bring. I also felt that I was doing much more than my share of child care, home care, yard care, and any other kind of care that was required.

When I revealed this to Doug he told me not to do anything until he and I had a chance to talk. We met a couple of nights later and he told the first thing I had to understand as a Christian, was that God hates divorce and that He had blessed this marriage even if we weren't believers when we were married. (We were married in a church but only because that's what you're supposed to do.) He also explained that the problem wasn't with Ginny but with me. I was being totally selfish. I wasn't giving any thought to what Ginny was going through. The pressures she faced each day, the fact that she wasn't getting to spend time with her husband or daughter, that she didn't have any time to herself, wasn't able to enjoy her home, time off, friends, and on, and on. And what would happen to Kathy if I left. What kind of life would she have with her mother working so much and her father not at home? What would happen to Ginny if she had these extra responsibilities on her? He explained that God expected me to stop looking out for myself but instead accept my responsibility to my family, buck up, and turn to God in prayer and accept His help and guidance.

¿CLUELESS CHRISTIANITY?

I met with Doug weekly after this and not much later accepted Jesus into my life. When I told Gin about my decision her first question was where that put her. I told her that if I had this right she was now on a higher pedestal than ever and that God expected me to put her welfare ahead of mine. She liked that answer and felt much better about my conversion. Not so much that she followed me into a relationship with Jesus, but maybe someday. The neat thing about this conversation was that Kathy was sitting in the back seat of the car and listening in. She didn't say anything but I can't help but think that God wanted her right there. The first time I testified?

Since then I've tried to keep maturing in my walk with God. I love to read and I've read numerous books about the Bible and Christianity. I've been in several fellowship situations including meeting with men's groups, Bible studies, meeting with several Christian brothers on a weekly basis, and other church related activities. Have I become a good Christian? That's for others to judge. My prayer life is quite weak and that often makes me feel that I haven't grown as I should. However I do look back to when I started and I no longer feel ignorant of the Bible. While I wouldn't feel real comfortable standing in front of a group and explaining how all of this works (maybe no one can) I'm very comfortable in my heart in my relationship with Christ. I sometimes worry that I haven't grown as much as I should have by now but there is a great peace in my life and so much is clearer than at any time in my life. And my marriage is better than ever!

3. How has your Christian faith evolved over the years?

¿CLUELESS CHRISTIANITY?

I believe that when I first became a Christian God's purpose for me was tied to Kathy. I truly believe that He has given her gifts that are tied to whatever plans He has for her. He wanted to get her on board and wanted a parental guidance and encouragement in developing a relationship with Christ. I've had little input in her spiritual education (hey-I've been stumbling through this myself) but God has used me in guiding us to Christ, and to Biblically centered churches where Kathy has met great teachers. Loving people in these churches have loved, encouraged, taught, and trusted her.

A few years ago Kathy went off to college and I've been wondering what God's doing with me. My wife is still an unbeliever and throughout my Christian walk I've tried to be an example of that "perfect" follower so as not to scare her off. I've come to realize that I'm not responsible for her coming to Christ; although I often wonder if there's something I'm supposed to be doing. Am I pushing too much? not enough? Am I misrepresenting some thing? Ah, if I would just crank up that prayer life and LISTEN!

4. How is God using you today versus 5-10-20 years go?

I think that right now God wants me to work within my church in whatever capacity I fit in. One of my spiritual gifts is that of "helps". Need chairs set up, taken down, kitchen cleaned up, wood hauled, someone to talk to— I'm your guy. Apparently that's been recognized by others as I'm now serving as a Deacon. I try to recognize a situation where I can lend support and pitch in.

I haven't mentioned my Christian life outside of my family and church. That's probably because so far I feel uncomfortable proactively expressing my beliefs. I pray that it's not because I'm ashamed, because I don't feel that I am, but I suppose it's due to my being timid about giving my opinions in general. Two of my coworkers are Christians and I talk freely with them about my beliefs. Other coworkers and my friends are aware of my beliefs but it's been through my actions more than anything I say. My oldest friend, Mark, is strongly anti-religion, and it bothered him greatly when I became a Christian. Every now and then we'll have discussions that lead to religion and he'll attack Christianity and I feel very comfortable stating my beliefs and pointing out how I think he would be helped by exploring it, but then I have a very good relationship with him. I need a confidence for outward expression of my faith.

5. What do you think of the shape of Christian faith in North America today?

I believe that the Christian faith of the US is stronger than people think. There are many signs to contrast that. People seem more accepting of life styles that are un-Biblical. Tolerance has become a word that is used to justify our wayward behaviors and when someone expresses disagreement with an un-religious act they are accused of being judgmental. Our religion-based morals are put aside when we're at work or play where a new set of morals are supplanted. "That's the way it's done in the business world." "If you want win you have to put everything else aside." We have become an "in your face", and instant gratification, society.

Despite these examples I still see a ground swell of people who realize that this country was founded on Judeo-

¿CLUELESS CHRISTIANITY?

Christian principles, and who also believe that this country has become great only through the gracious blessings of God. They realize that people have to come freely to a belief in the American system, just as they have to come freely to a relationship with God. And just as Christians are always under attack so is the American way of life. When people feel threatened enough they tend to act. I believe that Christians are starting to recognize current attacks as seriously threatening their faith and way of life. There seems to be a growing wave against abortion, a disgust with the immoral actions of government officials and corporate executives. I also wonder if the current crisis in the Catholic church isn't driving people to a closer examination of their beliefs, an action that often opens one to hearing God again. But then I'm an optimist.

I've also noticed how accepting this country is of expressions of faith during times of disaster. Following slaughters at schools, the attacks of September 11, disasters in the space program, whatever calamity, the nation appears to turn to God. Prayers for help and understanding are freely expressed and presented in the media. Public mourning services are held in churches and clergy asked to lead them. Yet during these times no plea for separation of state and church is raised.

In the Oct 02 issue of "The Atlantic Monthly", Philip Jenkins wrote an article about "The Next Christianity". He describes the growth of Christianity in the Third World, in particular the Southern Hemisphere. The figures he uses projects into a majority of the Christians in the world being from these countries within a few decades. He explains that because these countries have so little access to many of the wonders of modern science and medicine they still remain strong in their understanding of the world as being a very spiritual place. They are still very strongly influenced by the Virgin Mary and the miracles performed by Jesus, leading to what is considered in the North as a very conservative religion. Jenkins speculates on the cultural pressures these Christians may place on the current Protestant and Catholic hierarchies. He compares the potential effect to being of Reformational proportions. It will be interesting to see what effect this has in the US.

6. What do you think God has in store for you next?

I have no idea what God has planned for me in the future. As I've noted I don't have the best prayer life and that's not conducive to letting God share his five year plan with me. He's left with that trusty attention getter— a two by four to the head.

When I do pray I ask that whatever God has planned for me, that I recognize it, submit myself to that task, and trust that God will provide the means for me to carry it out. I'll keep plugging along hoping that I'm doing God's will and helping to carry out his work here on earth, and pray that in some small way I'm also helping to bring about His glory.

INTERVIEW SET #3- THIRTY-SOMETHING NOW (30-40 GROUP)

Bob Dunne, 37- Department of Environmental Protection Agent, Worcester, MA

¿CLUELESS CHRISTIANITY?

1. When did you become a Christian?

In the Fall of 1983 as a 21-year old student at UMass, Amherst (University of Massachusetts).

2. Why did you become a Christian?

A[1]: Theological Answer: Because God wanted me to. He chose me and granted me faith and repentance to believe and be saved when I heard the words of the Gospel.

A[2]: Anthropological Answer: Because I was looking for THE truth and for answers to the Big questions in life. Becoming a Christian made sense out of life and I saw, for the first time, what life was really all about. I had never been told that I could know that all my sins could be forgiven forever and know for sure that I'd have life forever in heaven with God. I saw that it was all about what God had done for me and not about what I could try to do for God. I was blown away that I could know God personally (and still am!). Did I have a choice??

3. How has your Christian faith evolved over the years?

I guess I would have to say that I have gone through 3 periods of growth/change in my Christian life. For the first five years I was involved with a great Bible-teaching church and Christian College Groups (esp. Navigators). I was really excited and just soaked up the Bible, learning all that I could. I explored all that I could of what God wanted me to be and I learned to trust Him more.

¿CLUELESS CHRISTIANITY?

For the next ten years I experienced a "dark ages" in my faith. I was tested in areas I didn't expect (marriage, house, kids, job). I shopped around trying to find a church that would feed us where we could make a difference. I was involved in a small group where we had good fellowship and some good teaching, but I felt like I was drifting. I began to get discouraged and got confused about what I believed. I spent more time on non-spiritual pursuits and had resigned myself to a life of spiritual mediocrity. Life got a little crazy and my faith just atrophied. I lost touch with the Scriptures as a basis for my faith.

For the last 4-5 years we've attended a new church and I've begun to go back to my roots. I now spend more time learning what the Bible teaches and my faith has once again begun to grow. I am trying to cultivate my life with Christ with the spiritual disciplines I had counted on as a young Christian (Bible reading & prayer) and am being stretched, trying to do new things that demand a greater trust in Christ to accomplish them. I'm seeking to know what I believe and why and to live out what I believe.

4. How is God using you today versus 5-10-20 years ago?

I am more focused in building up my family in the faith and learning and teaching what I've learned to others. I am trying to become more outward oriented. I am finding out what my strengths are and how I can use them to build the body of Christ and live among and communicate to those outside the church.

5. What do you think of the shape of Christian faith in North America today?

¿CLUELESS CHRISTIANITY?

I think in the evangelical movement there are two main currents heading in increasingly diverse directions. One is the one that says, "Experience is king" the other says, "The Bible is king". The two extremes are becoming more polarized and pretty soon people will have to choose sides. I think it is becoming what the liberal/fundamentalist debate was in the early 1900's. Both are equally sincere and evangelistic but the methods of getting there are completely different. There is a lot of confusion out there and I think we are in a period of tremendous change.

6. What do you think God has in store for you next?

You mean besides a large bank account, mansion in the Berkshires, & world-wide fame?

Other than that, I am somewhat unclear other than just trying to build a base of faith in God's word and His power at work in the world around us. He wants to make me more like Christ so there are a lot of areas that need a lot of change. I'm trying to be open to what He wants rather than what I want or the world around us wants. We'll see... the adventure continues!

Carrie Herbert, 36- IVCF staff, Alberta, Canada

1. When did you become a Christian?

I slipped into the Christian faith sometime in 1984. I was 19 years old and living with my fiancé. We asked the local minister to marry us and started to meet with her. I then started to meet with her alone because she was the first person in my life who asked me questions that caused me to wonder about who I was. Thus began a quest for identity that continues to this day. She invited me to take part in her confirmation classes and after the assurance that if I didn't value the input I would not be asked to come again, I agreed. Writing a statement of faith was one of the exercises in the class. I studied, asked questions, prayed, wrote and re-wrote my statement. The day of our confirmation arrived. I stood in the pulpit and glanced nervously at the crowd, cleared my throat, and began to read my statement. When I finished I was aware of a hush, then the realization that I really believed what I had wrote crashed in on me like a wave on the ocean shore.

2. Why did you become a Christian?

In my encounters with this minister, I tasted a quality of life I had never experienced before. She was real, honest, in touch with herself, courageous and seemed to have a vital, living relationship with Jesus. I was surprised by her acceptance because my impression was that Christians had a lot of rules that I was not following. This didn't make any difference to her and I felt a genuine love for me flowing from her. I wanted to be like her.

3. How has your Christian faith evolved over the years?

The evolution of my Christian faith has been similar to the development of a child. Initially I had so much to learn. I fell down often and experienced loving arms lifting me back up and encouraging me to try again. I've had times of rebellion and intense doubt in which I thought I was crazy to believe. The grace in this is that, even if it wasn't true, I still had a better quality of life than anything I had experienced before this. I am currently in a time that feels a bit like late adolescence. I wrestle between being too dependent upon God and too independent. I sense the call to walk beside Jesus as a companion more often. Many factors have played in my Christian evolution from people to books, times of solitude to great celebrations, from intense sorrow and deep joy, from stark contrasts of beauty and despair.

4. How is God using you today versus 5-10-20 years go?

I'm often unaware of how God is using me. What I know is God has always been very respectful of who I am, therefore how He has poured His love through me has taken various forms. Early in my walk of faith I had a job as a waitress in a bar. I was known affectionately as Sister Carrie by the patrons and was unashamed of this. Did God use that to speak into their lives? I trust God had His way. God had so much work to do in me in those early years as I journeyed towards wholeness. I was constantly surrounded by people, planning youth group, singing in the choir, going on missions, church stuff. I find that today my life is much more characterized by one to one interactions with people and solitude. If I'm centered in Christ I am much more able to hear, listen, see, love, embrace. I am slowly accepting the fact that

¿CLUELESS CHRISTIANITY?

God has and is making me into one who needs large amounts of space for solitude that He/I speak out of.

    5.   What do you think of the shape of Christian faith in North America today?

I think in most places it takes the shape of a ruler that is used to punish, measure, be precise, bar the door in, separate. It is indeed taxing to fight the battle of darkness both within and without the community of believers. I sense sparks of hope, "holy sparks" in the words of Annie Dillard, in various places. I grieve the loss of compassion, grace, forgiveness with one another that characterizes Jesus. I grieve as I watch generations at war with one another about inconsequential things, meanwhile people are longing for a comrade on the road, someone who will simply walk with them. I'm reminded of how many times Jesus simply walked down the road with people. I wonder if we are not so busy doing God's "work" that we miss Jesus in the midst of it?

    6.   What do you think God has in store for you next?

I find myself pregnant with holy anticipation. I do not know what God is birthing in me, however I do know the One who is knitting it together and I trust Him with my whole heart. So I wait and pray. I rest in the knowing of God holding me, those I love and those I will come to love. I am giving myself space for God to emerge and myself space to see. See what, you ask? The love between a newborn and its mother, the shadow of sun on snow, a fly caught in a desperate struggle in a spider's web, a tear in the eye of a friend.

INTERVIEW SET #4- MILLENNIAL MATRIX FAITH (18-30 GROUP; MILLENNIALS RISING)

Joy McDowell, 20- Wheaton College, Wheaton, IL, basketball 1,000 pointer!

1. When did you become a Christian?

I became a Christian when I was probably four or five. I barely remember it. I just recall sitting on my bed, looking out the window, and saying "those words."

2. Why did you become a Christian?

I guess I did it because the rest of my family was Christian. I looked up to my older siblings so much that I just wanted to be like them in every way, and this was one of the ways.

3. How has your Christian faith evolved?

I think the answer to that question would vary depending on which day you asked me. One day I would probably say it hasn't at all, that I have more doubts, more questions, than when I first gave my life to Christ. Other days I would tell you it has evolved immensely. I think all I can say at this point is that I know where I need to be, I know where I want to be, it is just hard to get there and stay in that spot. I know the answers and I know what to say in order to please others. I've heard all the Bible stories and verses and lessons, ever since I was a little girl. But I am really trying to learn everyday how to apply my faith. If my faith has evolved at all, it is into that of a discerning adult instead of a worry-free child.

I have messed up so much. I have found myself in most ungrateful, unbelieving, unsatisfying places in my walk with God lately. Those are the times at which the questions have overpowered the answers. Those are times at which I don't pay attention to those regurgitated verses in my head. At times like those I feel my faith has not evolved at all.

But it has. I know it has. I don't believe God would allow me to just sail adrift in this world like that. If there's anything I have come to better understand it is that faith can't just be a good feeling. What I mean by this is I've always heard Christians talk about how they've "heard" God, or had this "feeling" and just know He is there. I guess I sort of assume if God were close to me and if I were walking with Him, I would get this nice, mushy feeling. When it hasn't come I have just felt my faith to be so unreal and so...useless.

I think a lot of people are like this. Our society is so based on feelings and emotions. I think so many divorces take place cause people don't want to work at relationships once the feeling isn't there, like it used to be. A relationship with God is like that. One must work at it even when the excitement is not there. Even when I don't always feel "on fire" for God, or even sure He is there, I can't just let Him go. That's not what He does to me. And that's where faith comes in.

4. How is God using you today versus earlier?

I think today God is using me to really reach out and love my friends. I go to a public high school where I am one of the

*only Christians. I feel like my ministry is especially to fellow
teammates on sports teams. In that circle, everyone gets to
know each other real well. There is so much opportunity for
encouragement, to set examples, be a motivator... I feel like in
junior high school I was so intent upon telling people about
God that I forgot the most basic, basic tool...love. It feels so
good to love people in a way in that Jesus does. It's not easy.
But I think God uses me to show love, something that not many
people have anymore. I don't think I have been setting the
best example for how a Christian should live. I mess up on
that way too many times. But Jesus loved people, and that's
what I am really trying to do.*

5. What do you think of the shape of the Christian faith in
North America?

*I think it's at a point where it could keep on descending
down the ladder of false beliefs and hypocrisy or it could just
erupt. I'm not sure which direction this country is going to go
in. This upcoming generation, the future leaders of our
country, seem to me to be a people so confident and outspoken
in their beliefs. It is displayed even in school during
assemblies, when students perform marches for peace, write
up petitions, and even walk out of school. I wonder if this is
good or bad. These people who are Christians or become
Christians might be the most influential, stubbornly
persuasive, outspoken people in history. Then again that same
stubbornness and persuasiveness could be used to negatively
impact the shape of the Christian faith in North America.*

6. What do you think God has in store for you next?

¿CLUELESS CHRISTIANITY?

I have absolutely no idea. I wish I did because I am at a point in my life when I could really use some clear answers. But I am so sure it will all work out. I am so sure that God knows what He is doing. I am so unafraid to face the future because I know I can pray to Him about anything and He is listening. And it is so great to be able to say that.

Chris Michaels, 25, FRESH RESOURCE Staff, DJ, Vancouver, Canada

1. When did you become a Christian?

I became a Christian when I was really young. In fact I don't really remember when I specifically became a Christian. I think I've always just been able to feel God, and so I've always known He was there. When you know He's there, it is pretty easy to follow Him.

2. Why did you become a Christian?

Cause I felt God close to me

3. How has your Christian faith evolved over the years?

As a child I always knew God was close to me. He was just always there. Then, when I was 19 I met God in a dramatic new way. Everything became alive. I felt Him closer than ever, and began to hear Him speak clearly. It was at this time He began stirring my passion. Recently, I've been learning a lot about identity, and how we need to surrender control. Anyways, that's another story... .

4. How is God using you today versus 5-10-20 years go?

¿CLUELESS CHRISTIANITY?

20 years ago, I was 3. God used me to eat and crap. 10 years ago, I was 13. God was using me to hit on girls (maybe not.) 5 years ago, I was 18. Then, I was in my first year of college, and leading worship at my church, and other churches around BC. Today God seems to have taken control of my life. I feel like I'm on a rollercoaster. I love the directions God has taken me in. He has made my life exciting and fun. I still lead worship a lot, although now I do it using turntables. In the past few years, God has taken me across North America, to England, to Zimbabwe, to Bangladesh, to Singapore, and a few other places. I'm only 23 now, and if this is an indication of what the rest of my life is going to be like, I think I'm in for a fun ride.

5. What do you think of the shape of Christian faith in North America today?

Depends where you look I think. Some places are really dead, while other places are vibrant. I love being in the environments that encourage freedom and creativity. I find I just don't really have too much time for legalism and stuff anymore.

6. What do you think God has in store for you next?

Who knows. Maybe lunch.

Johanna Beers, 30, Project Assistant, EMD Pharmaceuticals.

1. When did you become a Christian?

This question is too definitive, as if "become a Christian" happens all at one point. When did I make a conscious decision to seek Christ's guidance in all areas of my life and seek to allow Him Lordship over my life? Dec. 27,

¿CLUELESS CHRISTIANITY?

1992. But becoming a Christian is a process that is still on going.

2. Why did you become a Christian?

> *At first, it was the only response I could have if I was truly going to live within the code I said directed my life – a life for a life (Jesus took my punishment so my life became His.) At the time, I had little understanding of God or Christianity lived out daily. Now, my reasons are different (thankfully!).*

3. How has your Christian faith evolved over the years?

> *Until returning from Taiwan, I think I could say my faith grew stronger in terms of my trust that He was directing my steps towards something better all the time. But my faith in the power of prayer to change things was very low. Now, I feel my understanding of Him was (and probably still is) way too narrow; and I question whether He is really bringing me to something really good, or if He is going to use me for a greater good, not necessarily something fun for me. I feel there is a strength in prayer but I am still not sure what its effect is on situations.*

4. How is God using you today versus 5-10-20 years go?

> *I do not know that He is using me any differently today than He did when I first started consciously and unconsciously looking to Him for guidance. What has changed has been the depth, knowledge and wisdom that He has taught me during each stage of the past 11 years and how much more effectively I am able to communicate about Him now. The heart of what I am doing has not changed. But I think I have moved from being mostly a student of His to*

continuing to be a student but also acting to build community and bridges for Him where these things do not exist.

5. What do you think of the shape of Christian faith in North America today?

Short, fat, and balding with a jolly smile. Oh wait, sorry, I thought you asked about my Christian father's shape. Shape? Hmm, form, function, expression... Expression I can answer. To me it is like a person oblivious to the fact that she has a bad cell phone connection. She just keeps talking with eloquence, feeling pleased with her strong conversational skills, wealth of information and tight-ass arguments, but the person on the other end of the phone is straining just to catch a word or two in every sentence. Finally, after trying without success to cut into the flow of words coming from the other side to let her know he cannot hear, he gives up in disgust and hangs up. Just like this woman, I feel that too often we in the church in the US are so busy speaking with passion that we fail to hear the other person trying to tell us they cannot even understand our words, let alone the content. But that is changing in exciting ways as God opens the eyes of more and more people within and outside the church who are growing frustrated with this expression and communication of the gospel and who are looking to ask and find deep answers to the pressing questions of our world.

6. What do you think God has in store for you next?

In store for me— in which area of my life? Spiritually, I think He wants continued growth towards the person He is creating me to be rather than the persona I have created for myself as a child. And a deepening understanding of His forgiveness. Other areas— a rich emerging into work and life that uses more and more of who God is making me to be, anything that brings more fulfillment than what I am currently involved in. I think God is ready to take me to a place where I am really using the gifts and skills He has been nurturing in me over the last few years.

CONNECTING WITH THE UNCONNECTED:
-real relationships

An Interview

PURPOSE: *To learn how to be yourself in relationships with the normal people around you.*

About Yourself:

1. Tell me about yourself.

2. What is most important to you in life (what do you value?)

• How do you pursue that?

3. What has been your religious experience and why/how has it been most helpful to you?

4. What has been your experience with Christians?

About Christianity:

1. How do you view Christianity as a whole?

2. If you could summarize the purpose of the Christian religion in a sentence how would you describe it?

3. What are the basic beliefs of the Christian religion?

4. Do you think Christianity is relevant to our society?

¿CLUELESS CHRISTIANITY?

5. What if anything do you believe Christianity has to offer?

6. Do you think Christianity has anything to offer to you personally?

7. If Christianity were to be viable to you, what would it offer or provide that you presently don't have?

8. If you sought answers to a life situation, why or why wouldn't you go to a Christian?

9. Have you ever known an individual Christian? What characteristics, good or bad, impressed you about this person?

10. Have you ever gone to a Christian church service? How did it feel? What made you feel that way?

11. What are your overall feelings about Church?

How Would You Like to See Christianity Change:

1. What problems do you see with Christianity?

• How would you correct them?

2. How would you change the Christian faith to make it more acceptable to our society?

Felt Need Questions:

1. If you could change something about your life what would that be?

2. If you were told you were dying in a week, what, if any, regrets would you have?

3. If you could make God to be exactly what you needed, wanted, what would He/It be to you?

4. What bothers you most about life?

5. Assuming the existence of God, if you could sit down with Him over a fine dinner and ask him any questions what would they be?

Or,

6. If you could have the answers to three questions about yourself, life, etc. answered, what would those questions be?

¿CLUELESS CHRISTIANITY?

ABOUT THE AUTHOR

Dr. Gary Davis and his wife, Starr (*actually, a dangerous woman*), have been married for 40 years. They have two grown children, Joshua and Bethany, who have long since flown the coop. Gary has a slew of academic degrees (five, so far), but his passion is loving people wherever they are in their journey and helping them create their future.

Starr and Gary live in Amherst, Massachusetts, but he travels way too much (UK, China, Canada/Mexico, Los Angeles), leaving Starr behind to tend the garden, shovel the snow, and take care of his 96 year old mother, Florence.

In his discretionary time he enjoys photography, hiking through mountains, and ogling exotic wrist watches. He also enjoys refined single malt Scotch whiskies…, and, oh, Volvos. (He bought his first one in 1961.)

He pleads guilty to being a genuine Christian who has little patience with Christianeze and the plastic façade of many church-goers. He insists that the Christian faith be expressed in the idioms and formats of the host-culture, no matter what or where that may be.

He neither judges nor holds stereotypical opinions of people who adhere to other life philosophies or faiths. He journeys alongside them as a fellow traveler seeking God, justice, mercy, and Truth. He believes he has found all four.

¿CLUELESS CHRISTIANITY?

BIBLIOGRAPHY

Arbor, A. (2010, Dec 1). PRAY TELL: *Americans stretching the truth about church attendance.* Retrieved May 3, 2011, from http://ns.umich.edu/htdocs/releases/story.php?id=8155

Armenian National Institute (1997, June 13). RESOLUTION. Retrieved on May 2011 from http://www.armenian-genocide.org/Affirmation.69/current_category.5/affirmation_detail.html

AVERT, 2010. The South African Department of Health Study, 2009. Retrieved on May 3, 2011 from, http://www.avert.org/safricastats.htm .

Barker, Joel Arthur. PARADIGMS: the business of discovering the future.
New York: Harper Collins Publishers, 1992.

Babbie, E., (1998), THE PRACTICE OF SOCIAL RESEARCH, 8th edition, Belmont, CA: Wadsworth Publishing,

Barna, G. (2001). BOILING POINT: Monitoring Cultural Shifts in the 21st Century. Regal Books, Ventura, CA

Bevans, Stephen. MODELS OF CONTEXTUAL THEOLOGY.
New York: Orbis Books, 2004.

¿CLUELESS CHRISTIANITY?

Bibby, Reginald W. RESTLESS GODS: the Renaissance of
  Religion in Canada.
  Toronto: Stoddart Press, 2002

Billings,M. (1997, June). THE INFLUENZA PANDEMIC OF 1918.
  Retrieved on May 3, 2011, from
  http://virus.stanford.edu/uda/

Blake, J., (2010, August 27). More teens becoming 'fake'
  Christians. Retrieved on May 11, 2011 from
  http://www.cnn.com/2010/LIVING/08/27/almost.chris
  tian/index.html

Brady, S., (2010 June 10). HEALTHNEWS, Retrieved on May
  11, 2011 from, http://www.healthnews.com/family-
  health/mental-health/antidepressant-use-rises-among-
  americans-4277.html)

Carey, James W., COMMUNICATION AS CULTURE:
  essays on media and society,
  New York/London: Routledge, 1999.

Canning, John. 100 GREAT EVENTS THAT CHANGED THE
  WORLD.
  New York: Hawthorne Books, Inc. Publishers, 1965.

Chew, R. (2011, May 2). GALILEO GALILEI.
  http://www.lucidcafe.com/library/96feb/galileo.html

¿CLUELESS CHRISTIANITY?

Christensen, C.E., (1997). INNOVATORS DILEMMA: when
 technologies cause great firms to fail. Harvard
 Business School Press, Cambridge

Clapp, Rodney. BORDER CROSSINGS: Christian trespasses
 on popular culture and public affairs. Grand Rapids:
 Brazos Press, 2000.

Einstein, A., Infeld, L. *(1938), THE EVOLUTION OF PHYSICS:
 from early concepts to relativity and quanta, New
 York: Simon and Schuster, p 92.*

ESV Bible [English Standard Version]

Ford, Kevin. JESUS FOR A NEW GENERATION: putting the
 Gospel in the language of Xers.
 Downers Grove: InterVarsity Press, 1995.

Garraty, John A. (ed.), COLUMBIA HISTORY OF THE WORLD.
 New York: Harper & Row, 1985.

Gibbs, Eddie. CHURCH NEXT: Quantum Changes in How
 We DO Ministry.
 Downers Grove: InterVarsity Press, 2000.

Gollub, James O. THE DECADE MATRIX: why the decade
 you were born into made you what you are today.
 Reading, MA: Addison-Wesley Publishing Company,
 1991.

¿CLUELESS CHRISTIANITY?

Grenz, Stanley J. A PRIMER ON POSTMODERNISM.
 Grand Rrapids: William B. Eerdmans Publishing
 Company, 1996.

Gruder, Darrell L., ed.. MISSIONAL CHURCH: a vision for
 the sending of the Church in North America. Grand
 Rapids: Wm. B. Eerdmans, 1998.

Guthrie, S. (2002, September 9). DOORS INTO ISLAM,
 Retrieved on May 11 2011 from
 www.christianitytoday.com/ct/2002/010/1.34.html

Hall, E. (2011, May 9). NATIONAL DEBT CLOCK.
 Retrieved on May 11, 2011 from
 http://www.brillig.com/debt_clock/

Herbst, Norton, and Gabe Lyons. ENGAGING
 postCHRISTIAN CULTURE: *our Mission in a New
 Context- participants guide with DVD*. Grand Rapids:
 Zondervan (Q Society Room), 2010.

Hoffman Brinker & Roberts (2010). CREDIT CARD DEBT
 STATISTICS. Retrieved on May 3, 2011, from
 http://www.hoffmanbrinker.com/credit-card-debt-
 statistics.html

Howard, P. K., (2003 March).LAWSUITS ARE DROWNING
 AMERICA. Retrieved on May 11, 2011 from,
 http://findarticles.com/p/articles/mi_m1272/is_2694_1
 31/ai_98829797/

304

¿CLUELESS CHRISTIANITY?

Howe, Neil, and William Strauss, MILLENIALS RISING: *the next great generation*.
New York: Random House, 2000.

Hunter, George, CHURCH FOR THE UNCHURCHED.
Nashville: Abingdon Press, 1996.

Klein, Juergen, "Francis Bacon", *The Stanford Encyclopedia of Philosophy* (Summer 2011 Edition), Edward N. Zalta (ed.), forthcoming URL = <http://plato.stanford.edu/archives/sum2011/entries/francis-bacon/>.

Kuhn, Thomas. THE STRUCTURE OF SCIENTIFIC REVOLUTION. Second edition, Enlarged,
Chicago: University of Chicago Press, 1970 (1962).

Lewis,C.S., MERE CHRISTIANITY, San Fransico: Harper (1952)

Long, Jimmy, GENERATING HOPE: a strategy for reaching the postmodern generation.
Downers Grove: InterVarsity Press, 1997.

McClaren, Brian D., A NEW KIND OF CHRISTIAN: *A tale of two friends on a spiritual journey*. San Francisco: Josse-Bass, 2001.

¿CLUELESS CHRISTIANITY?

Middleton, J. Richard and Brian J. Walsh, TRUTH IS
        STRANGER THAN IT USED TO BE: *Biblical faith
        in a postmodern age*. Downers Grove: Inter Varsity
        Press, 1995.

Mohler, R.A. Jr., (2004, July 15). MINISTRY IS STRANGER
        THAN IT USED TO BE. Retrieved on July 15, 2004
        from, www.albertmohler.com

NIV Bible [New International Version]

NKJV Bible [New King James Version]

O'Malley, M. and Smith, R.L., (2009, February 23).
        CATHOLIC CHURCH CLOSINGS HIT HOME.
        Retrieved on May 11, 2011 from,
        http://www.allbusiness.com/society-social-assistance-
        lifestyle/religion-spirituality/12155796-1.html

Parade, (2010, March) THE RISE OF HYPOCHONDRIA.
        Retrieved on May 11, 2011 from,
        http://www.parade.com/health/2010/03/31-rise-of-
        hypochondria.html)

Phillip LM, (2010, June 22). 3,000,000 iPads in 80 Days.
        Retrieved on May 11, 2011 from
        http://www.ipadinsider.com/tag/ipad-sales-figures/.

POSTMODERNISM: ON THE END OF
POSTMODERNISM AND THE RISE OF REALISM.
*Absolute Truth from True Knowledge of Physical
Reality. Postmodern Definition and Quotes.* (1997).
On Truth and Reality, Retrieved on May 11, 2011
from, http://www.spaceandmotion.com/Philosophy-
Postmodernism.htm

Ratzinger, Joseph. (Pope Benedict XVI). CHRISTIANITY
AND THE CRISIS OF CULTURES.
San Francisco: Ignatius Press, 2006.

Report of Teen Research Unlimited Study, (2000 January 3).
Discount Store News

Richardson, Rick. EVANGELISM OUTSIDE THE BOX
Downers Grove: Inter Varsity Press, 2000.

Robinson, B.A. (2007, Aug 10). ONTARIO CONSULTANTS ON
RELIGIOUS TOLERANCE. Retrieved May 3, 2011, from
http://www.religioustolerance.org/rel_rate.htm

Robnoxious, (2003, Jan 20). THE YEAR IS 1902. Retrieved on
May 3, 2011, from
http://www.goofball.com/jokes/facts/death_life_differ
ence_The_Year_Is_1902

Rogers, J. (2008, March). REVIVAL - EDWARDS AND WESLEY.
Retrieved on May 11, 2001 from,
http://www.forerunner.com/forerunner/X0609_Reviva
l_Edwards_and.html

Roxburgh, Alan J., REACHING A NEW GENERATION.
Downers Grove: InterVarsity Press, 1993.

RULES FOR THE STUDY OF NATURAL PHILOSOPHY, Newton
1999, pp. 794-6, from the General Scholium, which
follows Book 3, The System of the World.

Samovar, Larry A., Richard E Porter, Edwin R. McDaniel.
COMMUNICATION BETWEEN CULTURES.
Boston: Wadsworth, 2010.

Simon, J.M. (2010, May 7). CONSUMER CREDIT CARD DEBT
KEEPS DROPPING. Retrieved on May 4, 2011, from
http://www.creditcards.com/credit-card-news/federal-
reserve-g19-consumer-credit-march-10-1276.php

THE NEXT RULING CLASS. (2001, April). The Atlantic
Monthly

Tillich, Paul J., THEOLOGY OF CULTURE New York:
Oxford University Press, 1959.

Treasury Direct. (2008, August 18). HISTORICAL DEBT OUTSTANDING - ANNUAL 1950 - 1999 http://www.treasurydirect.gov/govt/reports/pd/histdebt /histdebt_histo4.htm

U.S. Department of Labor. (2007, November). *EMPLOYMENT STATUS OF WOMEN AND MEN IN 2008.* Retrieved on May 11, 2011, from http://www.dol.gov/wb/factsheets/Qf-ESWM08.htm.

U.S. Census Bureau. (2008, January 12). US DEPARTMENT OF HEALTH AND HUMAN SERVICES. Retrieved May 3, 2011 from http://www.census.gov/prod/2009pubs/p95-09-1.pdf

Wilkinson, P. ILLUSTRATED DICTIONARY OF MYTHOLOGY. NY: DK, 1998.
Butler, C. (2007). The Decline & fall of the Greek Polis. Retrieved May 3, 2011, from http://www.flowofhistory.com/units/birth/3/FC24

Wikipedia. (2011, May 14). GREEK GENOCIDE. Retreived on May 15, 2011 from http://en.wikipedia.org/wiki/Greek_massacre

¿CLUELESS CHRISTIANITY?

END NOTES—

Chapter 1

[i] The Conservative/Liberal controversy antagonized both camps, but positioned the conservatives as anti-intellectual anti-cultural, and anti-progress, thus granting a position of greater influence to the more liberal spectrum of Christianity.

[ii] Note: With the twenty-first century barely underway the resurgence of terrorism, now on a global level, has taken center stage as the key player promoting world instability. Al Qaeda, "the list," has crisscrossed the world with its network of local cells waiting for the word to activate their mission of vengeance on non-Islamic peoples everywhere.

[iii] But there were a lot of abuses of Christian expression within their worship services that disturbed more traditional Christian groups. There were scenes of extensive emotionalism to the negation of solid Biblical instruction; charismatic personalities were adored as spiritual icons; and a great deal of money was extracted from people, in the name of God, that actually went into the coffers of "the ministry."

[iv] For those of you in a more reserved age category, these last four are names of Christian music groups.

[v] During the first Great Awakening in North America, 1736-1742, Jonathan Edwards, a pastor in Northampton, Massachusetts got into trouble for his emphasis on *religious affections* as being just as essential a part in conversion as mental acceptance of the Truth.

[vi] In more academic terms, this is known as a **social construction of reality**— a vital part of our world. When we experience something we look to others to help us define what happened and how we should interpret it and respond; what it means, in part, is defined by those around us.

[vii] Paradigm, paradigm blending. The terms *paradigm, paradigm shift* were popularized by Thomas Kuhn in his 1962 work THE STRUCTURE OF SCIENTIFIC REVOLUTION. A *paradigm* is a way of perceiving life. A *paradigm shift* is a change from one way of thinking or perceiving to another. A *paradigm*

blending is a cultural phenomena where varying approaches to viewing life are intermingled to form a composite.

viii Http://www.religioustolerance.org/rel_rate.htm Ontario Consultants on Religious Tolerance. How many North Americans attend religious services (and how many lie about going)? 2007.

ix Diane Swanbrow, "*Study of worldwide rates of religiosity, church attendance*," University of Michigan news release at: www.umich.edu/newsinfo/Releases/1997/

x Independent surveys conducted in 1998, 2000, 2003 & 2007. Summary correlation.

Chapter 2

xi A new generation comes into influence about every 20 years. Fads seem to come around every 4-5 years. Look at your old ties. What, you don't have any old ties? You don't have a tie at all? Five years out, you will.

xii This kind of *visual intuition*, as I call it, will be dealt with more in chapter 5, Rethinking Thinking.

xiii The gods ruled the fates of women, too; but that wasn't important thing. This was a far less *politically correct* environment 4,000 years ago; before agricultural development and the Fertile Crescent.

xiv Wilkinson, Philip. *Illustrated Dictionary of Mythology*. NY: DK, 1998. P 24

xv The root of the word "*pagan*" referred to those who lived in the countryside, rural areas, outside of the mainstream of civilization culture. It grew to refer to *those who held onto the older religions.* http://www.etymonline.com/index.php?term=pagan.

xvi [Constant infighting between Greek city-states weakened their cumulative military strength; economic instability drew former soldiers to the countryside to take up farming; and the rise of Macedon to the north under Phillip II, Father of Alexander the Great).] http://www.flowofhistory.com/units/birth/3/FC24

xvii John Canning. 100 Great Events that Changed the World. Hawthorne Books, Inc. New York, 1965.

[xviii] I do not want to slight Oriental, African, and Mesoamerican cultural development intentionally, but this book seeks to address the development of the Christian faith in western cultural arenas. Please forgive me.

[xix] The first book printed in the English language was "The Recuyell," printed in Brussels in 1474 by William Caxton.

[xx] A set of gears in which many teeth make contact at once, reducing the strain on the teeth, allowing more pressure to be put on the mechanism.

[xxi] This led to Galileo's excommunication and a threat of being executed unless he recanted his belief of a heliocentric solar system. He recanted and was held in house arrest the remainder of his life. http://www.lucidcafe.com/library/96feb/galileo.html

[xxii] Available at http://plato.stanford.edu/entries/francis-bacon/ .

[xxiii] He also said *"t is not enough to have a good mind. The main thing is to use it well."* Discours de la Méthode, 1637.

[xxiv] First ascribed to Aristotle; then Ibn Sina (Islamic philosopher), Ibn Tufail (Andalusian-Islamic). It was also picked up by Sigmund Freud in his theories of psychoanalysis.

Chapter 3

[xxv] [www.goofball.com/jokes/facts/death_life_difference_The_Year_Is_1902

[xxvi] For you Mac/Apple Computer users, this is an unknown. You should be thankful you can utilize such a reliable CPU. Of course, having everything proprietary does limit one's ability for diversification.

[xxvii] Commuting to work 1950-1960- take a bus. Commuting to work 1970- drive yourself. Commuting to work 1980- Car-pool it. Commuting to work 1990-2000- grab yourself a latte, sit down at your laptop, log-on… in your bunny slippers.

[xxviii] Sorry. Sheep shot.

[xxix] Federal Reserve's G.19 report on consumer credit, May 2010.

http://www.creditcards.com/credit-card-news/federal-reserve-g19-consumer-credit-march-10-1276.php xxx Albeit, studies show that Americans seem more prone to this misuse than Canadians. As for south of the border, don't even think about it.

xxxi Followed soon after by VH1.

xxxii U.S. Census, 1980.

xxxiii To be fair, in China, it also stabilized the population to more appropriately fit the ability of the government, not to mention the land, to sustain such an exponentially expanding people.

xxxiv The original transatlantic cable, laid in 1857-1866, served to connect Europe and North America for about 2 weeks..., then failed. First fishing line, maybe?

xxxv Molly Billings, June, 1997 modified RDS February, 2005. http://virus.stanford.edu/uda/ change dates to 1918-1919

xxxvi Molly Billings, June, 1997 modified RDS February, 2005. http://virus.stanford.edu/uda/ change dates to 1918-1919

xxxvii Garraty, John A. (ed.), Columbia History of the World. New York: Harper & Row, 1985. Pg.1011.

xxxviii Roughly 1946-1954, a search for the potential Communists among the American populace. Many teachers, professors, and businessman were blacklisted by Senator Joseph McCarthy (WI) in what has been termed a "witch hunt."

xxxix Everyone was a Communist; or at least, you were supposed to be suspicious of everyone who expressed anything other than what you thought.

xl AVERT, 2010. http://www.avert.org/safricastats.htm . The last statistic for South Africa, for example, in 2007 reported that 28% of the population was infected with AIDS. 1,000 a day died.

xli The 24th Amendment protected African-Americans from discrimination in voting. It was ratified in 1964.

xlii 1999-2010, Hoffman Brinker & Roberts 42211 Garfield Rd, Ste. 302, Clinton Township, MI 48038. http://www.hoffmanbrinker.com/credit-card-debt-statistics.html

xliii http://www.treasurydirect.gov/govt/reports/pd/histdebt/histdebt_histo4.htm [US Government]

¿CLUELESS CHRISTIANITY?

xliv National Debt Clock. http://www.brillig.com/debt_clock/

xlv http://www.dol.gov/wb/factsheets/Qf-ESWM08.htm. Women are out earned by men by @ 20%. [Table 5. U.S. Department of Labor | Frances Perkins Building, 200 Constitution Ave., NW, Washington, DC]

xlvi *"Those who forget the past are condemned to repeat it."* George Santiano

xlvii Please, don't quibble about the "official" turn-of-the-century. We lost that one when we began celebrating virtually *all* holidays on weekends, no matter their official date.

xlviii The amazing phenomenon of suburban dwellers getting tired of living out of town, moving back into the city into rundown neighborhoods, purchasing row houses, turning them into town houses, upgrading them, and turning their value upside down, forcing the departure of neighbors too poor to now pay the increase in taxes and services.

xlix Technology played no small role in the increase of the velocity of change. To see how technology affected U.S. businesses take a look at INNOVATORS DILEMMA: *when technologies cause great firms to fail*, by Clayton M. Christensen. (Harvard Business School Press, Cambridge, 1997).

l Earl Babbie, The Practice of Social Research, 8th edition, Belmont, CA: Wadsworth Publishing, 1998. Pg.21.

li "Scientific"— to write on the meanings and implications of this word would indeed be another book. I simply use the word at face value, as commonly accepted, as involving some theory, consistent method, research, control groups, and postulated conclusions. Science's evolution to a philosophical position by of its authoritarian stance will not be dealt with in this work, believe me!

lii Of course the Chinese invention of paper helped a bit.

liii This didn't last long. By the time she turned 19 her spirit was quite different. Reality bites.

liv *"The Next Ruling Class,"* The Atlantic Monthly, April 2001.

lv This is somewhat limited to those who go on for further education following high school. The high school set will have a harder time making ends meet. They must therefore work more for their own preservation than those who have college and beyond degrees.

¿CLUELESS CHRISTIANITY?

Chapter 4

[lvi] "[4] Rules for the study of natural philosophy", Newton 1999, pp. 794-6, from the General Scholium, which follows Book **3**, *The System of the World*.

[lvii] Einstein, Albert; Infeld, Leopold *(1938), The Evolution of Physics: from early concepts to relativity and quanta, New York: Simon and Schuster,* (ISBN 0-671-20156-5) *p 92.*

[lviii] Paul McCartney, The Beatles, The White Album. 1968.

[lix] Ken Myers, MARS HILL AUDIO newsletter, May 2002.

[lx] R. Albert Mohler, Jr. MINISTRY IS STRANGER THAN IT USED TO BE. www.albertmohler.com July 15, 2004

[lxi] Applying postmodern thought to religion is not entirely precise. It is actually postmodern thought applied ONLY to Christianity. No other traditional religion (Islam, Hinduism, Budhism, Judism) would allow postmodern thought to be applied to it. They are not concerned with the effects postmodernism has on them as yet. They stand outside the circle of influence of the shift. Some retain their traditions fiercely; others simply hang in a sort of limbo, culturally. But their children will have some concern. There will be little difference between a postmodern Jew, Muslim, Budhist, or Hindu. Will there be that much distinction for the postmodern Christian? Hummmm.

[lxii] John 1:14. NIV Bible.

[lxiii] Romans 1:18-19. NKJV Bible.

[lxiv] cf- C.S. Lewis, Mere Christianity, Ch. 3 *The Reality of the Law.*

[lxv] John 14:1-11, NKJV Bible.

[lxvi] Hebrews 4:12, NIV Bible

Chapter 5

[lxvii] If you think this idea calling for a non-balanced faith to be radical or novel you are in good company. An account of the revival of religion in Northampton in 1740-1742 was reported in "*The State of Religion at Northampton in the County of Hampshire, About 100 Miles Westward of*

Boston." The letter was published in *The Christian History*, January 14, 21, and 28, 1743. Written by Rev. Jonathan Edwards, it recounted the moving of the Spirit of God upon the towns-people and their highly emotional responses, which resulted in their repenting and turning to Christ for salvation. Edwards was eventually removed from his church because of his insistence that conversion be more than a renewing of the mind: it must also be a change in the heart.
See= [http://www.jonathanedwards.com/text/jeaccnt.htm]

Chapter 6

[lxviii] First World- Europe/China. Second World- the Americas, Australia. Third World- Africa, Latin America. Fourth World- recovering/emerging former Soviet nations.

[lxix] Teens themselves spent $105 billion and influenced their parents to spend, on them, an additional $48 billion, for a total of $153 billion annually. "Report of Teen Research Unlimited Study," *Discount Store News*, January 3, 2000. Statistic for fiscal year 1999.

[lxx] I am well aware that to employ the phrase "churches generally," is impossible. What is at stake here is the general reaction of unchurched youth to traditional Christian worship, whether or not they employ more contemporary worship music.

[lxxi] MTV also offers a similar show called *Road Rules*. The difference being a travel ingredient.

[lxxii] Neil Howe and William Strauss, MILLENNIALS RISING: the next great generation, (Randon House; New York, 2000), 41 (with some modification).

[lxxiii] Howe and Strauss, 40

[lxxiv] Ibid., 40

[lxxv] Woodruff's dates differ slightly from Howe and Strauss in Millennials Rising, but his analysis and choice of representations for each generation are notably on target.

[lxxvi] Well, with the exception of RAP. I'm sorry; I just can't get into it. But I do like Country!

[lxxvii] See Appendix- Generational Interviews.

lxxviii The structure of theology experienced just as massive an overhaul between the premodern and modern eras. It was called the Protestant reformation.

Chapter 7

lxxix Phillip LM, IpadInsider, http://www.ipadinsider.com/tag/ipad-sales-figures/.

lxxx Authors William Strauss and Neil Howe have been very influential in defining American generations in their book *Generations: The History of America's Future, 1584 to 2069* (1991) and are frequently cited in books and articles on the subject. Howe and Strauss maintain that they use the term *Millennials* in place of *Generation Y* because the members of the generation themselves coined the term, not wanting to be associated with Generation X. Almost a decade later, they followed up their large study of the history of American demographics with a new book specifically on that generation, titled *Millennials Rising: The Next Great Generation* (2000). http://en.wikipedia.org/wiki/Millenials

lxxxi Note: Sociologically speaking, churches have always lagged behind because they are the most conservative institutions in society – which means they adopt any social changes last. They were the last to accept integrated congregations after the Civil Rights movement.

lxxxii See Neil Howe & William, Millennials Rising: *the next great generation*. Random House, New York, 2000.

lxxxiii I am not sure the "rugged American" image is as true for Canadian Christians. If anything, Canadian Christians seem to be more aware of their marginalization outside of the mainstream of society and have adapted appropriately.

Chapter 8

lxxxiv In Christianity Today, mid- 2002, George Barna laments the fact that he has failed to motivate the church to action with all the information and insight he has provided over the past decade.

¿CLUELESS CHRISTIANITY?

lxxxv Ecclesiastes 1:9 (New International Version) "What has been will be again, what has been done will be done again; there is nothing new under the sun."

lxxxvi Non-western cultures experience cultural paradigm shifts either every 50-75 years or every 300-500 years. Some, like aboriginals in Australia, seek to retain their old ways and remain as their ancestors.

lxxxvii You'll find a 1945 performance at—
http://www.youtube.com/watch?v=Watf8_Rf58s.

lxxxviii Attributed to General Douglas McArthur.

Chapter 9

lxxxix Not her real name.

xc Not her real name either.

xci Not his real name.

xcii Postmodernism: On the End of Postmodernism and the Rise of Realism. Absolute Truth from True Knowledge of Physical Reality. Postmodern Definition and Quotes.   http://www.spaceandmotion.com/Philosophy-Postmodernism.htm

xciii ADBUSTERS #30, June/July 2000.

xciv Antidepressants have risen to the top spot as the most commonly prescribed class of medications in the U.S. and, according to a new survey by Consumer Reports, it is a preferred method of treatment for people battling depression. After all, it is much easier to take a pill than sit in a therapist's office and talk for an hour. (Susan Brady, HealthNews, June 10, 2010) (http://www.healthnews.com/family-health/mental-health/antidepressant-use-rises-among-americans-4277.html)

xcv BNet, The CBS Interactive Business Network, (http://findarticles.com/p/articles/mi_m1272/is_2694_131/ai_98829797/)

xcvi Hypochondriacs have an overwhelming belief that any symptom, no matter how innocuous, will lead to a serious disease," says Dr. Arthur Barsky, a professor of psychiatry at Harvard, who says that an estimated 5% to 12% of patients who see doctors every year are hypochondriacs. The Internet hasn't helped. Hundreds of medical sites have produced a new

319

strain of hypochondria dubbed " cyberchondria."
(http://www.parade.com/health/2010/03/31-rise-of-hypochondria.html)

[xcvii] Michael O'Malley and Robert L. Smith, CATHOLIC CHURCH CLOSINGS HIT HOME. In LexisNexis. Feb 23, 2009. (http://www.allbusiness.com/society-social-assistance-lifestyle/religion-spirituality/12155796-1.html0)

[xcviii] Dean, Kenda, Creasy. Almost Christian: *what the faith of our teenagers is telling the American Church.* Oxford University Press, June, 2010. Also see— John Blake, *More teens becoming 'fake' Christians.* August 27, 2010. CNNLiving.
(http://www.cnn.com/2010/LIVING/08/27/almost.christian/index.html)

[xcix] In my own interactions with "normal" people I have been constantly surprised by their preconditioned response to the word "Christian" and their surprise when they discover that a genuine Christian has been in their midst all along, talking from his own Biblical presuppositional base.

[c] John 17- English standard Version

Chapter 10

[ci] "Generational Dominance" refers to the overall influence any particular generation, or subculture within that generation, exerts over a regional or national culture in general.

[cii] George Barna. BOILING POINT: Monitoring Cultural Shifts in the 21st Century.

(Regal Books, Ventura, CA) 2001.

[ciii] George Barna. BOILING POINT: Monitoring Cultural Shifts in the 21st Century.

(Regal Books, Ventura, CA) 2001. p.20.

[civ] Though this might be true of Christians within western culture. It was not so with her missionaries to other cultures. They, of a truth, were extreme risk takers. Praise God.

[cv] Christianity Today, Stand Guthrie, Doors into Islam, September 9, 2002, Vol. 46, No. 10. www.christianitytoday.com/ct/2002/010/1.34.html

¿CLUELESS CHRISTIANITY?

[cvi] The following description of Euclid Djefaris comes partly from my many conversations with him as well as a refresher conversation with his incredible sister, Sophia Henry, of Washington, DC.

[cvii] Armenian Massacres (Armenian Genocide)— refers to the deliberate and systematic destruction of the Armenian population of the Ottoman Empire during and just after World War I. It was implemented through wholesale massacres and deportations, with the deportations consisting of forced marches under conditions designed to lead to the death of the deportees. The total number of resulting Armenian deaths is generally held to have been between one and one and a half million. [June 13, 1997, gathering of Armenian Scholars in Montreal. (Armenian National Institute. 1334 G Street, NW Suite 200 Washington, DC 20005)]

(http://www.armenian-genocide.org/Affirmation.69/current_category.5/affirmation_detail.html)

[cviii] During World War I and its aftermath (1914–1923), the government of the Ottoman Empire instigated a violent campaign against the Greek population of the Empire. The campaign included massacres, forced deportations involving death marches, and summary expulsions. According to various sources, several hundred thousand Ottoman Greeks died during this period. Some of the survivors and refugees, especially those in Eastern provinces, took refuge in the neighboring Russian Empire. After the end of the 1919–22 Greco-Turkish War, most of the Greeks remaining in the Ottoman Empire were transferred to Greece under the terms of the 1923 population exchange between Greece and Turkey.
[http://en.wikipedia.org/wiki/Greek_massacre]

Made in the USA
Charleston, SC
22 October 2011